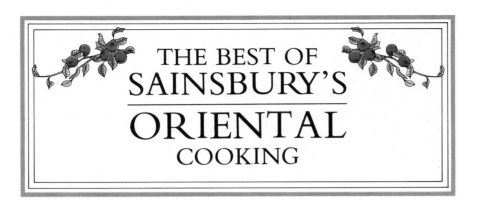

THE BEST OF
SAINSBURY'S

ORIENTAL
COOKING

THE BEST OF
SAINSBURY'S
ORIENTAL
COOKING

CONTENTS

CONTRIBUTORS

Main authors: Caroline Ellwood, Naomi Good, Yvette Stachowiak

Other contributing authors: Clare Ferguson, Clare Gordon-Smith,
Carole Handslip

NOTES

Standard spoon measurements are used in all recipes
1 tablespoon=one 15 ml spoon
1 teaspoon=one 5 ml spoon
All spoon measures are level.

Size 3 eggs should be used unless otherwise stated.

Ovens should be preheated to the specified temperature.

For all recipes, quantities are given in both
metric and imperial measures. Follow either
set but not a mixture of both, because they
are not interchangeable.

Published exclusively for
J Sainsbury plc
Stamford House
Stamford Street
London SE1 9LL
by Cathay Books
59 Grosvenor Street
London W1

First published 1987

© Cathay Books 1987
ISBN 0 86178 495 2

Printed in Italy

INTRODUCTION

We hear a great deal about the mystery of the East – but as anyone who has taken the time to learn about this fascinating part of the world will know, this is a vast area, different in so many ways from the West.

To start with, there are many delicious and intriguing cuisines in the lands of the East – each developed from a different combination of history, religion, economics, geography and cultural influences. One influence that is common to the whole of the Orient, however, is the view of food as an object of artistic and philosophic merit. Far Eastern cultures do not generally regard food as simply fuel, but rather as a forum for creative development and self-expression.

It is for that reason that the diverse cuisines in the region are not just limited to one in each country. China, for example, has an estimated 55 ethnic minorities, each contributing something different to the culinary quilt which covers this immense country.

In addition to the variety of ingredients that this huge geographical patchwork dictates, you will also note a lack of emphasis on meat dishes – as meat is often difficult to obtain. There is a far greater concentration on fresh vegetables and spices to provide culinary alternatives to overcome the scarcity of meat.

A good starting point when looking at Oriental cooking is to identify the major forms of cuisine in the region. Other than the well-known dishes of India, China and Japan, they also include quite distinct dishes from Thailand, Vietnam and several other nations in the region.

Thai cuisine, for example, combines salty, sour, sweet and hot flavours in an enticing melange. Indonesia, meanwhile, is heavily influenced by its geography for it is a chain of some 3,000 islands encompassing numerous racial groups, religions and languages. The Indians first arrived in Indonesia for trading purposes and then the spice race was on. The Arabs, Chinese, Dutch and Portuguese have all swept through this region in search of valuable spices and other commodities. Singapore and Malaysia share the same tropical monsoon climate and vegetation and their cuisine is very similar to that of Indonesia.

The beauty of East Asian cooking is that there is no need to invest in expensive equipment – a wok, and a bamboo steamer are both relatively cheap, but can also be improvised with equipment already existing in Western kitchens. For example, a frying pan with high sides can be used instead of a wok.

Although some specialist ingredients are used in the recipes, these are becoming more and more available in supermarkets. So keep looking and you will find that a whole new and exciting culinary world is open to you.

And once you have your equipment and ingredients in hand, prepare for our tasty tour through the Orient as you move through the chapters that follow . . .

INDIAN COOKING

REGIONAL COOKING

India is a large country with many regional variations in climate, custom, religion and food. The country has been invaded and colonized many times, and each time changes have taken place in the eating habits of the local population.

When the Moguls descended on northern India in the sixteenth century they brought with them their rich meat-based cuisine. From central Asia, too, came the *tandoor*, the clay oven, which gives its name to those delectable dishes now served in every Indian restaurant.

The north is a wheat-growing, bread-eating area. The preferred cooking fat is concentrated butter or ghee, although substitutes are used. Generally speaking the food is mild; it gets progressively hotter and spicier the further south you go.

The population of India is predominantly Hindu and vegetarian. When Hindus eat meat it is usually lamb – never beef, for the cow is sacred. There are, of course, many meat-eating minorities: the Goans from the ex-Portuguese colony on the west coast for whom pork is a speciality; the Muslims who eat beef and lamb but never pork; the Parsees who are omnivorous.

The more southern states grow rice as their staple food, use oil in preference to ghee and tend to be vegetarian. In Bengal on the east coast the food is again different, as they have plenty of fish – especially plump king-size prawns and lobsters – in the tidal waters of the Hooghly river. Mustard seeds and mustard oil are popular here too. But best of all are their sweets – little white and brown spheres floating in syrup and fudge-like pink, white and green squares.

All Indians love sweets but leave the making of them to the professionals. Those sweets that are simple enough to be made at home require patience rather than skill and the full attention of the cook or the results will be disappointing.

EQUIPMENT

In India the traditional method of grinding spices to a paste or powder is in a large mortar or on a flat stone using a heavy rolling-pin shaped stone. Here an electric blender with a strong motor or a food processor will make quick work of puréeing spices.

To grind small quantities of dry spices a coffee grinder is ideal – but you will not be able to use it for grinding coffee again. If you do not have a blender, a mezzaluna (a curved blade with two handles), a garlic press and a grater will give very satisfactory results.

In India saucepans do not have handles. They used to be made of heavy copper with tinned interiors and curved bottoms, but now they are often made from aluminium and are flat bottomed.

For frying, a large heavy wok-like pan is used and for making bread a slightly curved, iron plate-like griddle. Any heavy frying pan can be used instead.

In a traditional Indian household plates are not used. Instead they serve food on *thalis*, round trays made from metal, usually brass although stainless steel is becoming more commonly used, especially in urban areas, and silver (by those who can afford it) for special occasions. Small bowls called *katoris* are placed on the tray

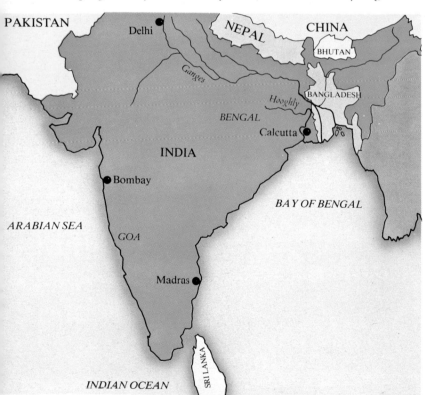

and filled with the various dishes. Chutneys and accompaniments are arranged on the *thali* itself, as are breads such as puris or chapatis. Rice is also served directly on to the tray. In the south banana leaves are sometimes used and make delightful disposable *thalis*.

At the end of a meal, especially if it has been a heavy one, *paan* is served as a *digestif* and an astringent mouth freshener. *Paan* is made from the leaf of the betel palm, spread with lime (calcium) paste and filled with chopped betel nut and a variety of spices such as cloves, cardamom seeds and aniseed. The leaf is then neatly folded into a triangle small enough to be popped whole into the mouth. It turns the mouth red when chewed and is addictive, especially when the ingredients include tobacco.

CHINESE COOKING

REGIONAL COOKING

There are four principal schools of Chinese cuisine: Cantonese (Kwangtung province), Huaiyang, Szechuan and Peking. Each region has its own specialities which depend on the climate and availability of local produce.

Cantonese cooking is influenced by the availability of locally caught fish, and seafood specialities are numerous. Stuffed vegetables are popular, often using shellfish for the filling. It is also from Canton that the delicious crispy pork recipes originate.

Huaiyang, with its centre at Yangchow, provides many of the steamed dishes, including savoury dumplings. The subtle-flavoured noodle recipes come from the banks of the Yangtze river delta in this area. Also in eastern China is Nanking, known for its duck dishes, and Shanghai – the trading centre – which has its own sophisticated cuisine.

In contrast, food from the Szechuan area is richly flavoured and piquant. Characteristic Szechuan dishes tend to be hot and peppery, mainly due to the use of chilli peppers, hot pepper oil and Szechuan peppercorns.

The Peking cuisine is the most varied of all. Over the centuries, chefs from the different regions of China have brought their own specialities to the capital city, making it the culinary centre. At the same time, Peking has its own cuisine; it is from here that the famous Peking Duck and Mongolian Hot Pot originate. The northern province of Honan on the Hwang Ho (Yellow River) is famous for its sweet-sour dishes.

PREPARING INGREDIENTS

In Chinese cooking the emphasis is on the preparation of food rather than cooking. This is the time-consuming part of the recipe – the actual cooking time is very short. Great care should be taken when cutting to ensure that all ingredients are a similar size and will therefore cook evenly.

Meat should be cut across the grain to help tenderise it. Normally, it is either sliced or shredded. Vegetables may be sliced straight or diagonally, shredded or diced.

To slice a vegetable diagonally, hold the knife or cleaver at a 45° angle to the vegetable, with the blade pointing away from you. To shred a vegetable, cut into diagonal slices then into thin strips. To dice, simply cut the food into 1 cm ($\frac{1}{2}$ inch) cubes. Always prepare each ingredient and put on one side before starting to cook.

COOKING METHODS AND EQUIPMENT

Frying, steaming and braising are the common methods.

Stir-frying: This is the most common Chinese cooking method. As the name implies, it is a technique of frying foods over a high heat, stirring constantly.

A small amount of oil is used and the food is stirred vigorously and constantly throughout cooking, which only takes a few minutes. This method ensures that the food is sealed and cooked quickly to hold in the flavour. A wok, with its round base and sloping sides, is perfect for stir-frying. If a wok is unavailable, use a deep frying pan instead.

Deep-frying: A wok or deep-fryer can be used for this method. The food is normally dipped into a batter of some sort before

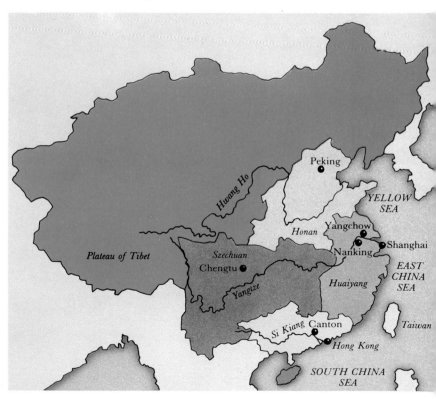

frying in hot oil. It is advisable to use a fat thermometer to check the temperature of the oil.

Steaming: Chinese steamers are made from bamboo in varying sizes to fit inside a wok or over a saucepan. They have a bamboo lid and are designed so that steam passes through the tiny holes in the bamboo to cook the food.

The food is arranged on an ovenproof plate, which is then placed on the perforated base of the steamer.

It is possible to use a metal steamer on top of a saucepan for smaller items, but bamboo steamers are readily available at reasonable cost and are worth buying.

Red braising: This is a unique Chinese style of cooking. The food is stewed in a mixture of soy sauce, water and sugar, with flavourings of root ginger, spring onions and sherry. The food takes on a reddish colour during cooking.

JAPANESE COOKING

Elegant simplicity and frugality are essential in the presentation of Japanese food – with emphasis on its aesthetic and seasonal qualities. The Japanese are less fond of strong tastes than most other Eastern peoples. Instead of the fiery chillies and pungent fish sauces used in other Oriental cuisines, they prefer light, almost ethereal flavours. However, they do enjoy wasabi, a horseradish paste used as a dip and hot pepper oils similar to Tabasco sauce.

Though Japan closed its ports to foreigners between 1600 and 1868, there are detectable Korean, Portuguese and American influences in its food. For example, tempura – deep-fried fish and vegetables in the lightest of batters – is said to have been introduced by Portuguese traders in the sixteenth century.

The staple foods of Japan include rice, seaweed, fish and soya beans in various forms such as miso paste, shoyu, (the Japanese version of soy sauce) and tofu, and at least one meal a day includes these items. Fish is of particular importance to the Japanese and sushi and sashimi, both made from raw fish, are a delectable example of Japan's culinary arts.

COOKING METHODS AND EQUIPMENT

One important aspect of Japanese cuisine is that cooking at the table plays a vital role for both practical and social reasons. The Japanese like to eat their food as soon as it is cooked (or in the case of sushi, prepared) and they also enjoy the traditions that go with eating certain foods. In sushi bars, it is considered best to sit in front of the chef so you get the freshest cut fish and besides, it is always fascinating to watch the art of sushi making.

Japanese culinary arts focus on deep-frying, plenty of grilling, quick stir-frying and steaming. Tempura, though not quintessentially Japanese, is a good example of deep-frying, while Yakitori Chicken and Teriyaki Beef demonstrate the fine technique of grilling.

Western tools are easily adapted to Japanese cuisine, so there is no need to buy a battery of new equipment. A fondue pot, an electric frying pan and a wok or even a sturdy cast-iron frying pan will adequately cover most needs.

SOUTH EAST ASIAN COOKING

Indonesia, Malaysia, Thailand and Burma are all part of South East Asia. Though there have been many political upheavals in this area throughout history it is worth noting that while outside influences have been assimilated, the different countries still retain their separate identities and traditions, and this is reflected in the distinctive cuisines.

All the countries in South East Asia share common ingredients. Rice, lemon grass, blachan (or shrimp paste), coconuts, fresh and dried fish, onions, garlic and chillies are found throughout this part of the world.

Religion has also left its mark on the culinary wealth. With the year-round religious festivals, colourful and vivid food is prepared to celebrate each occasion. Elaborate food decoration, in the shape of carved fruits and vegetables, has reached a level unattained by Western chefs.

COOKING METHODS AND EQUIPMENT
In South East Asia, there are few ovens or grills as Westerners know them and an open charcoal stove is used for all culinary tasks. Meat and fish are frequently barbecued, occasionally wrapped in banana leaves to seal in the flavour. Woks are a necessary item and are used for frying, boiling, simmering and steaming.

A pestle and mortar for grinding spices with various other ingredients is essential as the resulting pastes form the foundation for most South East Asian dishes. Nuts, onions, garlic, blachan, ginger and chillies are the most common ingredients; they are fried or simmered before being added to a dish. An electric coffee grinder specifically reserved for spices can be used instead of a pestle and mortar.

SPECIALIST INGREDIENTS

The following are available from Asian, Chinese and Japanese food stores or some supermarkets:

Abalone: A smooth-textured shellfish available in cans.
Asafoetida (heeng): A strong-flavoured brown resin used in Indian cooking. Available ground, it should be used in very small quantities. Keep tightly covered.
Bamboo Shoots: Crunchy cream-coloured shoots of the bamboo plant. Available in canned and dried form. (Dried bamboo shoots should be soaked before use.)
Bean Paste, Sweet: Thick, red soy bean paste with added sugar, sold in cans. Used as a dip and as a base for sweet sauces.
Bean Sauce, Yellow/Black: A thick sauce made from black or yellow soy beans, sold in cans.
Bean Sprouts: Tiny, crunchy shoots of mung beans. Bean sprouts are available fresh and should be eaten on day of purchase. Also sold in cans, but fresh ones are recommended.
Blachan (trasi): A strong-smelling, salty shrimp paste from South East Asia. Available in cans or packets. It has a very pungent smell, so keep tightly sealed in the refrigerator once opened. It must be well fried or wrapped in foil and roasted before use.
Black Beans: Salted, fermented black beans with a strong, salty flavour. Sold in packs or by weight. Must be soaked for 5 to 10 minutes before use.
Bonito flakes: Also known as flaked katsuobushi. Bonito flakes come from a tuna-like fish which is skinned, boned, dried for up to 3 years, then finely flaked.
Cardamom (elaichi): An aromatic seed pod which comes in three varieties: white, green (more perfumed than the white) and large black (not always available). The whole pod is used to flavour rice and meat dishes and then discarded, or the pod is opened and the seeds removed and crushed for sprinkling on sweets or vegetables.
Cayenne pepper or chilli powder: Powdered dried red chillies. The strength varies from batch to batch. Use with caution.
Chestnuts, dried: Require soaking before use. Fresh chestnuts may be used instead, without soaking.
Chillies, hot fresh green (hari mirch): Use with care. For a less pungent result slit the chillies and discard the seeds. Do not touch your face or rub your eyes while handling chillies, and wash your hands immediately afterwards.
Chillies, dried red (sabat lal mirch): These add a good flavour when tossed in whole with other frying spices. The smaller ones are very pungent so add them cautiously. They can also be crumbled between finger tips, if preferred. Handle with the same care as green chillies (above).
Chinese Leaves: Also called Chinese cabbage, it has a slightly sweet flavour. Can be eaten raw in salads, or cooked.
Chinese Mushrooms, dried: Need to be soaked in warm water for 15 to 20 minutes and stalks must be removed before use. Continental dried mushrooms can be used instead.
Cinnamon (dalchini): Available in stick and ground form. The stick should be discarded before the dish is served.
Coconut (narial): Used in many sweet and savoury dishes. When buying a coconut choose one that is heavy for its size. To open it, pierce the 'eyes' with a skewer and pour away the liquid. Put the coconut in a preheated moderately hot oven, 190°C (375°F), Gas Mark 5, for 15 minutes, then place on a sturdy table or on the floor and give it a sharp tap with a mallet or hammer; it will break in two. Using a sharp knife, prise away the flesh from

the shell, then peel off the brown skin and cut the coconut into pieces. If the coconut is already open put it in the oven for 15 to 20 minutes or until you hear the shell cracking. The flesh will then be easy to remove. Grate the coconut in a food processor or by hand and use as required.

Coconut milk is an infusion used to flavour and thicken many dishes, particularly in Southern India and South East Asia. To make it, place the grated coconut in a bowl, pour over about 600 ml (1 pint) boiling water, just to cover and leave for 1 hour. Strain through muslin, squeezing hard to extract as much 'thick' milk as possible. To make 'thin' coconut milk pour another 600 ml (1 pint) of boiling water over the coconut flesh from which the thick milk has already been extracted, and repeat the process.

Creamed coconut, which can be bought in packets from many supermarkets and healthfood shops, is a very useful substitute. It is very quick to make into coconut milk by following the directions on the packet.

Concentrated butter or Ghee: A good cooking fat from India. It is better than butter because it can be heated to a higher temperature without burning. Ghee can be bought in tins or made at home. To make ghee, place 250 g (8 oz) unsalted butter in a small pan over low heat. Bring to just below simmering point and cook for 20 to 30 minutes or until it has stopped sputtering and is beginning to change colour. Strain through several thicknesses of muslin. Keep in a screw-topped jar in a cool place – refrigeration is not necessary. 250 g (8 oz) butter makes 175–200 ml (6–7 fl oz) ghee. Larger quantities take a little longer to make.

Coriander, fresh green (hara dhanya): A delicate, fragrant herb. Parsley may be substituted, but it does not have the same flavour.

Coriander seeds (dhanya): Come whole or ground. Used a lot in ground form. Very fragrant.

Cumin seeds (zeera): There are many varieties of this strong flavoured, caraway-like seed. The black variety is best. Comes ground or whole.

Curry leaves (kari patta): Aromatic leaves of the sweet Nim tree, available dried. Release an appetizing smell when cooked.

Fennel seeds (sonf): These aniseed-flavoured seeds are often chewed as a digestive. They add a fine flavour to many dishes.

Fenugreek seeds (methre): Small ochre brown seeds with a powerful bitter-sweet flavour used in Indian vegetable and pulse dishes. Use sparingly.

Fish sauce: Used in various forms throughout South East Asia as a flavouring agent and as popular as soy sauce in China and Japan. Various types are available here, so experiment until you find one to your taste.

Five Spice Powder: A Chinese mixture of five spices – anise pepper, star anise, cinnamon, cloves and fennel seeds. It is strong and pungent and should be used sparingly.

Garam Masala: A ground spice mixture used in many Indian recipes. You can buy it or prepare your own: the flavour is better when it is freshly ground. To make it, place 2 tablespoons black peppercorns, 1 tablespoon black cumin seeds, 1 small cinnamon stick, 1 teaspoon whole cloves, $\frac{1}{4}$ nutmeg, 2 teaspoons cardamom seeds and 2 tablespoons coriander seeds in a coffee grinder and grind to a powder. Store in a screw-topped jar.

Ginger, fresh (adrak): A khaki-coloured, knobbly rhizome. Should be smooth and fresh looking. Keep in a plastic bag in the refrigerator. Always peel before using. It can be grated, finely chopped or puréed in an electric blender or food processor.

Ginger, dried (sonth): Sold whole or powdered. Does not give as good a flavour as fresh ginger.

Gram flour (bessan): Ground chick peas or split peas. Excellent for making batter and used in India in place of flour.

Harusame: Japanese 'spring rain' noodles, fine and almost transparent, made from rice or potato flour.

Hoisin Sauce: A thick, brownish-red soy-based sauce. Used in China as a condiment and in cooked dishes.

Hot Pepper Oil: A hot tasting oil, made from hot chillies.

Kamaboko: Japanese ready-cooked pounded white fish sausage, with a firm texture. It has a sweet-mild flavour, with a very faint undertone of fish.

Kemiri nuts: Also known as candlenuts and used frequently in Malaysian and Indonesian cookery. Macadamia nuts or almonds may be used instead.

Ketjap manis: Indonesian sweetened soy sauce. To make your own, bring 150 g (5 oz) firmly packed demerara sugar and 250 ml (8 fl oz) of water to a simmer, stirring constantly until the sugar dissolves. Increase the heat to high and continue cooking until syrup reaches 100°C (200°F) on a sugar thermometer. Reduce the heat to low and stir in 7 tablespoons black treacle, 1 teaspoon grated fresh ginger, $\frac{1}{2}$ teaspoon ground coriander and freshly ground black pepper. Simmer 3 minutes. Keeps for 2 to 3 months, tightly sealed, in the refrigerator.

Kombu: Dried seaweed. Used to make *dashi*, the foundation Japanese stock.

Krupuk wafers: Indonesian pounded dried shrimp and tapioca 'crisps' or crackers. Deep-fried to quickly puff up into light curly crisps three times their size. Chinese prawn crackers can be used instead.

Laos root: A pungent ginger-like root, with a slightly medicinal taste, usually only available fresh in the Far East. It can be bought here in powder or dried form. There is no real substitute, so it can be omitted.

Lemon grass: Known also as *citronelle*, lemon grass is an aromatic tropical grass, with a lemon flavour. It is also sold dried, sometimes under the name of *sereh powder*. A strip of pared lemon rind may be substituted. Common in South East Asian cooking.

Lotus Leaves: Used as a wrapping for foods to be cooked to impart flavour. Dried lotus leaves are sold in packages; soak in warm water for 20 minutes before use.

Macadamia nuts: Originally from Australia, macadamia nuts are used in Malaysian and Indonesian recipes. Almonds can be used instead.

Mirin: A sweetened version of sake, used only for cooking. Dry sherry may be used as an alternative.

Mooli or Daikon: Giant Japanese white raddish. A mild white turnip or cucumber may be substituted.

Mustard seeds (sarson): Small, round reddish-black seeds. When fried for a few seconds they sputter with the heat and give out a delicious smell.

Nam pla: A salty, spiced, fermented fish mixture which is the Thai fish sauce. The Chinese type, which is easier to find, can be used instead.

Oyster Sauce: A light sauce made from oysters and soy sauce. Used for flavouring meat and vegetables.

Panir (Indian cheese): A curd cheese used in cooking. To make panir, bring 1.2 litres (2 pints) milk to the boil, remove from heat and stir in a bare $\frac{1}{4}$ teaspoon tartaric acid dissolved in 120 ml (4 fl oz) hot water. Stir gently until the milk curdles, then leave for 30 minutes. Line a sieve with muslin and strain the curdled milk, squeezing out all the liquid. Form the remaining curds into a rough rectangle about 1–1.5 cm ($\frac{1}{2}$–$\frac{3}{4}$ inch) deep in the same cloth and wrap it tightly round. Place this packet between two flat surfaces and place a 2.5 kg (5 lb) weight on top. Leave for 2 to 3 hours. 1.2 litres (2 pints) milk makes 125 g (4 oz) panir.

Peppercorns, Szechuan: Used whole or ground, in marinades and cooked dishes.

Pickled Cabbage: Usually yellow-green in colour, packed in brine in jars.

Pickled Vegetables, Szechuan: Hot and spicy in flavour, they are added to meat, fish and vegetable dishes.

Pulses (dhals): These form an important part of the Indian diet. There are nearly 60 varieties in India but the most commonly used are mung, both olive green and yellow; *masoor* or Egyptian lentils – the common salmon pink lentils available in every supermarket; *channa* – split peas; *kabli channa* or Bengal gram – chick peas; *tur* – the vari-coloured pigeon-pea; *lobia* – black-eyed peas; *dhal*-lentils; and *rajma* – red kidney beans.

Rice Stick Noodles: These are long sticks, like noodles, made from rice flour. They do not require soaking before use.

Rice vinegar: Vinegar made from rice but with far less bite than Western varieties. Cider vinegar may be used at a pinch, but the flavour will not be the same.

Rice wine: The Chinese and Japanese versions can be used interchangeably. Use dry sherry if rice wine is not available.

Saffron (kesar): Available in threads and in powdered form. The threads are soaked in hot water or milk before using. Saffron gives food a lovely yellow colour and a fine aroma and taste.

Saifon: Japanese dried soy flour noodles which can be used instead of harusame noodles.

Sake: Japanese rice wine used both in cooking and, warmed, as a beverage. An equal amount of Chinese rice wine can be a replacement in cookery.

Sansho: Japanese fragrant pepper, made from the leaf of the prickly ash. Freshly ground black pepper may be substituted.

Sesame Seed Oil: A nutty-flavoured oil, generally used in small quantities at the end of cooking.

Sesame Seed Paste: Rather like peanut butter in texture and flavour.

Sesame Seeds: Tiny, flat seeds, used in both sweet and savoury recipes. Tahini (the Middle-Eastern equivalent) may be substituted.

Shichimi: Japanese dried blend of hot spices, also known as Seven-Flavours Spice. Includes pepper leaf, rape seed, poppy seed, hemp seed, dried tangerine peel and sesame seeds. Used as a flavouring or garnish. There are several bottled proprietary brands available in this country.

Shiritaki noodles: Japanese transparent noodles made from sweet potatoes and used in sukiyaki or soups. They have a firm texture, but little taste.

Shrimps, dried: These have a strong, salty flavour.

Soba noodles: Japanese buckwheat noodles, used in soups.

Soy Sauce: The common dark variety is used unless otherwise stated. Light soy sauce is often used as an accompaniment.

Star anise: A Chinese spice with a distinctive liquorice flavour, shaped like a star with eight points.

Straw Mushrooms: Chinese. Small round type of mushroom. Available in cans.

Szechwan peppercorns: A reddish-brown Chinese peppercorn with a specially pungent flavour. Usually dry roasted in a frying pan before cooking to develop its full flavour.

Tamarind (imli): Pods from the tamarind tree, used as a souring agent. Sold as pods or pulp – pulp is easier to use. Both must be soaked in hot water, then squeezed and strained before use. Vinegar or lemon juice may be used instead.

Tofu: Ground soya bean curd is pressed and set into cakes, 7.5 cm (3 inches) square. Can be used in sweet and savoury dishes. Only use fresh tofu for cooking.

Transparent Noodles: Also called cellophane noodles, these are semi-transparent. Soak in hot water for 5 minutes before use.

Turmeric (haldi): A rhizome commonly used in its powdered form for its earthy taste and yellow colour. It stains clothing and work surfaces so be careful not to spill it.

Udon noodles: Japanese wheat noodles available in various thicknesses.

Water Chestnuts: Available in cans, these have a crunchy texture.

Water Chestnut Flour: Made from water chestnuts, this has a distinctive flavour.

Wonton Skins: Thin yellow dough from China, packed in cellophane.

Wooden Ears: Black Chinese fungi with a delicate flavour. Soak in warm water for 20 minutes before use.

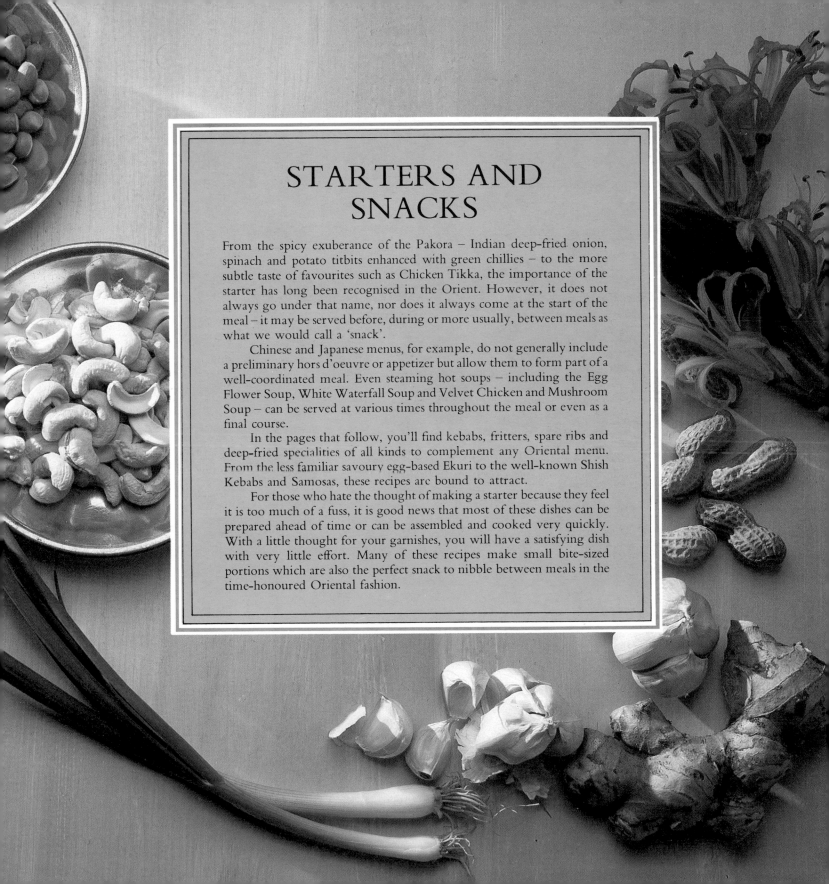

STARTERS AND SNACKS

From the spicy exuberance of the Pakora – Indian deep-fried onion, spinach and potato titbits enhanced with green chillies – to the more subtle taste of favourites such as Chicken Tikka, the importance of the starter has long been recognised in the Orient. However, it does not always go under that name, nor does it always come at the start of the meal – it may be served before, during or more usually, between meals as what we would call a 'snack'.

Chinese and Japanese menus, for example, do not generally include a preliminary hors d'oeuvre or appetizer but allow them to form part of a well-coordinated meal. Even steaming hot soups – including the Egg Flower Soup, White Waterfall Soup and Velvet Chicken and Mushroom Soup – can be served at various times throughout the meal or even as a final course.

In the pages that follow, you'll find kebabs, fritters, spare ribs and deep-fried specialities of all kinds to complement any Oriental menu. From the less familiar savoury egg-based Ekuri to the well-known Shish Kebabs and Samosas, these recipes are bound to attract.

For those who hate the thought of making a starter because they feel it is too much of a fuss, it is good news that most of these dishes can be prepared ahead of time or can be assembled and cooked very quickly. With a little thought for your garnishes, you will have a satisfying dish with very little effort. Many of these recipes make small bite-sized portions which are also the perfect snack to nibble between meals in the time-honoured Oriental fashion.

PAKORA

125 g (4 oz) gram
  flour★
1 teaspoon salt
½ teaspoon chilli
  powder★
about 150 ml (¼
  pint) water
2 green chillies★,
  finely chopped
1 tablespoon finely
  chopped coriander
  leaves★
1 teaspoon melted
  concentrated butter
  or ghee★
2 onions, cut into
  rings
oil for deep-frying
8 small spinach leaves
2–3 potatoes, par-
  boiled and sliced

Sift the flour, salt and chilli powder into a bowl. Stir in sufficient water to make a thick batter and beat well until smooth. Leave to stand for 30 minutes.

Stir the chillies and coriander into the batter, then add the melted butter or ghee. Drop in the onion rings to coat thickly with batter.

Heat the oil in a deep pan, drop in the onion rings and deep-fry until crisp and golden. Remove from the pan with a slotted spoon, drain on kitchen paper and keep warm.

Dip the spinach leaves into the batter and deep-fry in the same way, adding more oil to the pan if necessary.

Finally, repeat the process with the potato slices.

Serve hot.
Serves 4

CHICKEN TIKKA

750 g (1½ lb) chicken
  breasts
MARINADE:
1 × 150 g (5 oz)
  carton natural
  yogurt
1 tablespoon grated
  root ginger★
2 cloves garlic,
  crushed
1 teaspoon chilli
  powder★
1 tablespoon ground
  coriander★
½ teaspoon salt
juice of 1 lemon
2 tablespoons oil
TO GARNISH:
1 onion, sliced
2 tomatoes, quartered
4 lemon twists

Skin, bone and cube the chicken breasts. Mix the marinade ingredients together in a bowl. Drop the chicken cubes into the marinade, cover and leave in the refrigerator overnight.

Thread the chicken on to 4 skewers and cook under a preheated hot grill for 5 to 6 minutes, turning frequently.

Remove the chicken from the skewers and arrange on individual serving plates. Garnish with onion, tomato and lemon to serve.
Serves 4

Pakora; Chicken Tikka

INDONESIAN SPICY BEEF CRÊPES

150 g (5 oz) plain
    flour
120 ml (4 fl oz)
    milk, at room
    temperature
120 ml (4 fl oz)
    water
2 eggs, at room
    temperature, lightly
    beaten
salt
2 to 3 tablespoons
    concentrated butter
    or ghee★
FILLING:
2 teaspoons oil
350 g (12 oz) lean
    . minced beef
50 g (2 oz) peas
1 clove garlic, crushed
1 teaspoon finely
    chopped root
    ginger★
½ teaspoon sugar
½ teaspoon freshly
    ground black
    pepper
¼ teaspoon freshly
    grated nutmeg
pinch chilli powder★
salt
2 teaspoons cornflour
1 tablespoon water
85 ml (3 fl oz)
    concentrated butter
    or ghee★
TO GARNISH:
6 × 1 x 13 cm (½ x 5
    inch) thin ribbons
    of blanched spring
    onion
6 × 1 x 13 cm (½ x 5
    inch) thin ribbons
    of blanched carrots

To make the crêpes, combine all the ingredients, except the butter, in a medium bowl. Mix until just smooth. Cover and stand at room temperature for 1 hour.

Heat 1 tablespoon of the butter in a 15 cm (6 inch) non-stick frying pan over a medium-low heat. Ladle 3 tablespoons of the batter into the pan, tilting the pan until the bottom is covered with a thin layer. Cook for 1 minute until the underside is light brown, shaking the pan frequently to prevent sticking. Turn out the crêpe on to kitchen paper and cover with waxed paper. Repeat with the remaining batter.

To make the filling, heat the oil in a large frying pan over a medium-high heat. Add the beef, peas, garlic, ginger, sugar, pepper, nutmeg, chilli powder and salt. Stir-fry for 4 minutes, until the beef is almost cooked through. Remove from the heat and pour away excess fat. Dissolve the cornflour in the water and stir the mixture into the beef.

Arrange 2 tablespoons of the filling in the centre of the cooked side of each crêpe. Fold the bottom edge over the beef. Fold the sides over slightly, then roll up to enclose the filling.

Heat the butter in a large frying pan over a moderate heat. Add the filled crêpes, in batches if necessary, seam side down. Cook on both sides for about 4 minutes until brown and crisp.

To serve, tie half the crêpes around the centre with the spring onion strips. Tie the remaining crêpes around the centre with the carrot strips. Serve immediately.
Makes 12

(Picture, page 12)

AMOTIK

50 g (2 oz)
    tamarind★
6 tablespoons hot
    water
4 tablespoons oil
750 g (1½ lb)
    monkfish or other
    firm white fish,
    cubed
flour for dusting
1 onion, chopped
4 green chillies★,
    finely chopped
2 cloves garlic,
    crushed
1 teaspoon ground
    cumin★
½–1 teaspoon chilli
    powder★
salt
1 tablespoon vinegar

Soak the tamarind in the water for 30 minutes, then strain, squeezing out as much water as possible. Discard the tamarind and reserve the water.

Heat the oil in a large pan. Lightly dust the fish with flour, add to the pan and fry quickly on both sides. Remove from the pan with a slotted spoon and set aside.

Add the onion to the pan and fry until soft and golden. Add the tamarind water, chillies, garlic, cumin, chilli powder, and salt to taste and cook for 10 minutes. Add the fish and any juices and the vinegar. Simmer, uncovered, for about 5 minutes; be careful not to overcook.
Serves 4

Amotik

EKURI

50 g (2 oz) butter
1 onion, finely
    chopped
2 green chillies★,
    finely chopped
8 eggs, lightly beaten
    with 2 tablespoons
    water
1 tablespoon finely
    chopped coriander
    leaves★
salt

Heat the butter in a pan, add the onion and fry until deep golden. Add the chillies and fry for 30 seconds, then add the eggs, coriander and salt to taste, and cook, stirring, until the eggs are scrambled and set. Serve hot.
Serves 4

SHISH KEBAB

500 g (1 lb) minced
    lamb
2 tablespoons finely
    chopped celery
    leaves
2 tablespoons
    chopped parsley
2 onions, finely
    chopped
1 teaspoon turmeric★
salt and pepper
TO GARNISH:
chopped parsley
finely chopped onion

Mix all the ingredients together very thoroughly, seasoning with salt and pepper to taste. Roll the mixture into thin sausage shapes and cook under a preheated moderate grill for about 10 minutes, turning several times. Serve garnished with parsley and chopped onion.
Serves 4

Ekuri; Shish Kebab

INDONESIAN CORN AND CRAB FRITTERS

1 × 326 g (11½ oz)
   can sweetcorn,
   drained
125 g (4 oz) cooked
   white crabmeat,
   flaked
2 eggs, beaten
2 small onions, finely
   chopped
2 spring onions,
   thinly sliced
1 green chilli pepper★,
   thinly sliced
1 tablespoon cornflour
salt and black pepper
50 ml (2 fl oz) oil

Combine all the ingredients, except the oil, in a large bowl and mix well. Set aside.

Heat the oil in a large frying pan over a medium-high heat. Drop 1 heaped tablespoon of the corn mixture into the hot oil, flattening it into an oblong with the back of the spoon. Cook on both sides for 3 minutes until brown. Repeat with the remaining fritter batter, in batches if necessary. Remove with a slotted spoon and drain on kitchen paper. Transfer the fritters to a heated serving platter and serve immediately.
Makes about 15

Fish Fritters

INDIAN KEBAB

750 g (1½ lb)
   minced beef
1 small onion, grated
2 cloves garlic,
   crushed
1 tablespoon tomato
   purée
juice of ½ lemon or
   1 lime
1 tablespoon plain
   flour
½ teaspoon each
   ground cumin★,
   chilli powder★ and
   ground coriander★
pinch each of ground
   cinnamon, ginger,
   nutmeg and cloves
salt and pepper
TO GARNISH:
few lettuce leaves,
   shredded
lemon twists
cucumber slices

Put the meat, onion, garlic, tomato purée, lemon or lime juice and flour into a bowl and mix well. Stir in all the spices and mix thoroughly. Season well with salt and pepper and mix until smooth.

Divide the mixture into 6 portions and shape around skewers to make long thin rissoles. Refrigerate if possible for 1 to 2 hours until firm.

Place under a preheated hot grill and cook for 15 to 20 minutes, turning occasionally, until well browned.

Arrange the kebabs on a bed of lettuce, garnish with lemon twists and cucumber slices, and serve hot, with rice.
Serves 6

FISH FRITTERS

6 tablespoons oil
2 onions, chopped
1 tablespoon ground
   coriander★
3 green chillies★,
   seeded and chopped
1 teaspoon salt
1 teaspoon pepper
750 g (1½ lb) cod
   fillets, skinned and
   cut into small
   pieces
2 tablespoons finely
   chopped coriander
   leaves★
BATTER:
125 g (4 oz) gram
   flour★
½ teaspoon chilli
   powder★
½ teaspoon salt
1 egg, beaten
7 tablespoons water

Heat 3 tablespoons of the oil in a pan, add the onions and fry until just soft. Stir in the coriander, chillies, salt and pepper, then add the fish. Fry for 2 minutes, then cover and cook on very low heat for 2 minutes. Break up the mixture with a fork and add the chopped coriander. Remove from the heat and set aside while making the batter.

Sift the flour, chilli powder and salt into a bowl. Add the egg and water and beat well to make a smooth batter. Leave to stand for 30 minutes, then stir in the fish mixture.

Heat the remaining oil in a frying pan and drop in small spoonfuls of the batter mixture. Fry on both sides until golden. Drain thoroughly and keep warm while frying the remainder.
Serves 4

MEAT PUFFS

3 tablespoons self-
  raising flour
3 eggs, beaten
5–6 tablespoons water
250 g (8 oz) minced
  beef
1 bunch of spring
  onions, finely
  sliced
1 green chilli★, finely
  chopped
1 teaspoon turmeric★
salt
oil for frying

Sift the flour into a bowl, add the eggs and beat well to combine. Gradually add enough water to make a thick creamy batter, beating well.

Stir in the minced beef, onions, chilli, turmeric, and salt to taste; the mixture should be like a stiff porridge. Leave in a warm place for 1 hour.

Heat about 1 cm (½ inch) depth of oil in a frying pan. When really hot, drop in spoonfuls of the meat mixture and fry on each side for 2 minutes. Drain well and keep warm while cooking the remainder, adding more oil as required. Serve hot.

Serves 4

BRINJAL CUTLETS

2 large aubergines
salt
3 tablespoons oil
1 onion, finely
  chopped
1 clove garlic, finely
  chopped
2 green chillies★,
  seeded and finely
  chopped
1 teaspoon turmeric★
500 g (1 lb) minced
  beef
1 egg, lightly beaten
2–3 tablespoons fresh
  breadcrumbs

Cook the whole aubergines in boiling salted water for 15 minutes or until almost tender. Drain thoroughly and cool.

Heat the oil in a pan, add the onion and fry until golden. Add the garlic, chillies and turmeric and fry for 2 minutes. Add the mince and cook, stirring, until brown all over. Add salt to taste and cook gently for 20 minutes, until the meat is tender.

Cut the aubergines in half lengthways. Carefully scoop out the pulp, add it to the meat mixture and mix well. Check the seasoning. Fill the aubergine shells with the mixture, brush with egg and cover with breadcrumbs. Cook under a preheated moderate grill for 4 to 5 minutes, until golden.

Serves 4

Meat Puffs; Brinjal Cutlets

PRAWNS IN GINGER SAUCE

8 spring onions,
  chopped
5 cm (2 inch) piece
  root ginger★, chopped
2 tablespoons dry
  sherry
2 tablespoons soy
  sauce★
150 ml (¼ pint)
  chicken stock
salt and pepper
12 peeled
  Mediterranean
  prawns

Put all the ingredients, except the prawns, into a saucepan, seasoning with salt and pepper to taste. Bring to the boil, then simmer for 2 minutes. Stir in the prawns, cover and cook for 3 minutes. Serve immediately, with rice or noodles.
Serves 4

Hot and Sour Soup

SWEET AND SOUR SPARE RIBS

1 kg (2 lb) lean
  spare ribs, cut into
  5 cm (2 inch)
  pieces
salt
2 tablespoons oil
1 piece root ginger★,
  finely chopped
1 clove garlic, crushed
SAUCE:
4 tablespoons clear
  honey
4 tablespoons malt
  vinegar
2 tablespoons soy
  sauce★
1 × 142 g (5 oz) can
  tomato purée
1 teaspoon mixed
  herbs
2 teaspoons chilli
  powder★
dash of Worcester-
  shire sauce
2 cloves garlic,
  crushed

Mix all the sauce ingredients together, cover and set aside.

Sprinkle the spare ribs with salt. Heat the oil in a wok or deep frying pan, add the ginger and garlic and fry for 1 minute. Add the spare ribs and fry quickly until browned. Lower the heat and cook for 10 minutes.

Spoon the sauce over the spare ribs and turn to coat them evenly. Cover the pan with foil or a lid and simmer gently for 25 to 30 minutes, until the meat is tender, stirring occasionally.

To serve, arrange the spare ribs on a warmed serving dish. Serve immediately.
Serves 4 to 6

HOT AND SOUR SOUP

4 dried Chinese
  mushrooms★
900 ml (1½ pints)
  stock
175 g (6 oz)
  shrimps, fresh or
  frozen and thawed
50 g (2 oz)
  Szechuan pickled
  vegetables★, sliced
50 g (2 oz) canned
  bamboo shoots★,
  drained and
  shredded
2 celery sticks, sliced
  diagonally
½ cucumber, cut into
  5 cm (2 inch)
  matchstick pieces
2 tablespoons sherry
2 tablespoons soy
  sauce★
1 tablespoon red
  wine vinegar
25 g (1 oz) ham,
  diced
1 spring onion,
  chopped

Soak the mushrooms in warm water for 15 minutes. Squeeze dry, discard the hard stalks, then slice the mushroom caps.

Bring the stock to the boil, add the shrimps, pickled vegetables, bamboo shoots, mushrooms and celery and simmer for 5 minutes.

Add the cucumber to the pan with the sherry, soy sauce, vinegar and ham and cook for 1 minute. Sprinkle with the spring onion and serve immediately.
Serves 4 to 6

Egg Flower Soup; Soup with Beef Balls

EGG FLOWER SOUP

4–5 wooden ears★
  (optional)
2 tablespoons soy
  sauce★
2 teaspoons cornflour
175 g (6 oz) pork
  fillet, shredded
900 ml (1½ pints)
  stock
1 teaspoon salt
2 eggs
2 spring onions,
  chopped
1 tablespoon chopped
  coriander leaves★

Soak the wooden ears in warm water, if using, for 10 minutes. Rinse and drain well, then chop roughly.

Blend the soy sauce and cornflour together. Add the pork and toss until evenly coated. Bring the stock to the boil, add the salt, pork and wooden ears, if using, and cook for 5 minutes.

Beat the eggs until frothy and pour into the boiling stock, stirring constantly. Remove from the heat, add the spring onions and coriander and serve immediately.
Serves 4 to 6

SOUP WITH BEEF BALLS

4–5 dried Chinese
  mushrooms★
350 g (12 oz) lean
  beef, minced
1 onion, finely
  chopped
1 tablespoon
  cornflour
1 egg
salt
900 ml (1½ pints)
  beef stock
1 bunch watercress,
  stalks removed
3 spring onions,
  finely chopped
1 tablespoon soy
  sauce★

Soak the mushrooms in warm water for 15 minutes. Squeeze dry and discard the hard stalks, then slice the mushroom caps.

Mix the beef, onion, cornflour and egg together. Add salt to taste and shape the mixture into small balls. Drop the meat balls into iced water for 15 minutes; drain thoroughly.

Meanwhile, heat the stock in a large pan. Add the meat balls and cook for 10 minutes. Add the mushrooms, watercress, spring onions and soy sauce and cook for 2 minutes. Serve hot.
Serves 4 to 6

SWEETCORN AND PRAWN SOUP

2 teaspoons finely
  chopped root
  ginger★
1 tablespoon dry
  sherry
250 g (8 oz) frozen
  peeled prawns,
  thawed
900 ml (1½ pints)
  chicken stock
1 × 326 g (11½ oz)
  can sweetcorn,
  drained
salt
50 g (2 oz) lean
  ham, diced
1 tablespoon chopped
  chives

Mix the ginger, sherry and prawns together. Bring the stock to the boil, then stir in the prawn mixture. Add the sweetcorn to the pan with salt to taste. Cook for 2 minutes, stirring occasionally.

Sprinkle with the ham and chives and serve immediately.

Serves 4 to 6

PORK SPARE RIB SOUP

1 tablespoon oil
500 g (1 lb) pork
  spare ribs, cut into
  2.5 cm (1 inch)
  pieces
2 teaspoons shredded
  root ginger★
1 clove garlic, sliced
2 spring onions,
  chopped
900 ml (1½ pints)
  beef stock
1 teaspoon salt
2 tomatoes, diced
250 g (8 oz) bean
  sprouts★

Heat the oil in a pan, add the spare ribs and fry for 5 minutes until golden brown. Add the ginger, garlic and spring onions and cook for 2 minutes. Add the stock and bring to the boil. Cover and simmer for 1 hour or until the meat is tender.

Add the remaining ingredients and cook for 1 minute. Serve hot.

Serves 4 to 6

Hot Peppery Soup; Sweetcorn and Prawn Soup; Pork Spare Ribs Soup

HOT PEPPERY SOUP

2 tablespoons oil
2 red or green
  chillies★, seeded
  and chopped
2 cakes tofu★, each
  cut into 10 pieces
125 g (4 oz) skinned
  chicken breast,
  minced
1 tablespoon cornflour
900 ml (1½ pints)
  chicken stock
8 crisp lettuce leaves,
  each torn into 3 or
  4 pieces
2 tablespoons soy
  sauce★
2 spring onions,
  chopped
125 g (4 oz) peeled
  prawns
1 tablespoon cider
  vinegar
pepper

Heat the oil in a wok or frying pan, add the chillies and fry briskly for about 30 seconds to extract all the oil and flavour; discard the chillies. Add the tofu to the pan and fry for 3 or 4 minutes until golden brown. Drain and set aside.

Mix the chicken and cornflour together.

Heat the stock in a large pan. Add the chicken and cornflour mixture and stir until evenly mixed. Add the lettuce, soy sauce, spring onions, prawns and cider vinegar. Bring to the boil, then add pepper to taste. Cook for 2 minutes. Add the tofu and serve hot.

Serves 4 to 6

HOT JUMBO PRAWNS

1 teaspoon root
　ginger★, chopped
3 spring onions,
　chopped
12 giant peeled
　Mediterranean
　prawns
3 tablespoons self-
　raising flour
pinch of salt
½–1 teaspoon chilli
　powder★
¼ teaspoon paprika
3 teaspoons dry sherry
1 egg, beaten
1 tablespoon chopped
　coriander leaves★
oil for deep-frying
coriander leaves and
　tomato flowers (see
　page 155) to
　garnish

Mix together the ginger, spring onions and prawns. Place the flour, salt, chilli powder and paprika in a bowl. Add the sherry and egg and beat to a smooth batter. Fold in the coriander and the prawn mixture.

Heat the oil in a wok to 160°C (325°F) and deep-fry half the battered prawns for 2 to 3 minutes, until golden brown. Drain on kitchen paper and keep hot while frying the remaining prawns.

Arrange on a warmed serving dish, garnish with coriander leaves and tomato flowers and serve immediately.
Serves 4

PRAWNS WITH ASPARAGUS

175 g (6 oz) fresh
　asparagus, cut into
　2.5 cm (1 inch)
　pieces
salt
4 tablespoons dry
　sherry
1 teaspoon light soy
　sauce★
500 g (1 lb) peeled
　prawns
2 tablespoons oil
2 cloves garlic, thinly
　sliced
2 teaspoons finely
　chopped root
　ginger★
4 spring onions,
　chopped

Blanch the asparagus in boiling salted water for 2 minutes; drain well and set aside.

Mix the sherry and soy sauce together in a large bowl. Stir in the prawns and leave to stand for 15 minutes.

Heat the oil in a wok and quickly stir-fry the garlic, ginger and half the spring onions. Add the prawns and marinade, and the asparagus and stir-fry for 1 to 2 minutes, until the ingredients are hot.

Transfer to a warmed serving dish and sprinkle with the remaining spring onions. Serve immediately.
Serves 4

CLAM AND ABALONE SOUP

8–10 dried Chinese
　mushrooms★
1.2 litres (2 pints)
　stock
50 g (2 oz)
　abalone★, thinly
　sliced
125 g (4 oz) boneless
　chicken breast,
　thinly sliced
1 cm (½ inch) piece
　root ginger★, diced
1–2 tablespoons dry
　sherry
1 tablespoon soy
　sauce★
1 × 227 g (8 oz) can
　clams, drained
chopped spring onion
　to garnish

Soak the mushrooms in warm water for 15 minutes. Squeeze dry and discard the hard stalks, then cut the mushroom caps into quarters.

Bring the stock to the boil and add the abalone, chicken and ginger. Simmer for 2 minutes, add the remaining ingredients and cook for 2 minutes.

Sprinkle with the spring onion and serve immediately.
Serves 4 to 6

Prawns with Asparagus; Hot Jumbo Prawns

SHREDDED PORK AND NOODLES IN SOUP

3–4 dried Chinese
  mushrooms★
  (optional)
250 g (8 oz) lean
  pork, shredded
1 tablespoon soy
  sauce★
1 tablespoon dry
  sherry
350 g (12 oz) egg
  noodles
900 ml (1½ pints)
  stock
4 spring onions,
  chopped
125 g (4 oz) canned
  bamboo shoots★,
  drained and
  shredded
few Chinese leaves★,
  shredded

Soak the mushrooms in warm water for 15 minutes, if using. Squeeze dry, discard the hard stalks, then slice the mushroom caps.

Put the pork into a bowl, add the soy sauce and sherry and leave to marinate for 10 to 15 minutes.

Cook the noodles in boiling salted water for about 5 minutes, or until cooked; drain.

Bring the stock to the boil, add the mushrooms, if using, pork, marinade, spring onions and bamboo shoots. Simmer for 2 to 3 minutes, then add the noodles and Chinese leaves. Cook for 2 minutes. Serve hot.

Serves 4 to 6

VELVET CHICKEN AND MUSHROOM SOUP

1 egg white
2 teaspoons cornflour
175 g (6 oz) chicken
  breast, cut into
  matchstick pieces
900 ml (1½ pints)
  chicken stock
50 g (2 oz) button
  mushrooms, sliced
75 g (3 oz) canned
  bamboo shoots★
  drained and
  shredded
1 teaspoon finely
  chopped root
  ginger★
2 spring onions,
  chopped
½ teaspoon salt
1 tablespoon soy
  sauce★

Put the egg white and cornflour into a bowl and mix well. Add the chicken and toss until evenly coated.

Bring the stock to the boil, add the chicken and remaining ingredients and simmer for 3 minutes. Serve hot.

Serves 4 to 6

PURE VEGETABLE SOUP

4 dried Chinese
  mushrooms★
25 g (1 oz)
  transparent
  noodles★
½ bunch watercress
900 ml (1½ pints)
  stock
2 courgettes, diced
1 small turnip, diced
50 g (2 oz) spinach,
  chopped
2 carrots, diced
1 teaspoon salt
1 tablespoon soy
  sauce★
2 spring onions,
  chopped

Soak the mushrooms in warm water for 15 minutes. Squeeze dry and discard the hard stalks, then slice the mushroom caps.

Soak the noodles in hot water for 10 minutes; drain. Remove the stalks from the watercress and divide the leaves.

Bring the stock to the boil. Add the courgettes, turnip, watercress, spinach and carrots. Simmer for 20 minutes.

Add the remaining ingredients and cook for 5 minutes. Serve hot.

Serves 4 to 6

Shredded Pork and Noodles Soup; Velvet Chicken and Mushroom Soup; Pure Vegetable Soup

WHITE WATERFALL SOUP

75 g (3 oz) pork
  tenderloin, cut into
  5 mm (¼ inch)
  slices
25 ml (1 fl oz) soy
  sauce★
1 tablespoon mirin★
  or dry sherry and
  1 teaspoon sugar
900 ml (1½ pints)
  clear chicken stock
1 carrot, sliced into
  matchstick pieces
25 g (1 oz) shirataki
  noodles★ or
  spaghettini
2 tablespoons sesame
  seed oil★
¼ teaspoon hot pepper
  oil★ or Tabasco
  sauce
salt
12 mange tout to
  garnish

Place the pork in a small bowl, then add the soy sauce and mirin. Stir to coat the pork completely. Cover and set aside.

Bring the stock to a simmer in a large saucepan over a moderate heat. Remove the pork from the soy sauce mixture with a slotted spoon and add to the stock. Add the carrot and noodles, then simmer for 3 minutes, skimming frequently. Stir in the sesame seed oil, hot pepper oil and salt. Divide the mange tout between four heated soup bowls, then ladle the soup into the bowls.

Serves 4

MISTY FRIED PRAWNS

75 g (3 oz)
  harusame★ or
  saifon★ noodles
30 × 50 g (2 oz) large
  uncooked prawns,
  peeled, deveined
  but tails left intact
50 g (2 oz) plain
  flour
¼ teaspoon sansho★
salt
2 egg whites
oil for deep-frying
lemon wedges to
  garnish
soy sauce★ for dipping

Using scissors cut the noodles into 1 cm (½ inch) pieces. Set aside.

Score the underside of the prawns to prevent curling. Combine the flour, sansho and salt in a plastic bag. Add the prawns to the flour mixture in batches and shake to coat lightly.

Beat the egg whites until foamy. Dip each prawn into the egg white, then pat on the noodles, covering the prawn completely.

Heat the oil in a wok or large saucepan to 180°C (350°F) or until a cube of bread turns brown in 30 seconds. Lower the prawns carefully into the oil in batches. Fry for about 3 minutes until opaque. The noodles should remain pale. Drain on kitchen paper. Serve hot with the lemon wedges and soy sauce.

Serves 8 as part of a Japanese meal

SUNOMONO

1 large cucumber,
  thinly sliced
salt
120 ml (4 fl oz) rice
  wine vinegar★ or
  cider vinegar
3 tablespoons caster
  sugar
1 tablespoon soy
  sauce★
TO GARNISH:
125 g (4 oz) peeled
  prawns
2 thin lemon slices,
  cut in half
4 parsley sprigs

Sprinkle the cucumber slices liberally with the salt and drain in a colander for 30 minutes. Press the slices gently to remove the excess moisture, then place in a medium bowl.

Stir the vinegar, sugar and soy sauce together in a small bowl until the sugar has dissolved. Pour over the cucumber slices and toss well.

To serve, lift the cucumber slices out of the dressing and arrange in four individual bowls. Garnish each one with an equal amount of the prawns, then top with the lemon slices and parsley sprigs. Serve immediately.

Serves 4

CURRIED FRIED SPARE RIBS

50 ml (2 fl oz) soy
  sauce★
2 tablespoons Chinese
  rice wine★ or dry
  sherry
1 tablespoon curry
  powder or to taste
2–3 cloves garlic,
  crushed
salt and black pepper
1 kg (2 lb) pork spare
  ribs, ribs separated
  and cut into 5 cm
  (2 inch) lengths
1 large egg (size 1 or
  2) lightly beaten
250 g (8 oz) cornflour
oil for deep-frying
fresh coriander sprigs★
  to garnish

In a large bowl, combine the soy sauce, rice wine, curry powder, garlic, salt and pepper. Add the ribs, tossing well to coat with the mixture. Cover and marinate for 1 hour.

Add the egg to the mixture, then toss the ribs again. On a large plate, dredge the ribs through the cornflour, shaking off the excess, and press the coating firmly on to the meat

Pour the oil into a wok or large frying pan and heat to 180°C (350°F) or until a cube of bread turns brown in 30 seconds. Add the ribs and deep-fry in batches if necessary, for 5 to 6 minutes, turning occasionally, until they are golden. Drain on kitchen paper.

Skim any particles from the surface of the oil. Heat the oil to 200°C (400°F). Add the ribs, and fry for 3 minutes, or until they are a deep golden colour. Drain on kitchen paper. Garnish and serve hot.

Serves 6

White Waterfall Soup; Sunomono

DEEP-FRIED SCALLOPS

12 scallops, fresh or
  thawed if frozen
½ teaspoon very
  finely chopped root
  ginger★
2 spring onions,
  finely chopped
3 tablespoons
  self-raising flour
pinch of salt
2 teaspoons dry
  sherry
1 egg, beaten
oil for deep-frying
TO GARNISH:
tomato flower (see
  page 155)
coriander leaves★

Cut the scallops in half. Parcook fresh
ones in boiling water for 1 minute;
drain thoroughly. Mix the scallops
with the ginger and spring onions.

Put the flour and salt into a bowl,
add the sherry and egg and beat to a
smooth batter. Fold in the scallops and
toss until evenly coated.

Heat the oil in a wok or deep-fryer
to 160°C (325°F) and deep-fry the
scallops for 2 to 3 minutes until golden
brown. Drain on kitchen paper.

Arrange on a warmed serving dish
and garnish with a tomato flower and
coriander leaves. Serve immediately.
Serves 4

QUICK-FRIED PRAWNS

125 g (4 oz) fresh
  asparagus, cut into
  2.5 cm (1 inch)
  pieces (optional)
4 tablespoons dry
  sherry
1 egg white
pinch of salt
500 g (1 lb) peeled
  prawns, fresh or
  thawed if frozen
1 tablespoon oil
1 teaspoon finely
  chopped root
  ginger★
2 spring onions,
  chopped

Cook the asparagus in boiling salted
water for 5 minutes, if using; drain
thoroughly.

Mix 2 tablespoons of the sherry
with the egg white and salt. Add the
prawns and toss until evenly coated;
drain.

Heat the oil in a wok or frying pan,
add the ginger and half the spring
onions and fry for 2 minutes. Add the
prawns and cook for 5 minutes, or
until they become pink. Add the
asparagus, if using, and remaining
sherry and cook for 1 minute.

Transfer to a warmed serving dish
and sprinkle with the remaining spring
onions. Serve immediately.
Serves 4 to 6

Deep-Fried Scallops; Quick-Fried Prawns

FRIED WONTON WITH SWEET AND SOUR SAUCE

3 tablespoons soy
  sauce★
1 tablespoon dry
  sherry
500 g (1 lb) minced
  pork
1 teaspoon brown
  sugar
1 clove garlic,
  crushed
1 piece root ginger★,
  finely chopped
250 g (8 oz) frozen
  spinach, thawed
  and squeezed dry
500 g (1 lb) wonton
  skins★, cut into 5
  cm (2 inch) squares
oil for deep-frying
spring onion flowers
  to garnish (see
  page 155)
SAUCE:
2 teaspoons
  cornflour,
1 tablespoon
  water
1 tablespoon oil
2 cloves garlic,
  crushed
2 tablespoons soy
  sauce★
2 tablespoons clear
  honey
2 tablespoons wine
  vinegar
2 teaspoons chilli
  sauce★
1 tablespoon dry
  sherry
2 tablespoons tomato
  purée

Put the soy sauce, sherry and pork into a bowl and mix well. Add the sugar, garlic, ginger and spinach and mix well. Spoon a little of this mixture on to the centre of each wonton skin. Dampen the edges and fold to form triangles, pressing the edges together firmly to ensure that the filling does not come out during frying.

Heat the oil in a wok or deep-fryer and fry the wonton, a few at a time, for about 5 minutes until golden brown. Drain on kitchen paper and keep hot.

To make the sauce: blend the cornflour with the water. Heat the oil in a pan, add the garlic and fry for 1 minute. Stir in the remaining ingredients, bring to the boil and simmer for 2 minutes. Spoon into a small serving bowl.

Arrange the wonton on a warmed serving dish, with the sauce bowl in the centre. Garnish with spring onion flowers. Serve immediately, dipping each wonton into the sauce before eating.
Serves 4 to 6

CRISPY SPRING ROLLS

250 g (8 oz) plain
  flour
pinch of salt
1 egg
300 ml (½ pint)
  water
  (approximately)
oil for deep-frying
FILLING:
1 tablespoon oil
250 g (8 oz) lean
  pork, shredded
1 clove garlic, crushed
2 celery sticks, sliced
125 g (4 oz) button
  mushrooms, sliced
2 spring onions,
  chopped
125 g (4 oz) bean
  sprouts★
125 g (4 oz) frozen
  peeled prawns,
  thawed
2 tablespoons soy
  sauce★

Sift the flour and salt into a bowl. Add the egg and beat in sufficient water to make a smooth batter.

Lightly oil a 20 cm (8 inch) frying pan and place over moderate heat. Pour in just enough batter to cover the base of the pan. Cook until the underside is pale brown, then turn and cook the other side. Remove from the pan and put on one side. Repeat with the remaining batter.

To make the filling: heat the oil in a pan, add the pork and brown quickly. Add the garlic and vegetables; stir-fry for 2 minutes. Mix in the prawns and soy sauce. Leave until cool.

Place 2 to 3 tablespoons of the filling in the centre of each pancake. Fold in the sides and form into a tight roll, sticking down the edge with a little flour and water paste.

Heat the oil in a wok or deep-fryer and deep-fry the spring rolls a few at a time until golden brown. Drain on kitchen paper. Serve immediately.
Serves 4 to 6

Crispy Spring Rolls

CRISPY PANCAKE ROLLS

250 g (8 oz) plain
    flour
pinch of salt
1 egg
300 ml (½ pint) water
FILLING:
1 tablespoon oil
1 teaspoon finely
    chopped root
    ginger★
2 cloves garlic,
    crushed
250 g (8 oz) boneless
    chicken breast,
    skinned and diced
2 tablespoons soy
    sauce★
1 tablespoon dry
    sherry
125 g (4 oz) button
    mushrooms, sliced
2 celery sticks, sliced
3 spring onions,
    chopped
50 g (2 oz) peeled
    prawns
1 tablespoon chopped
    coriander leaves★

Sift the flour and salt into a bowl, add the egg and beat in sufficient water to give a smooth batter.

Lightly oil a 20 cm (8 inch) frying pan and place over a moderate heat. Pour in just enough batter to cover the base and cook until the underside is golden. Turn and cook the other side; set aside. Repeat with the remaining batter.

To make the filling, heat the oil in a wok or deep frying pan, add the ginger and garlic and cook for 30 seconds. Add the chicken and brown quickly. Stir in the soy sauce and sherry, then the mushrooms, celery and spring onions. Increase the heat and cook for 1 minute, stirring. Stir in the prawns and coriander off the heat, and leave until cool.

Place 2 or 3 tablespoons of the filling in the centre of each pancake. Fold in the sides and form into a tight roll, sealing the edge with a little flour and water paste. Deep-fry the rolls a few at a time for 2 to 3 minutes. Drain and serve.
Serves 4 to 6

DEEP-FRIED DRUMSTICKS

8 chicken drumsticks
50 g (2 oz) plain
    flour
1 egg (size 2) beaten
oil for deep-frying
MARINADE:
2 tablespoons dry
    sherry
2 tablespoons soy
    sauce★
pinch of sugar
4 cloves garlic,
    crushed
2 teaspoons finely
    chopped root
    ginger★
4 spring onions,
    chopped
TO GARNISH:
lemon slices
parsley sprigs

Make the marinade by putting the sherry, soy sauce, sugar, garlic, ginger and spring onions into a bowl; add the chicken and turn to coat. Leave for 30 minutes. Remove the chicken; reserve the marinade.

Sift the flour into a bowl and beat in the egg. Gradually beat in the marinade, to form a smooth paste. Dip the chicken into the batter and turn to coat evenly. Heat the oil in a wok or deep frying pan and deep-fry the chicken for 12 to 15 minutes, until golden brown and cooked through. Drain on kitchen paper.

Serve immediately, garnished with lemon and parsley.
Serves 4

Crispy Pancake Rolls; Deep-Fried Drumsticks

TEMPURA

900 ml (1½ pints) oil
 for deep-frying
12 peeled
 Mediterranean
 prawns, with tails
 left on
500 g (1 lb) plaice or
 sole fillets, skinned
 and cut into small
 pieces
8 button mushrooms
1 bunch spring onions,
 cut into 3.5 cm (1½
 inch) lengths
1 red and 1 green
 pepper, cored,
 seeded and sliced
1 large onion, cut into
 wedges
½ small cauliflower,
 broken into florets
½ small aubergine,
 thinly sliced
BATTER:
1 egg
150 ml (¼ pint) water
125 g (4 oz) plain
 flour
50 g (2 oz) cornflour
pinch of salt
DIPPING SAUCE:
300 ml (½ pint)
 canned chicken
 consommé
4 tablespoons sweet
 vermouth or sherry
4 tablespoons light soy
 sauce★

For the batter, lightly beat the egg in a large bowl. Beat in the water until frothy. Sift the flour, cornflour and salt together and fold in gradually. Heat the oil in a wok or deep frying pan. Dip the fish and vegetables in the batter, then deep-fry in batches until golden. Drain on kitchen paper; keep warm.

Heat the sauce ingredients together, then pour into a warmed serving bowl. Serve with the Tempura.
Serves 4–6

TEMPURA
Tempura is one of the most celebrated Japanese dishes. Deep-fried foods are noted for their delicacy, with the crisp batter so thin that the colours and textures of the food show through. The addition of sesame oil to the frying oil gives the food a distinctive nutty flavour. For best results the fish and vegetables should be ice-cold before coating, and the batter made at the last minute.

Crispy Vegetables

CRISPY VEGETABLES

500 g (1 lb) mixed
 vegetables, e.g.
 cauliflower, beans,
 mushrooms, mange
 tout, peppers, cut
 into small pieces
oil for deep-frying
AVOCADO DIP:
1–2 cloves garlic,
 roughly chopped
1 small onion,
 roughly chopped
4 tomatoes, skinned,
 seeded and chopped
1 teaspoon chilli
 powder★
2 avocados, peeled
 and stoned
1 tablespoon chopped
 coriander leaves★
pinch of ground
 coriander★
1 tablespoon lime or
 lemon juice
BATTER:
125 g (4 oz) plain
 flour
pinch of salt
1 tablespoon oil
150 ml (¼ pint) water
2 egg whites, stiffly
 whisked

Put the dip ingredients into a food processor or electric blender and work until smooth. Spoon into a serving dish, cover with cling film and chill for not more than 30 minutes.

For the batter, sift the flour and salt into a bowl, gradually beat in the oil and water, then fold in the egg whites. Heat the oil in a wok or deep frying pan. Drop the vegetables into the batter, then deep-fry in batches for 2 to 3 minutes, until golden. Drain on kitchen paper. Serve with the avocado dip.
Serves 6

CHINESE TEA EGGS

10 large eggs
1.2 litres (2 pints)
  water
25 g (1 oz) Chinese
  black tea leaves
25 ml (1 fl oz)
  Chinese rice wine★
  or dry sherry
2 thin slices root
  ginger★, crushed
7.5 cm (3 inch)
  cinnamon stick★
¾ tablespoon salt
½ tablespoon soy
  sauce★
2 whole star anise★

Place the eggs in a large saucepan with enough cold water to cover them by 2.5 cm (1 inch). Bring the water to the boil over a moderate heat, then simmer for 10 minutes. Drain the eggs in a colander and refresh under cold running water.

In the saucepan, combine all the remaining ingredients with the measured water. Bring the mixture to the boil over a moderate heat. Cover, then simmer for 15 minutes.

With the back of a spoon, tap the eggs lightly all over to crack the shells but do not peel. Add the eggs to the tea mixture. Cover and simmer gently for 45 minutes.

Remove the pan from the heat and let the eggs remain in the liquid until they are cool enough to handle. Carefully peel the eggs, then transfer to a serving dish. Serve hot, at room temperature or chilled.
Makes 10

EGG AND COCONUT CURRY

2–3 tablespoons oil
5 cm (2 inch) stick
  cinnamon★
6 cardamom pods★
6 cloves
2 onions, finely
  chopped
2 cloves garlic, finely
  chopped
2.5 cm (1 inch) piece
  root ginger★, grated
4 green chillies★, 2
  finely chopped and
  2 slit
450 ml (¾ pint) thick
  coconut milk★
salt
¼ teaspoon freshly
  grated nutmeg
6 hard-boiled eggs,
  halved

Heat the oil in a saucepan and add the cinnamon, cardamom pods and cloves. Fry for a few seconds and as they change colour add the onions, garlic, ginger and chopped chillies. Fry gently, stirring, until soft and golden.

Pour in the coconut milk and bring to the boil. Add the salt, nutmeg and the slit green chillies and simmer for 10 minutes or until the sauce is thick. Add the eggs and simmer for a further 5 minutes.

Transfer to a warmed serving dish.
Serves 4

EGGS IN CHILLI SAUCE

⅓–1 teaspoon small
  dried red chillies★
2 onions, chopped
4 cloves garlic
15 g (½ oz) unsalted
  peanuts
1 teaspoon powdered
  lemon grass★ or
  grated lemon rind
1 teaspoon blachan★
  or shrimp paste
1 teaspoon salt
1 teaspoon sugar
2 tablespoons oil
300 ml (½ pint) thick
  coconut milk★
6 curry leaves★
6 hard-boiled eggs

Put the first 8 ingredients into a food processor or electric blender and work until smooth.

Heat the oil in a wok or frying pan and fry the spice paste for 3 to 4 minutes; stir well and add a little water if it gets too dry. Stir in the coconut milk and curry leaves and bring to the boil. Add the eggs and simmer for 15 minutes or until the sauce thickens.

Transfer to a warmed serving dish.
Serves 4

Eggs in Chilli Sauce; Egg and Coconut Curry

COCONUT PRAWN BALLS

500 g (1 lb) fresh
   peeled prawns
2 eggs, beaten
50 g (2 oz) grated
   fresh coconut★
1 tablespoon cornflour
1 teaspoon ground
   coriander★
salt
250 ml (8 fl oz) oil

Place the prawns in a food processor or electric blender and grind coarsely. Transfer to a large bowl. Add all the remaining ingredients, except the oil, and stir until well mixed. Cover and chill for 1 hour.

Heat the oil in a wok or large frying pan over a medium-high heat. Spoon heaped teaspoons of the prawn mixture into the hot oil and cook for 3 minutes, turning occasionally, until lightly browned. Remove with a slotted spoon and drain on kitchen paper. Repeat with the remaining prawn mixture. Transfer to a heated serving platter and serve immediately.
Makes about 30

POACHED EGG CURRY

3 tablespoons oil
1 teaspoon mustard
   seeds★
6 curry leaves★
4 onions, finely
   chopped
2 cloves garlic,
   crushed
2–4 green chillies★,
   finely chopped
3.5 cm (1½ inch) piece
   root ginger★, grated
1 teaspoon turmeric★
1 tablespoon ground
   coriander★
1 teaspoon chilli
   powder★
salt
1 × 397 g (14 oz) can
   tomatoes, sieved
4 eggs

Heat the oil in a large frying pan and add the mustard seeds and curry leaves. When the seeds begin to pop, add the onions, garlic, chillies and ginger. Fry, stirring, until soft and golden.

Add the turmeric, coriander, chilli powder and salt to taste and fry, stirring, for 2 to 3 minutes. Stir in the tomatoes and cook for 15 to 20 minutes; add a little water if the curry becomes too thick.

Adjust the quantity of salt if necessary. Break the eggs into the curry and cook gently until they are cooked to your liking. Serve immediately.
Serves 4

EGG CURRY WITH YOGURT

50 g (2 oz) butter
2 cloves garlic,
   crushed
1 tablespoon finely
   grated root ginger★
1 onion, chopped
¼ teaspoon turmeric★
1 teaspoon chilli
   powder★
5 tablespoons strained
   yogurt
1 × 227 g (8 oz) can
   tomatoes, chopped
salt
6 hard-boiled eggs
1 tablespoon chopped
   coriander leaves★
   (optional)

Melt the butter in a large frying pan, add the garlic, ginger and onion and fry over low heat until soft and golden. Add the turmeric and chilli powder and fry, stirring, for a few seconds.

Stir in 1 tablespoon of the yogurt. When it has been absorbed stir in the next spoonful. When all the yogurt has been incorporated, stir in the tomatoes with their juice.

Add salt to taste and the eggs. Spoon the sauce over the eggs, cover the pan and simmer for 10 minutes.

Sprinkle the coriander over the top, if using, and simmer for a further 5 minutes. Serve immediately.
Serves 4

Poached Egg Curry; Egg Curry with Yogurt

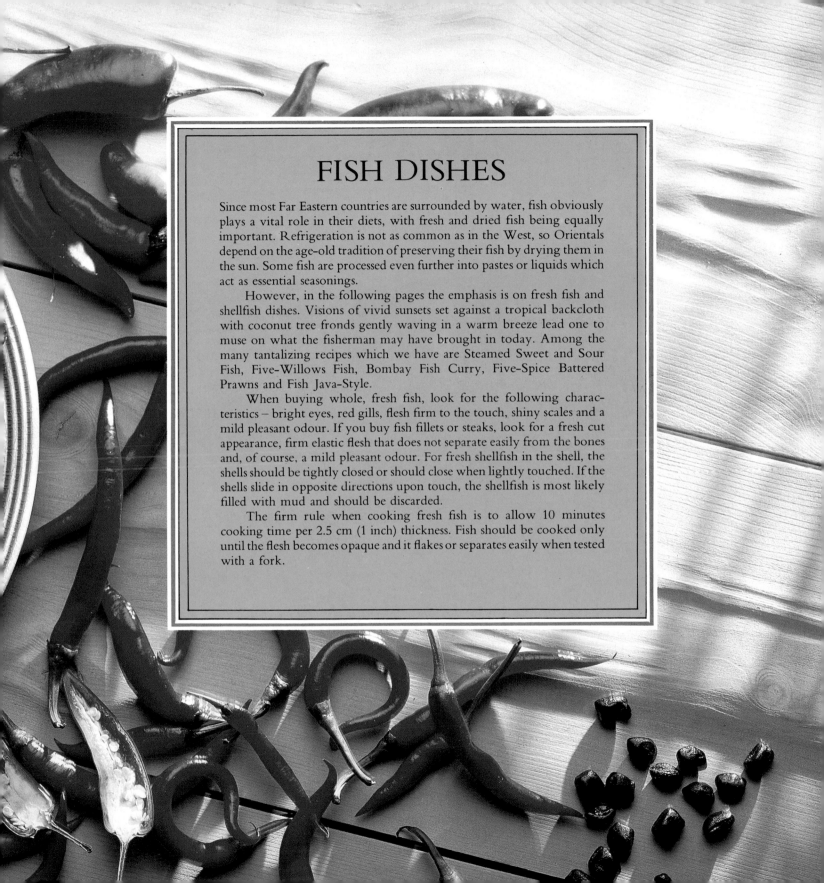

FISH DISHES

Since most Far Eastern countries are surrounded by water, fish obviously plays a vital role in their diets, with fresh and dried fish being equally important. Refrigeration is not as common as in the West, so Orientals depend on the age-old tradition of preserving their fish by drying them in the sun. Some fish are processed even further into pastes or liquids which act as essential seasonings.

However, in the following pages the emphasis is on fresh fish and shellfish dishes. Visions of vivid sunsets set against a tropical backcloth with coconut tree fronds gently waving in a warm breeze lead one to muse on what the fisherman may have brought in today. Among the many tantalizing recipes which we have are Steamed Sweet and Sour Fish, Five-Willows Fish, Bombay Fish Curry, Five-Spice Battered Prawns and Fish Java-Style.

When buying whole, fresh fish, look for the following characteristics – bright eyes, red gills, flesh firm to the touch, shiny scales and a mild pleasant odour. If you buy fish fillets or steaks, look for a fresh cut appearance, firm elastic flesh that does not separate easily from the bones and, of course, a mild pleasant odour. For fresh shellfish in the shell, the shells should be tightly closed or should close when lightly touched. If the shells slide in opposite directions upon touch, the shellfish is most likely filled with mud and should be discarded.

The firm rule when cooking fresh fish is to allow 10 minutes cooking time per 2.5 cm (1 inch) thickness. Fish should be cooked only until the flesh becomes opaque and it flakes or separates easily when tested with a fork.

CANTONESE WHOLE FISH

4 dried Chinese
   mushrooms★
1 × 1–1.25 kg (2–2½ lb)
   trout, mullet or
   bass, cleaned
2 × 1 cm (½ inch) root
   ginger★
2 spring onions
50 g (2 oz) ham
50 g (2 oz) canned
   bamboo shoots★,
   drained
MARINADE:
2 spring onions,
   chopped
1 clove garlic, sliced
3 tablespoons soy
   sauce★
2 tablespoons dry
   sherry
2 tablespoons
   chicken stock
2 teaspoons cornflour

Soak the mushrooms in warm water for 15 minutes. Squeeze dry, discard the hard stalks, then slice the mushroom caps.

Score the flesh of the fish by making 3 diagonal cuts on each side. Place in a shallow dish.

Mix all marinade ingredients together and spoon over the fish. Leave to marinate for 30 minutes.

Finely shred the ginger, spring onions, ham and bamboo shoots and mix together with the mushrooms.

Place the fish on a heatproof plate. Pour over the marinade and place in a steamer. Sprinkle with the mushroom mixture and steam vigorously for 15 to 20 minutes, until tender. Transfer to a serving platter and garnish with cucumber and spring onions, if desired. Serve immediately.
Serves 4 to 6

BATTERED PRAWNS

4 tablespoons
   self-raising flour
pinch of salt
½ teaspoon 5-spice
   powder★
1 cm (½ inch) piece
   root ginger★, finely
   chopped
1 egg
4–5 tablespoons
   water
oil for deep-frying
500 g (1 lb) peeled
   Mediterranean
   prawns
TO GARNISH:
shredded spring
   onions
lemon twists

Sift the flour, salt and 5-spice powder into a mixing bowl, then add the ginger. Make a hollow in the centre and add the egg. Beat thoroughly, adding sufficient water to make a smooth light batter.

Heat the oil in a deep-fryer. Dip each prawn into the batter, then deep-fry 2 or 3 at a time for 2 to 3 minutes, until golden brown. Drain on kitchen paper; keep warm.

Arrange on a warmed serving dish and garnish with spring onions and lemon. Serve immediately.
Serves 4 to 6

Cantonese Whole Fish; Battered Prawns

SALMON STEAKS BAKED IN FOIL

1 tablespoon oil
4 × 175 g (6 oz)
    salmon steaks
2 tablespoons sake★ or
    dry sherry
2 tablespoons soy
    sauce★
salt and black pepper
1 small onion, sliced
    into thin rings
1 lemon, thinly sliced
fresh dill sprigs
    (optional)

Grease four 20 cm (8 inch) squares of foil with the oil, then place 1 salmon steak on each one. Season each steak with ½ tablespoon of the sake, ½ tablespoon of the soy sauce and salt and pepper. Arrange 4 or 5 onion rings on each slice and then 2 lemon slices. Top with the dill sprigs, if using, then seal the packages tightly. Cook in a preheated hot oven, 200°C (400°F), Gas Mark 6, for 20 minutes.
    Serve, unwrapped, on heated plates.
Serves 4

STEAMED SWEET AND SOUR FISH

1 large whole fresh or
    frozen plaice,
    cleaned
salt
2 × 1 cm (½ inch)
    pieces root ginger★,
    shredded
3 spring onions,
    sliced
SAUCE:
150 ml (¼ pint) fish
    or chicken stock
1 tablespoon soy
    sauce★
1 tablespoon sugar
1 tablespoon wine
    vinegar
1 tablespoon dry
    sherry
1 tablespoon tomato
    purée
1 teaspoon chilli
    sauce★
pinch of salt
1 tablespoon
    cornflour
2 tablespoons water

Score the fish by making 3 diagonal cuts on each side. Rub the fish with salt and sprinkle with the ginger and spring onions. Put on an ovenproof plate and place in a steamer. Steam for 12 to 15 minutes until tender.
    Meanwhile, make the sauce. Mix all the ingredients, except the cornflour and water, together in a small saucepan, bring to the boil and cook for 1 minute. Blend the cornflour with the water and stir into the sauce. Cook, stirring, until thickened.
    Carefully lift the plaice onto a warmed serving dish. Spoon over the sauce and serve hot.
Serves 4

PAPER-WRAPPED FISH

4 × 125 g (4 oz)
    plaice or sole fillets
pinch of salt
2 tablespoons dry
    sherry
1 tablespoon oil
2 tablespoons
    shredded spring
    onion
2 tablespoons
    shredded root
    ginger★
oil for deep-frying
spring onion
    flowers to garnish
    (see page 155)

Cut the fish fillets into 2.5 cm (1 inch) squares. Sprinkle with salt and toss in the sherry.
    Cut out 15 cm (6 inch) squares of greaseproof paper and brush with the oil. Place a piece of fish on each square of paper and arrange some spring onion and ginger on top. Fold into envelopes tucking in the flaps to secure.
    Heat the oil in a wok or deep-fryer to 180°C (350°F). Deep-fry the wrapped fish for 3 minutes. Drain on kitchen paper and arrange on a warmed serving dish. Garnish with spring onion flowers and serve immediately. Each person unwraps his own parcels with chopsticks.
Serves 4

Paper-Wrapped Fish

FISH MOLEE

750 g (1½ lb) cod
  fillet, skinned and
  cut into 4 pieces
2 tablespoons plain
  flour
4 tablespoons oil
2 onions, sliced
2 cloves garlic,
  crushed
1 teaspoon turmeric★
4 green chillies★,
  finely chopped
2 tablespoons lemon
  juice
175 ml (6 fl oz) thick
  coconut milk★
salt

Coat the fish with the flour. Heat the oil in a frying pan, add the fish and fry quickly on both sides. Remove with a slotted spoon and set aside.

Add the onion and garlic to the pan and fry until soft and golden. Add the turmeric, chillies, lemon juice, coconut milk, and salt to taste and simmer, uncovered, for 10 minutes or until thickened.

Add the fish and any juices, spoon over the sauce and cook gently for 2 to 3 minutes, until tender.
Serves 4

Fish Molee; Baked Spiced Fish

BAKED SPICED FISH

4 tablespoons oil
125 g (4 oz) grated
  coconut★
5 cm (2 inch) piece
  root ginger★,
  chopped
1 large onion,
  chopped
4 cloves garlic, finely
  chopped
2 green chillies★,
  seeded and chopped
1 teaspoon chilli
  powder★
2 tablespoons finely
  chopped coriander
  leaves★
4 tablespoons lemon
  juice
salt
1 kg (2 lb) cod steaks

Heat the oil in a pan, add the coconut, ginger, onion, garlic, chillies and chilli powder and fry gently until the onion is translucent. Add the coriander, lemon juice and salt to taste and simmer for 15 minutes or until the coconut is soft.

Oil the bottom of a baking dish just large enough to hold the fish. Arrange the fish steaks side by side and pour over the spice mixture.

Bake in a preheated moderate oven, 160°C (325°F), Gas Mark 3, for 25 minutes or until tender.
Serves 4

TROUT WITH SALTED CABBAGE

2 tablespoons oil
1 onion, chopped
2 × 1 cm (½ inch)
    pieces root ginger★,
    finely shredded
4 trout, cleaned
150 ml (¼ pint)
    chicken stock
25 g (1 oz) pickled
    cabbage★, chopped
25 g (1 oz) canned
    bamboo shoots★,
    drained and sliced
1 tablespoon soy
    sauce★
2 teaspoons dry sherry

Heat the oil in a wok or deep frying pan, add the onion and ginger and cook for 1 minute. Add the trout and fry for 1 minute on each side, until browned.

Stir in the stock, then add the cabbage, bamboo shoots, soy sauce and sherry. Cook for 10 minutes, basting the fish occasionally.

Transfer to a warmed serving dish and garnish with lemon twists and coriander, if desired. Serve immediately.
Serves 4

FIVE-WILLOWS FISH

1 small cucumber
2 carrots
1 cm (½ inch) piece
    root ginger★, sliced
3 spring onions,
    chopped
2 cloves garlic,
    1 crushed and
    1 sliced
120 ml (4 fl oz)
    vinegar
1 grey mullet, carp
    or bass, cleaned
4 tablespoons oil
1 tablespoon hoisin
    sauce★
2 tablespoon sugar
1 tablespoon sesame
    seed oil★
cucumber fan and
    carrot flower (see
    page 155) to
    garnish

Cut the cucumber in half lengthways and discard the soft centre. Slice the cucumber flesh and carrots into 5 cm (2 inch) long matchstick pieces.

Put the cucumber, carrots, ginger, spring onions, crushed garlic and vinegar in a bowl and mix well. Leave to marinate for 30 minutes.

Score the fish by making 3 diagonal cuts on both sides. Heat the oil in a wok or deep frying pan, add the sliced garlic and fry for 1 minute. Add the fish and fry for 1 minute on each side until golden brown.

Add the vegetables and marinade, stir in the hoisin sauce and sugar and cook for 2 minutes; sprinkle with the sesame seed oil.

Transfer the fish to a warmed serving dish and spoon over the vegetables and sauce. Garnish with the cucumber fan and carrot flower and serve immediately.
Serves 4 to 6

Trout with Salted Cabbage; Five-Willows Fish

HADDOCK IN CHILLI SAUCE

4 tablespoons oil
2 large onions, sliced
3 cloves garlic,
    crushed
750 g (1½ lb) haddock
    fillets, cut into
    chunks
2 tablespoons plain
    flour
1 teaspoon turmeric★
4 green chillies
    (seeded if liked)★,
    thinly sliced
2 tablespoons lemon
    juice
175 ml (6 fl oz) thick
    coconut milk★
salt
chilli flowers to
    garnish (see page
    155, optional)

Heat the oil in a wok or deep frying pan, add the onions and fry until soft and golden. Add the garlic and cook for 30 seconds. Remove from the pan with a slotted spoon and set aside.

Toss the fish in the flour, add to the pan and brown quickly on all sides. Drain on kitchen paper.

Return the onions and garlic to the pan, stir in the turmeric and chillies and cook for 1 minute. Stir in the lemon juice, coconut milk and salt to taste and simmer, uncovered, for 10 minutes, stirring until the sauce has thickened.

Return the fish to the pan and heat for 2 to 3 minutes. Spoon into a warmed serving dish and garnish with chilli flowers, if using.
Serves 4

SPICED PRAWNS IN COCONUT

4 tablespoons oil
1 large onion, thinly
    sliced
4 cloves garlic, thinly
    sliced
2 teaspoons ground
    coriander★
1 teaspoon turmeric★
1 teaspoon chilli
    powder★
½ teaspoon ground
    ginger★
½ teaspoon salt
pepper
2 tablespoons vinegar
200 ml (⅓ pint)
    coconut milk★
2 tablespoons tomato
    purée
500 g (1 lb) peeled
    prawns
TO GARNISH:
whole prawns in shell
lemon slices

Heat the oil in a wok or deep frying pan, add the onion and garlic and fry gently until soft and golden brown.

Mix the spices together in a bowl, add the salt and pepper, stir in the vinegar and mix to a paste. Add to the pan and fry for 3 minutes, stirring constantly.

Stir in the coconut milk and tomato purée and simmer for 5 minutes.

Stir in the prawns and heat thoroughly for 2 to 3 minutes, until they are coated in the sauce.

Spoon into a warmed serving dish and garnish with whole prawns and lemon slices.
Serves 4

Haddock in Chilli Sauce; Spiced Prawns in Coconut

FISH WITH PIQUANT SAUCE

1 × 1.25 kg (2–2½ lb)
mullet, bass or trout,
cleaned

2 × 2.5 cm (1 inch)
pieces root ginger★,
finely chopped

3 spring onions,
chopped

50 g (2 oz) lean
bacon, derinded and
diced

50 g (2 oz) canned
bamboo shoots★,
drained and
shredded

2 tablespoons chopped
coriander leaves★

PIQUANT SAUCE:

1 tablespoon
cornflour

2 tablespoons water

150 ml (¼ pint) fish
stock or water

1 tablespoon each dark
soy sauce★, soft
light brown sugar,
wine vinegar, dry
sherry and tomato
purée

2 tablespoons chilli
sauce★

TO GARNISH:

coriander leaves★

tomato flowers (see
page 155)

Make 3 diagonal cuts on each side of
the fish. Mix together the ginger,
spring onions, bacon, bamboo shoots
and coriander and press into the cuts.
Place on a heatproof plate, lower into
a wok and steam vigorously for 15
minutes, or until tender.

Meanwhile, blend the cornflour
with the water and put with the other
sauce ingredients in a small pan and
mix well. Bring to the boil and cook,
stirring, for 2 minutes, until thickened.

Carefully lift the fish on to a
warmed serving plate, garnish with the
coriander and tomato flowers, and
serve with the Piquant sauce.
Serves 4

CHINESE STEAMED TROUT

1 tablespoon sesame
seed oil★

1 tablespoon light soy
sauce★

1 tablespoon dry
sherry

2 rainbow trout, about
1 kg (2 lb) total
weight, cleaned

4 cloves garlic, thinly
sliced

6 spring onions,
shredded★

2 × 2.5 cm (1 inch)
pieces root ginger★,
shredded

2 tablespoons dry
white vermouth

2 tablespoons oil

Mix together the sesame seed oil, soy
sauce and sherry and use to brush the
inside and the skin of each fish.

Mix together garlic, spring onions
and ginger and put a quarter of the
mixture inside each fish.

Place the fish on a heatproof plate,
scatter over the remaining garlic
mixture and pour over the vermouth
and oil. Put the plate in a wok and
steam vigorously for 15 minutes, or
until the fish is tender.

Arrange the fish on a warmed
serving plate, spoon over the juices
and serve immediately.
Serves 4

Fish with Piquant Sauce; Chinese Steamed Trout

STEAMERS

The bamboo steamer is among the most ancient of Chinese
cooking utensils. It comes in several sizes and is designed to fit
inside a wok or over a saucepan. One of the advantages of the
design is that several steamers may be stacked on top of each
other for multiple cooking.

If you do not have a steamer, place the food on a heatproof
plate which fits into a wok with a lid. Place a strip of foil
under the plate to enable it to be lifted in and out of the wok.

SOLE WITH SATÉ SAUCE

25 g (1 oz) butter
1 small onion, very
   finely chopped
1 tablespoon each
   chopped chives,
   tarragon and
   parsley
grated rind of ½ lemon
8 Dover or lemon sole
   fillets
1 egg, beaten
4–5 tablespoons fresh
   breadcrumbs
lime or lemon wedges
   to garnish
SATÉ SAUCE:
1 teaspoon each
   coriander★, cumin★
   and fennel seeds★
2 cloves garlic,
   crushed
125 g (4 oz) crunchy
   peanut butter
1 teaspoon dark soft
   brown sugar
2 green chillies★,
   seeded and finely
   chopped
150 g (5 oz) creamed
   coconut★, dissolved
   in 450 ml (¾ pint)
   hot water
3 tablespoons lemon
   or lime juice

First make the sauce: heat a wok or deep frying pan, add the crushed seeds and stir-fry for 2 minutes. Add the garlic, peanut butter, sugar, chillies and coconut milk, stir well and cook gently for 7 to 8 minutes. Stir in the lemon or lime juice; keep warm.

Melt the butter in a pan, add the onion and cook for 1 minute. Stir in the herbs and lemon rind. Cool slightly, then divide between the fish. Roll up each fillet, secure with wooden cocktail sticks, dip in the beaten egg, then coat in the breadcrumbs. Deep-fry for 4 to 5 minutes, until golden. Drain on kitchen paper and arrange on a warmed serving dish. Serve with the Saté sauce and lime or lemon wedges.
Serves 4

MONKFISH IN HERB SAUCE

750 g (1½ lb)
   monkfish, skinned
150 ml (¼ pint) dry
   white wine
1 bouquet garni
salt and pepper
125 g (4 oz) butter
2–3 small onions,
   finely chopped
2 small leeks, finely
   sliced
2 tablespoons each
   chopped parsley,
   thyme, watercress
   and marjoram
bunches of fresh herbs
   to garnish

Place the monkfish in a wok or deep frying pan, pour over the wine, add the bouquet garni and season with salt and pepper to taste. Slowly bring to the boil, then cover with a lid or foil and simmer gently for 8 to 10 minutes, until the fish is tender. Remove from the heat and leave to cool.

Using a slotted spoon, lift the fish from the pan; drain well and remove the bones.

Discard the bouquet garni, then boil the liquid rapidly until reduced by half. Pour off the liquid and reserve for later.

Wipe the pan with kitchen paper. Melt the butter in the clean pan, add the onions and leeks and fry for 5 minutes, without browning. Stir in all the chopped herbs.

Return the fish and reserved liquid to the pan and heat through gently. Season to taste with salt and pepper and serve immediately, garnished with fresh herbs.
Serves 4

Sole with Saté Sauce; Monkfish in Herb Sauce

PRAWNS IN CHILLI SAUCE

1 tablespoon oil
3 spring onions,
 chopped
2 teaspoons finely
 chopped root
 ginger★
250 g (8 oz) peeled
 prawns
125 g (4 oz) mange
 tout
¼ teaspoon chilli
 powder★
1 teaspoon tomato
 purée
¼ teaspoon salt
½ teaspoon sugar
1 tablespoon dry
 sherry
½ teaspoon sesame
 seed oil★
whole prawns in shell
 to garnish

Heat the oil in a wok or deep frying pan, add the spring onions and ginger and stir-fry for 30 seconds. Add the prawns, mange tout, chilli powder, tomato purée, salt, sugar and sherry and stir-fry briskly for 5 minutes. Sprinkle over the sesame seed oil and arrange on a warmed serving dish. Serve immediately, garnished with whole prawns.
Serves 4

CRAB IN BLACK BEAN SAUCE

2 tablespoons oil
2 tablespoons salted
 black beans★,
 coarsely chopped
2 cloves garlic,
 crushed
2 tablespoons chopped
 root ginger★
4 spring onions,
 chopped
250 g (8 oz) lean
 finely minced pork
1 large cooked crab,
 cut into pieces
2 tablespoons dry
 sherry
300 ml (½ pint)
 chicken stock
 preferably
 homemade
2 eggs, beaten
1–2 teaspoons sesame
 seed oil★

Heat the oil in a wok or deep frying pan, add the black beans, garlic, ginger and spring onions and stir-fry briskly for 30 seconds. Add the pork and brown quickly for 1 minute. Add the crab, sherry and stock and boil rapidly for 8 to 10 minutes.

Combine the eggs and sesame oil and stir into the wok. Stir for 30 seconds, until the egg has cooked into strands. Transfer to a warmed serving dish, garnish with spring onion flowers, if desired, and serve immediately.
Serves 4

Crab in Black Bean Sauce; Prawns in Chilli Sauce

BRAISED FISH WITH BLACK BEAN SAUCE

3 tablespoons black
 beans★
2 tablespoons oil
2 spring onions,
 chopped
1 cm (½ inch) piece
 root ginger★, finely
 chopped
1 small red pepper,
 seeded and diced
2 celery sticks,
 chopped
2 tablespoons soy
 sauce★
2 tablespoons dry
 sherry
4 × 150 g (5 oz) cod
or haddock cutlets
shredded spring onion
 to garnish

Soak the black beans in warm water for 10 minutes; drain.

Heat the oil in a wok or deep frying pan, add the spring onions, ginger, red pepper and celery and stir-fry for 1 minute. Stir in the soy sauce and sherry. Place the fish on top of the vegetables and simmer for 5 to 10 minutes until almost tender, depending on the thickness of the fish. Spoon over the black beans and cook for 2 minutes.

Arrange the fish on a warmed serving dish and spoon the sauce over. Serve hot, garnished with spring onion.
Serves 4

FISH JAVA-STYLE

3 tablespoons
  cornflour
1 teaspoon salt
750 g (1½ lb) thick
  haddock fillets,
  skinned and cut
  into fingers
4–6 tablespoons oil
2 onions, sliced
3 cloves garlic, finely
  chopped
2.5 cm (1 inch) piece
  root ginger★, finely
  chopped
300 ml (½ pint) water
2 tablespoons dark soy
  sauce★
1 teaspoon sugar
¼ teaspoon grated
  nutmeg
2 tablespoons lemon
  juice

Mix the cornflour with the salt on a
plate. Lightly roll the fish pieces in the
mixture.

Heat half the oil in a wok or frying
pan, add the fish and fry lightly. Lift
out and set aside on a plate.

Rinse out the pan and return to the
heat with the remaining oil. Add the
onions, garlic and ginger and fry until
soft and golden. Stir in the water, soy
sauce, sugar, nutmeg and lemon juice.
Return the fish to the pan and
simmer, uncovered, for 5 to 10
minutes or until the fish is cooked.

Transfer to a warmed serving dish.
Serves 4

SPICY FRIED PRAWNS

2 tablespoons oil
2 small onions, sliced
2 red chillies★, finely
  chopped (optional)
500 g (1 lb) raw
  peeled prawns
300 ml (½ pint) water
juice of 1 lemon
SPICE PASTE:
1–1½ teaspoons chilli
  powder★
4 small onions,
  quartered
2 cloves garlic
2.5 cm (1 inch) piece
  root ginger★,
  chopped
1 teaspoon blachan★
1 teaspoon sugar
1 teaspoon salt
pared rind of 1 lemon

First make the spice paste: put all the
ingredients into a food processor or
electric blender and work until
smooth.

Heat the oil in a wok or deep frying
pan, add the onions and chillies and
fry, stirring, until soft and golden.
Add the spice paste and fry, stirring,
for 5 minutes. Stir in the prawns.
After a few minutes, when they turn
pink, add the water and lemon juice.
Add more salt if necessary and cook
for 15 to 20 minutes or until the sauce
is thick.

Transfer to a warmed serving dish.
Serves 4

Fish Java-Style; Spicy Fried Prawns

MACHI MUSSALAM

1 kg (2 lb) cod steaks
1 teaspoon salt
1 × 150 g (5 oz)
    carton natural
    yogurt
4 tablespoons oil
2 onions, finely sliced
2.5 cm (1 inch) piece
    root ginger★, finely
    sliced
4 green chillies★
2 cloves garlic
1 teaspoon fenugreek
    seeds★
coriander leaves★ to
    garnish (optional)

Sprinkle the fish with the salt and marinate it in the yogurt for an hour or so, turning once or twice.

Heat 1 tablespoon of the oil in a pan, add one of the onions and fry until crisp. Place this, together with the remaining onion, the ginger, chillies and garlic, in an electric blender or food processor and work to a smooth paste.

Heat the remaining oil in a large frying pan with a lid. Fry the fenugreek seeds for 30 seconds, then add the prepared paste and fry until it starts to brown. Now add the fish and yogurt. Stir carefully and spoon the mixture over the fish. Cover and simmer for 5 to 10 minutes, or until cooked through; if drying too fast add 2 tablespoons water; if too liquid, uncover and allow to dry out.

Transfer to a warmed dish and garnish with coriander, if using, to serve.

Serves 4

COCONUT FISH

2 tablespoons oil
4 green chillies★,
    seeded and chopped
2 cloves garlic, finely
    chopped
2.5 cm (1 inch) piece
    root ginger★, finely
    chopped
125 g (4 oz) creamed
    coconut★
1 kg (2 lb) thick
    haddock fillets,
    skinned and cubed
salt
juice of 2 lemons

Heat the oil in a large frying pan, add the chillies, garlic and ginger and fry gently for 3 minutes. Add the creamed coconut and, when bubbling, add the fish and salt to taste. Stir well.

Cook for 3 to 4 minutes, stirring and breaking up the fish as it cooks. As soon as all the fish is cooked through, pour in the lemon juice, stir well and serve.

Serves 4

Machi Mussalam; Coconut Fish

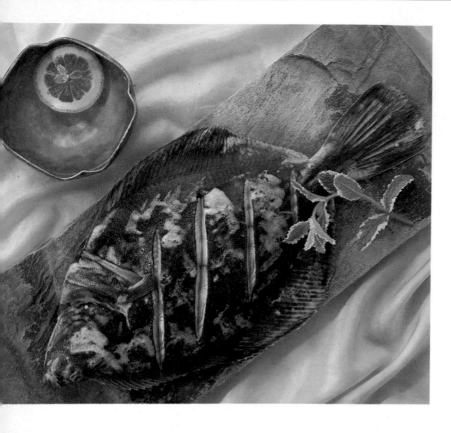

JAPANESE MARINATED FISH

3 tablespoons oil
3 tablespoons rice vinegar★
2 tablespoons soy sauce★
1 tablespoon mirin★ or dry sherry
1 teaspoon grated fresh root ginger★
1 clove garlic, crushed
black pepper
4 × 150 g (5 oz) fish steaks or fillets

Combine the oil, rice vinegar, soy sauce, mirin, ginger, garlic and pepper in a shallow dish. Add the fish, cover and marinate for 30 minutes.

Remove the fish from the marinade, reserving the marinade. Grill for about 10 minutes under a preheated grill, basting frequently with the marinade, until the fish flakes easily. Serve the fish on a heated serving dish.
Serves 4

GRILLED SPICED FISH

2 large or 4 small plaice, cleaned
150 g (5 oz) natural yogurt
2 cloves garlic, crushed
1 teaspoon ground coriander seeds★
½ teaspoon chilli powder★
1 teaspoon garam masala★
1 tablespoon vinegar
1 tablespoon oil
salt
TO GARNISH:
2 tablespoons finely chopped parsley
1 lemon, quartered

Slash the fish on both sides and place in separate shallow dishes. Mix the remaining ingredients together, adding salt to taste, and divide between the fish. Spoon it all over one side and leave for 1 hour, then turn and spoon over the juice that has collected in the dish. Leave for another hour.

Cook under a preheated moderate grill for 3 to 4 minutes. Turn and baste with any juices collected in the grill pan, then cook for a further 3 or 4 minutes.

Serve sprinkled with the parsley and accompanied by lemon quarters.
Serves 4

Grilled Spiced Fish

PRAWNS WITH TAMARIND

1 small red pepper, cored, seeded and coarsely chopped
25 g (1 oz) small onions, coarsely chopped
2 cloves garlic, coarsely chopped
1 red chilli, seeded and chopped
1 tablespoon ground dried lemon grass★
6 tablespoons oil
4 teaspoons caster sugar
2 teaspoons lime juice
salt
500 g (1 lb) unpeeled Mediterranean prawns, heads left on and deveined through the shell
watercress to garnish
TAMARIND PASTE:
250 g (8 oz) tamarind★
120 ml (4 fl oz) water

To make the tamarind paste, place the tamarind and water in a small saucepan and bring to the boil. Cover and simmer gently for 10 minutes. Remove from the heat and stand, covered, for 1 hour. Mash the tamarind with the water and pass it through a fine sieve into a bowl. Reserve 3 tablespoons of the paste. Use the remaining paste for another recipe; it will keep in the refrigerator for 2 weeks.

Place the red pepper, onions, garlic, chilli and lemon grass in a food processor or liquidizer and blend.

Heat the oil in a wok or large frying pan over a medium-high heat until hot. Add the pepper mixture and stir-fry for 5 minutes. Gradually blend in the tamarind paste, sugar, lime juice and salt to taste. Add the prawns and stir-fry for 5 minutes, or until the prawns are just firm to the touch. Transfer the prawns to a heated serving platter and garnish with the watercress.
Serves 4

(Picture, page 32)

BOMBAY FISH CURRY

2 tablespoons oil
2 tablespoons finely
 chopped onion
2 cloves garlic,
 crushed
1 tablespoon finely
 chopped root
 ginger★
½ teaspoon chilli
 powder★
4 green chillies★
300 ml (½ pint) thin
 coconut milk★
salt
4 fish cutlets (halibut,
 cod, etc.)

Heat the oil in a pan, add the onion, garlic, ginger and chilli powder and fry until the onion is soft. Add the chillies, coconut milk and salt to taste and simmer until thickened. Add the fish, spooning the sauce over, and cook, uncovered, for about 5 minutes or until tender.
Serves 4

PRAWN KEBAB

2 tablespoons oil
1 tablespoon lemon
 juice
2 cloves garlic,
 crushed
1 teaspoon paprika
½ teaspoon chilli
 powder★
½ teaspoon salt
½ teaspoon turmeric★
1 tablespoon finely
 chopped coriander
 leaves★
12 peeled giant
 Mediterranean
 prawns

Put all the ingredients into a shallow dish, stirring to coat the prawns thoroughly. Cover and chill for several hours, stirring occasionally.

Thread the prawns on skewers, or place in the grill pan, and cook under a preheated moderate grill for 3 to 4 minutes on each side, or until cooked. Spoon over the pan juices when turning.
Serves 4

PRAWN CHILLI FRY

3 tablespoons oil
3 onions, sliced
2 green chillies★,
 chopped
2.5 cm (1 inch) piece
 root ginger★,
 chopped
½ teaspoon chilli
 powder★
½ teaspoon turmeric★
salt
1 × 227 g (8 oz)
 packet frozen
 prawns

Heat the oil in a pan, add the onions and fry until soft and golden. Add the chillies, ginger, chilli powder, turmeric and salt to taste and fry for 2 minutes.

Add the prawns and cook, uncovered, for about 3 minutes or until all the moisture has evaporated.
Serves 4

Prawn Kebab; Prawn Chilli Fry

MASALA MACHI

4 herrings or
   mackerel, boned
   and cleaned
1 teaspoon salt
2 tablespoons lemon
   juice
2 cloves garlic
4 green chillies★,
   seeded
4 tablespoons
   coriander leaves★
1 teaspoon ground
   coriander seeds★
3 tablespoons oil
1 onion, chopped
lemon wedges to
   garnish

Slash the fish, sprinkle a little salt inside each one and set aside.

Put the lemon juice, garlic, chillies, coriander leaves and seeds and remaining salt into an electric blender or food processor and work to a paste.

Heat 2 tablespoons oil in a pan, add the onion and fry until golden. Add the blended spices and fry gently, stirring, for 5 minutes, until the mixture is thick and smooth.

Spread the paste inside each fish and brush lightly with the remaining oil.

Cook under a preheated moderate grill for about 4 minutes on each side. Or wrap in foil and cook in a preheated moderate oven, 180°C (350°F), Gas Mark 4, for about 20 minutes, until tender.

Garnish with lemon wedges.
Serves 4

PICKLED HADDOCK STEAKS

4 tablespoons oil
4 × 250 g (8 oz)
   haddock steaks,
   cleaned
2 onions, chopped
2 cloves garlic
2.5 cm (1 inch) piece
   root ginger★
1 tablespoon
   coriander seeds★
4 green chillies★,
   seeded
5 tablespoons wine
   vinegar
½ teaspoon turmeric★
4 curry leaves★
salt

Heat the oil in a large frying pan, add the fish and fry on both sides until browned. Remove with a slotted spoon and set aside. Add the onions to the pan and fry until soft.

Put the garlic, ginger, coriander seeds, chillies and 1 tablespoon of the vinegar into an electric blender or food processor and work to a paste. Add to the pan with the turmeric, curry leaves, and salt to taste and fry for 3 to 4 minutes.

Add the remaining vinegar, bring to simmering point, stir well and add the fish. Cook, uncovered, for 3 to 4 minutes, until tender.

Place the fish in a dish, pour over all the juices and leave to cool. Cover and keep in the refrigerator for at least 12 hours. Serve cold.
Serves 4

Pickled Haddock Steaks

PRAWN AND EGG CURRY

4 tablespoons oil
1 large onion, chopped
1 clove garlic, chopped
2.5 cm (1 inch) piece
   root ginger★,
   chopped
1 tablespoon ground
   coriander★
2 teaspoons ground
   cumin★
1 teaspoon chilli
   powder★
1 tablespoon tomato
   purée
300 ml (½ pint) water
salt
6 hard-boiled eggs,
   halved
1 × 227 g (8 oz)
   packet frozen
   prawns
25 g (1 oz) creamed
   coconut★

Heat the oil in a saucepan, add the onion and fry until golden. Add the garlic and ginger and fry for 1 minute. Add the remaining spices and fry gently for 2 minutes, stirring occasionally; if the mixture becomes too dry, add 1 tablespoon water. Add the tomato purée, mix well, then add the water and salt to taste. Cover and simmer for 10 minutes.

Add the eggs, spooning some mixture over them, cover and cook for 15 minutes, stirring occasionally.

Stir in the prawns. When the curry starts to simmer again, stir in the creamed coconut. Let the mixture come to simmering point once more, then serve immediately.
Serves 4

TANDOORI SOLE

½ teaspoon chilli
    powder★
½ teaspoon turmeric★
½ teaspoon ground
    coriander★
½ teaspoon ground
    cumin★
1 teaspoon ground
    ginger★
½ teaspoon garam
    masala★
¼ teaspoon salt
pepper
300 g (10 oz) natural
    yogurt
2 cloves garlic,
    crushed
2 drops of red food
    colouring
2 lemon sole, skinned
    and filleted
TO GARNISH:
coriander leaves★
lime wedges

Mix all the spices together, adding the salt and pepper to taste. Add to the yogurt with the garlic and red food colouring and stir until well mixed. Pour into a large bowl, add the fish, turn to coat thoroughly and leave to marinate for 1 hour.

Pour boiling water into a roasting pan to come halfway up the sides. Put a grill rack in the pan and place the marinated fish on the rack. Pour any remaining marinade over the fish.

Cook in a preheated moderate oven, 180°C (350°F), Gas Mark 4, for 15 minutes.

Garnish with coriander and lime wedges and serve immediately.
Serves 2

STIR-FRIED FISH WITH VEGETABLES

500 g (1 lb) cod fillet,
    skinned and cut
    into 2.5 cm (1
    inch) wide strips
1 teaspoon salt
1 tablespoon oil
2 rashers back bacon,
    derinded and
    shredded
50 g (2 oz) frozen
    peas, cooked
50 g (2 oz) frozen
    sweetcorn, cooked
6 tablespoons chicken
    stock or water
2 teaspoons dry sherry
2 teaspoons soy sauce★
1 teaspoon sugar
1 teaspoon cornflour
1 teaspoon water
spring onion brushes,
    to garnish (see
    page 155)

Sprinkle the fish fillets with the salt and leave for 15 minutes.

Heat the oil in a frying pan, add the fish and bacon and stir-fry for 3 minutes. Add the remaining ingredients, except the cornflour and water, and bring to the boil. Blend the cornflour and water and stir in. Cook for 1 minute.

Garnish with spring onion brushes and serve immediately.
Serves 4

Tandoori Sole; Stir-Fried Fish with Vegetables

MEAT DISHES

The traditions of Oriental cookery have always encouraged creative ways with meat. Both meat and poultry have always been scarce and difficult to obtain in large quantities, and this has led to the invention of imaginative dishes which cunningly stretch meagre supplies to the full.

You'll find delicious examples of this in the Braised Chicken with Peppers and Corn dish, brimming with the flavour imparted by additions such as soy sauce, ginger and dry sherry. In contrast we have Aloo 'Chops' from India, in which a spicy minced beef mixture is enclosed in a mashed potato coating.

There is even a mouth-watering recipe for the classic Chinese favourite – Peking Duck – complete with instructions on how to prepare the spring onion 'flower' garnish and the Mandarin Pancakes in which the crispy duck is wrapped.

Pork – braised, sweet and sour, barbecued and even teamed with pumpkin – features prominently, as well as lamb prepared in the Chinese 'Red Cooked' style, Roghan Ghosht, a lamb curry from north India and Kofta Curry, a dish of spicy meatballs.

China and India, however, are not the only countries contributing to this fascinating range of recipes. You can also sample curries from Thailand, spicy chicken from Indonesia and lamb in a 'Hot Pot' from Mongolia – all without boarding a single plane. So fasten your culinary seatbelts and turn the page . . .

CHICKEN WINGS WITH OYSTER SAUCE

500 g (1 lb) chicken
   wings
2 tablespoons oil
2 leeks, sliced
3 tablespoons oyster
   sauce★
radish flowers★ (see
   page 155)
cucumber slices
MARINADE:
4 spring onions,
   chopped
1 cm (½ inch) piece
   root ginger★,
   shredded
1 clove garlic, sliced
1 tablespoon soy
   sauce★
2 tablespoons dry
   sherry

Trim the tips off the chicken wings, then cut the wings in half at the joints.

Make the marinade: put the spring onions, ginger, garlic, soy sauce and sherry into a bowl. Add the chicken wings and stir well to coat, then leave to marinate for 15 minutes.

Heat the oil in a wok or deep frying pan, add the chicken and marinade and stir-fry for 15 minutes. Add the leeks and oyster sauce and cook for a further 3 to 4 minutes.

Serve immediately, garnished with radish flowers and cucumber slices.
Serves 4 to 6

JAPANESE-STYLE GRILLED CHICKEN

4 × 150 g (5 oz)
   boneless chicken
   breasts, skinned and
   cut into 2.5 cm
   (1 inch) cubes
8 spring onions,
   including 7.5 cm (3
   inch) of the green
   tops, cut into 2.5
   cm (1 inch) pieces
TERIYAKI SAUCE:
250 ml (8 fl oz)
   mirin★ or 175 ml
   (6 fl oz) dry
   sherry and 1
   tablespoon sugar
250 ml (8 fl oz) soy
   sauce★
250 ml (8 fl oz)
   chicken stock
3 tablespoons sugar
2 teaspoons finely
   chopped root
   ginger★
1 clove garlic, crushed

To make the teriyaki sauce, place the mirin in a medium saucepan over a moderate heat and bring to simmering point. Carefully ignite the mirin and shake the pan constantly until the flames die down. Stir in the remaining sauce ingredients, then bring to the boil, stirring occasionally. Remove from the heat and let cool.

Place the chicken in a shallow dish, then pour over the sauce. Cover and chill for at least 3 hours, or overnight, turning the chicken pieces occasionally.

Remove the chicken from the sauce and reserve the sauce. Loosely thread the chicken cubes on to 8 thin skewers, alternating each cube with a piece of spring onion. Dip the chicken into the sauce and place the skewers 10 cm (4 inches) below a preheated grill and cook for 3 to 4 minutes. Dip the skewers into the sauce again and cook the other side for 2 to 3 minutes, or until the chicken is firm to the touch.

To finish, moisten each skewer with a few teaspoons of the marinade and serve immediately.
Serves 4

SERVING JAPANESE FOOD

Raised oblong wood or laquer serving dishes, wicker trays and small china bowls, are all traditionally used for serving Japanese food. Serving and eating utensils consist almost solely of chopsticks, even with soup. Soup is drunk directly from the bowl and chopsticks are used to pick up the various garnishes in the soup.

All the food is generally placed on the table at the same time, with little formality about the order in which it is eaten. A semi-formal meal, though, would include several small appetizer courses, followed by soup and perhaps a boiled vegetable. A meat or fish dish would be next, accompanied by a small dish of raw vegetables or fish with a rice vinegar dressing. Plain boiled rice, pickles and green tea would conclude the meal.

Chicken Wings with Oyster Sauce

DEEP-FRIED CHICKEN LEGS

8 chicken drumsticks
50 g (2 oz) plain
    flour
1 egg (size 2), beaten
oil for deep-frying
MARINADE:
2 tablespoons sherry
2 tablespoons soy
    sauce★
1 teaspoon sugar
1 cm (½ inch) piece
root ginger★,
    finely chopped
2 cloves garlic,
    crushed
TO GARNISH:
radish flowers (see
    page 155)
chilli flowers (see
    page 155)
cucumber slices

To make the marinade: put the sherry, soy sauce, sugar, ginger and garlic into a bowl and mix well. Add the drumsticks, turn to coat and leave to marinate for 1 hour. Remove the chicken and reserve the marinade.

Put the flour into a bowl, beat in the egg, then gradually mix in the marinade, stirring well to form a smooth paste. Dip the chicken into the mixture and turn to coat evenly.

Heat the oil in a wok or deep-fryer and deep-fry the chicken legs for 12 to 15 minutes until golden brown. Drain on kitchen paper.

Serve hot, garnished with radish flowers, placed in chilli flowers, and cucumber slices.
Serves 4 to 6

BRAISED CHICKEN WITH PEPPERS AND CORN

1 tablespoon oil
3 spring onions,
    chopped
2 × 1 cm (½ inch)
pieces root ginger★,
    shredded
500 g (1 lb) boneless
    chicken breast,
    shredded
2 tablespoons light
    soy sauce★
2 tablespoons dry
    sherry
2 green peppers,
    cored, seeded and
    sliced
1 × 425 g (15 oz)
    can baby corn or
    sweetcorn, drained

Heat the oil in a wok or frying pan, add the spring onions and ginger and fry for 1 minute. Add the chicken and brown lightly. Pour in the soy sauce and sherry and cook for a further 1 minute. Stir in the peppers and corn and stir-fry for 2 minutes.

Pile the mixture on to a warmed serving dish and serve immediately.
Serves 4 to 6

Deep-Fried Chicken Legs; Braised Chicken with Peppers and Corn

CHICKEN
WITH CHESTNUTS

125 g (4 oz) dried
    chestnuts★
500 g (1 lb) boneless
    chicken breast,
    cubed
½ teaspoon salt
2 tablespoons oil
2 cloves garlic, sliced
1 cm (½ inch)
    piece root ginger★,
    finely chopped
4 spring onions, each
    cut into 4 pieces
2 tablespoons soy
    sauce★
2 tablespoons sherry
2 teaspoons sugar
1 tablespoon
    cornflour
2 tablespoons water

Soak the dried chestnuts in warm
water for 1 hour; drain.

Toss the chicken cubes in the salt.
Heat the oil in a wok or frying pan,
add the garlic and fry until browned.
Add the ginger, spring onions and
chicken and stir-fry for 1 minute. Add
the chestnuts and cook for 2 minutes.
Add the soy sauce, sherry and sugar.

Blend the cornflour with the water.
Stir into the pan and cook, stirring, for
1 minute.

Spoon into a warmed serving dish
and serve immediately.
Serves 4 to 6

CHICKEN IN FOIL

1 tablespoon soy
    sauce★
1 tablespoon dry
    sherry
1 tablespoon sesame
    seed oil★
500 g (1 lb) boneless
    chicken breast, cut
    into 16 equal pieces
4 spring onions, each
    cut into 4 pieces
2 × 1 cm (½ inch)
    pieces root ginger★,
    shredded
1 celery stick,
    shredded

Mix the soy sauce, sherry and sesame
seed oil together. Add the chicken and
toss well to coat, then leave to
marinate for 15 to 20 minutes.

Cut out 16 pieces of foil large
enough to enclose the pieces of
chicken generously. Brush the foil
with oil, place a piece of chicken in
the centre and top with a piece of
spring onion, some ginger and celery.
Fold the foil over to enclose the
chicken and seal the edges well. Place
in a steamer and steam for 10 to 12
minutes.

Serve hot in the foil.
Serves 4 to 6

CHICKEN
WITH CASHEW NUTS

3 tablespoons dry
    sherry
1 egg white
1 teaspoon cornflour
2 boneless chicken
    breasts, cut into
    small pieces
2 tablespoons oil
2 spring onions,
    chopped
1 green pepper,
    cored, seeded and
    diced
125 g (4 oz) canned
    bamboo shoots★,
    drained and
    shredded
1 tablespoon soy
    sauce★
125 g (4 oz)
    unsalted cashew
    nuts

Mix 2 tablespoons of the sherry, the
egg white and cornflour together. Add
the chicken and toss well until evenly
coated.

Heat the oil in a wok or frying pan,
add the spring onions and stir-fry for
30 seconds. Add the chicken and cook
for 3 minutes. Add the remaining
ingredients and cook for 2 minutes.

Pile into a warmed serving dish and
serve immediately.
Serves 4

*Chicken with Cashew Nuts; Chicken with Chestnuts; Chicken in
Foil*

PEKING DUCK

1 × 1.75–2 kg
  (4–4½ lb)
  oven-ready duck
2 tablespoons soy
  sauce★
2 tablespoons dark
  brown sugar
MANDARIN
  PANCAKES:
500 g (1 lb) plain
  flour
pinch of salt
300 ml (½ pint)
  boiling water
  (approximately)
sesame seed oil★
TO SERVE:
1 small cucumber, cut
  into 5 cm (2 inch)
  matchstick pieces
1 bunch spring
  onions, cut into
  5 cm (2 inch)
  matchstick pieces
8 tablespoons hoisin
  sauce★
spring onion flower
  (see page 155)

Immerse the duck in a pan of boiling water for 2 minutes, then drain thoroughly. Hang up the duck to dry in a well ventilated room overnight.

Mix the soy sauce and sugar together and rub over the duck. Hang for 2 hours until the coating is dry.

Place the duck on a rack in a roasting pan and cook in a preheated moderately hot oven, 200°C (400°F), Gas Mark 6, for 1½ hours.

Meanwhile, make the pancakes. Sift the flour and salt into a mixing bowl. Gradually add the boiling water, mixing to make a stiff dough. Knead and shape into a roll, 5 cm (2 inches) in diameter. Cut into 1 cm (½ inch) slices, then roll out into thin 15 cm (6 inch) diameter pancakes. Brush one side of each pancake with sesame seed oil and sandwich the pancakes together in pairs.

Place an ungreased frying pan over a high heat. When hot, lower the heat slightly and place a pancake 'sandwich' in the pan. When it starts to puff up, turn and cook the other side until lightly browned.

Pull the 2 pancakes apart and fold each in half. Place on a warmed serving dish and cover with foil to prevent them drying out; keep warm.

Cut off all the crispy skin from the duck and arrange on a warmed serving dish. Garnish with cucumber. Remove all the meat and arrange on another warmed serving dish. Garnish with spring onion. Place the hoisin sauce in a small bowl. Garnish the pancakes with a spring onion flower.

To eat, spread a little hoisin sauce over a pancake. Cover with a piece of duck skin and meat, then top with a few pieces of cucumber and spring onion. Roll up the pancake.
Serves 4 to 6

Peking Duck

PLEASURE-BOAT DUCK

1.75 kg (4 lb) duck
4 dried Chinese
　mushrooms★
2 tablespoons oil
4 spring onions,
　chopped
1 cm ($\frac{1}{2}$ inch) piece
　root ginger★, finely
　chopped
125 g (4 oz) lean
　pork, shredded
50 g (2 oz) broad
　beans, cooked
GLAZE:
3 tablespoons soy
　sauce★
1 tablespoon dry
　sherry
1 tablespoon sesame
　seed oil★
TO GARNISH:
turnip flowers (see
　page 155)
radishes
mint leaves

Immerse the duck in a pan of boiling water for 2 minutes, then drain well.

Soak the dried mushrooms in warm water for 15 minutes. Squeeze dry, discard the hard stalks, then slice the mushroom caps.

Heat the oil in a wok or frying pan, add the spring onions, ginger and pork and fry for 2 minutes. Add the beans and cook for a further minute. Add the mushrooms.

Leave to cool, then use to stuff the duck; sew up securely.

Mix the glaze ingredients together and brush over the duck. Place in a roasting pan and cook in a preheated hot oven, 220°C (425°F), Gas Mark 7, for 1$\frac{1}{4}$ to 1$\frac{1}{2}$ hours, basting occasionally with the glaze.

Transfer to a warmed serving dish and garnish with turnip flowers with radish centres, and mint leaves. Serve immediately.
Serves 4 to 6

Pleasure-Boat Duck; Soy-Braised Duck

SOY-BRAISED DUCK

1 × 1.5–1.75 kg
　(3–4 lb) duck
4 × 1 cm ($\frac{1}{2}$ inch)
　pieces root ginger★,
　finely chopped
1 large onion, finely
　chopped
1 teaspoon salt
6 tablespoons soy
　sauce★
3 tablespoons malt
　vinegar
1 tablespoon oil
4 spring onions, each
　cut into 3 pieces
150 ml ($\frac{1}{4}$ pint)
　chicken stock
1 tablespoon
　cornflour
2 tablespoons water
1 × 227 g (8 oz) can
　pineapple slices,
　halved
3 tablespoons dry
　sherry
TO GARNISH:
pineapple slices
shredded spring onions

Prick the skin of the duck all over. Mix the ginger and onion with the salt and rub inside the duck. Put into a large bowl and add the soy sauce and vinegar. Leave for 1 hour, basting occasionally. Transfer to a roasting pan. Cook in a preheated oven, 220°C (425°F), Gas Mark 7, for 30 minutes.

Heat the oil in a pan, add the spring onions and fry until lightly browned. Remove and set aside.

Remove the duck from the oven and pour off any excess fat. Lower oven temperature to 190°C (375°F), Gas Mark 5. Sprinkle the duck with the spring onions, remaining marinade and stock. Cover with foil. Cook in oven for 1 hour, basting occasionally.

Place the duck on a board, joint and chop into 16 pieces. Reassemble on a warmed serving dish; keep hot.

Blend the cornflour and water. Put the pineapple and juice in a pan. Stir in the sherry, blended cornflour and duck juices. Cook for 2 minutes and serve in a sauce bowl.

Garnish and serve.
Serves 4 to 6

BALINESE ROASTED AND STIR-FRIED DUCK

50 g (2 oz) salted macadamia nuts★
2 large cloves garlic, crushed
1 teaspoon ground coriander★
½ teaspoon grated root ginger★
250 ml (8 fl oz) chicken stock
1 × 2 kg (4½ lb) oven-ready duck
250 ml (8 fl oz) boiling water
2 tablespoons oil
2 green chillies★, seeded and finely chopped
1 tablespoon lemon juice
salt
TO GARNISH:
coriander sprigs
chilli powder

(Picture, page 48)

Combine the nuts, garlic, coriander, ginger and 25 ml (1 fl oz) of the stock in a food processor or electric blender. Liquidize to a smooth paste, adding a bit more stock if the mixture is too dry. Cover and set aside.

Pierce the duck all over with a fork, then place on a rack in a roasting pan and pour in the boiling water. Cook in a preheated hot oven, 220°C (425°F), Gas Mark 7, for 45 minutes.

Remove the pan from the oven and pour away the fat and juices. Return the duck to the oven and cook for 45 minutes, or until done. Let the duck cool slightly. Remove all the fat, skin and bones and discard. Cut the meat into bite-sized pieces.

Heat the oil in a wok or large frying pan over a high heat; add the nut mixture and stir-fry for 30 seconds. Add the duck and chillies. Stir-fry for 1 minute. Blend in remaining stock, lemon juice and salt. Stir-fry for 5 minutes, until the sauce is slightly thickened. Garnish and serve immediately.
Serves 4

NANKING SPICED DUCK

2 tablespoons rock salt
3 teaspoons Szechuan peppercorns★
1 × 1.75–2 kg (4–4½ lb) oven-ready duck
TO GARNISH:
chilli flowers (see page 155)
cucumber twists and slices

Put the salt and peppercorns into a frying pan over high heat for 10 minutes to brown; cool.

Rub this mixture thoroughly over the inside and outside of the duck. Wrap lightly in foil and store in the refrigerator for 3 days.

Remove the foil and place the duck on a rack in a roasting pan. Cook in a preheated moderately hot oven, 200°C (400°F), Gas Mark 6, for 1¼ to 1½ hours, until golden brown.

Garnish and serve immediately.
Serves 4 to 6

DUCK WITH ALMONDS

500 g (1 lb) lean duck meat, cut into small chunks
2 slices root ginger★, shredded
1 clove garlic, crushed
3 tablespoons oil
3–4 dried Chinese mushrooms★ (optional)
4 spring onions, sliced
125 g (4 oz) canned bamboo shoots★, drained and sliced
3 tablespoons soy sauce★
2 tablespoons sherry
2 teaspoons cornflour
1 tablespoon water
25 g (1 oz) flaked almonds, toasted

Put the duck into a bowl with the ginger and garlic. Pour over 1 tablespoon of the oil and leave to marinate for 30 minutes.

Soak the mushrooms in warm water for 15 minutes, if using. Squeeze dry, discard the hard stalks, then slice the mushroom caps.

Heat the remaining oil in a wok or deep frying pan, add the spring onions and stir-fry for 30 seconds. Add the duck and cook for 2 minutes. Add the mushrooms, bamboo shoots, soy sauce and sherry and cook for 2 minutes. Blend the cornflour with the water and stir into the pan. Cook for 1 minute, stirring, until thickened.

Stir in the toasted almonds and serve immediately.
Serves 4 to 6

Duck with Almonds

DEEP-FRIED BEEF SLICES

500 g (1 lb) rump
    steak, thinly sliced
oil for deep-frying
soy sauce★ to serve
MARINADE:
4 spring onions,
    chopped
pinch of salt
1 tablespoon dry
    sherry
1 cm ($\frac{1}{2}$ inch) piece
    root ginger★, finely
    chopped
1 tablespoon chilli
    sauce★
1 green chilli★, seeded
    and finely chopped
BATTER:
4 tablespoons plain
    flour
pinch of salt
1 egg
3–4 tablespoons water
TO GARNISH:
coriander leaves★
lemon slice

Make the marinade: put the spring onions, salt, sherry, ginger, chilli sauce and chilli into a bowl and mix well. Add the steak, toss well to coat and leave to marinate for 20 to 25 minutes.

Meanwhile, make the batter. Sift the flour and salt into a bowl, break in the egg and beat well, adding sufficient water to make a smooth batter.

Heat the oil in a wok or deep-fryer. Dip the steak slices into the batter and deep-fry in hot oil until golden brown. Drain on kitchen paper.

Arrange the meat on a warmed serving dish and garnish with coriander and a lemon slice. Serve immediately, with soy sauce handed separately.

Serves 4 to 6

Deep-Fried Beef Slices

RED-COOKED BEEF WITH BROCCOLI

1 kg (2 lb) lean
    stewing steak, cut
    into 2.5 cm (1
    inch) cubes
1 cm ($\frac{1}{2}$ inch) piece
    root ginger★, finely
    chopped
2 cloves garlic,
    crushed
6 tablespoons soy
    sauce★
3 tablespoons dry
    sherry
50 g (2 oz) sugar
    crystals
1 teaspoon 5-spice
    powder★
600 ml (1 pint) beef
    stock
500 g (1 lb) broccoli,
    broken into florets

Put the meat cubes into a saucepan. Add the ginger, garlic, soy sauce and sherry. Sprinkle over the sugar and 5-spice powder.

Pour in the stock and bring to the boil, then cover and simmer for 1 to 1$\frac{1}{2}$ hours, until the meat is tender.

Add the broccoli to the pan. Boil vigorously, uncovered, until the broccoli is just cooked and the stock reduced and thickened.

Arrange the meat and broccoli on a warmed serving dish. Serve immediately.

Serves 4 to 6

STEAK TERIYAKI

120 ml (4 fl oz) soy
    sauce★
50 ml (2 fl oz)
    mirin★
50 ml (2 fl oz) sake★
    or dry sherry
2 tablespoons caster
    sugar
4 × 200 g (7 oz)
    sirloin steaks
4 spring onions
    brushes (see page
    155) to garnish

Combine the soy sauce, mirin, sake and sugar in a small saucepan. Bring to the boil over a moderate heat, stirring occasionally. Cool for 10 minutes.

Place the steaks in a shallow dish and pour the mixture over to coat completely. Cover and marinate for 1 hour at room temperature or for 4 hours in the refrigerator, turning the steaks occasionally.

Remove the steaks from the marinade, reserving the marinade, and transfer them to a grill pan. Brush with the reserved marinade, place under a preheated grill and cook for 3 minutes on each side for medium rare or 6 minutes each side for well-done meat. Brush the steaks frequently with the marinade while grilling.

Garnish and serve immediately.

Serves 4

BRAISED PORK WITH PUMPKIN

4 tablespoons soy sauce★

3 tablespoons dry sherry

350 g (12 oz) lean pork, cut into 1 cm (½ inch) slices

2 tablespoons oil

500 g (1 lb) pumpkin, cut into 2.5 cm (1 inch) cubes

4 spring onions, each cut into 3 pieces

1 cm (½ inch) piece root ginger★, shredded

2 cloves garlic, sliced

Put the soy sauce and sherry in a bowl and add the pork. Mix well and leave to marinate for 20 minutes.

Heat the oil in a wok or frying pan, add the pumpkin and fry quickly until browned. Add the spring onions, ginger and garlic and cook for 1 minute. Add the pork and marinade and cook for 12 to 15 minutes, until the pork and pumpkin are tender.

Spoon the mixture on to a warmed serving dish. Serve immediately.

Serves 4 to 6

CASSEROLE OF LION'S HEAD

750 g (1½ lb) finely minced pork

1 teaspoon salt

2 cloves garlic, crushed

2 × 1 cm (½ inch) pieces root ginger★, finely chopped

4 tablespoons soy sauce★

3 tablespoons dry sherry

4 spring onions, finely chopped

1 tablespoon cornflour

oil for deep-frying

300 ml (½ pint) beef stock

750 g (1½ lb) spinach

chopped spring onion to garnish

Put the pork into a bowl, stir in the salt, garlic, ginger, 1 tablespoon each of the soy sauce and sherry, and 2 of the spring onions. Mix in the cornflour, then form the mixture into balls, the size of a walnut.

Heat the oil in a wok or deep-fryer, add the meat balls and deep-fry until golden brown. Drain on kitchen paper. Put the meat balls in a pan and add the remaining soy sauce, sherry and spring onions. Spoon over the stock, cover and simmer for 15 to 20 minutes.

Meanwhile, cook the spinach, with just the water clinging to the leaves after washing, for 5 to 10 minutes until tender. Transfer to a warmed serving dish, arrange the meat balls on top and garnish with spring onion. Serve immediately.

Serves 4 to 6

TUNG-PO LAMB

2 tablespoons oil

750 g (1½ lb) lean lamb, thinly sliced

250 g (8 oz) carrots, sliced diagonally

4 celery sticks, sliced diagonally

3 tablespoons soy sauce★

4 tablespoons dry sherry

2 leeks, sliced

4 cloves garlic, thinly sliced

4 spring onions, each cut into 3 pieces

2 × 1 cm (½ inch) pieces root ginger★, shredded

1 teaspoon lightly crushed black peppercorns

2 teaspoons sugar

TO GARNISH:
lemon slices
coriander leaves★

Tung-Po Lamb

Heat the oil in a wok or deep frying pan, add the lamb and brown on both sides. Lower the heat, add the carrots and celery and stir-fry for 2 minutes. Stir in the soy sauce and sherry. Cover and cook for 15 minutes, until the vegetables are tender.

Add the leeks, garlic, spring onions and ginger and cook for 1 minute. Add the peppercorns and sugar and heat through until the sugar dissolves.

Spoon the Tung-Po on to a warmed serving dish, garnish with lemon and coriander and serve immediately.

Serves 4 to 6

BRAISED LEG OF PORK

1.5–1.75 kg (3–4 lb)
  leg of pork
salt
6 spring onions, each
  cut into 3 pieces
2 × 1 cm (½ inch)
  pieces root ginger★,
  chopped
150 ml (¼ pint) soy
  sauce★
6 tablespoons dry
  sherry
50 g (2 oz) soft
  brown sugar
radish flowers★,
  turnip flowers (see
  page 155) and
  spring onions to
  garnish

Rub the pork with salt; do not score the skin. Put the spring onions and ginger into a large pan, pour over the soy sauce and sherry, then stir in the sugar. Put the pork in the pan, turning to coat with the soy sauce mixture. Bring to the boil, cover and simmer for 2 to 2½ hours, until very tender, turning occasionally.

Remove the pork from the pan and keep hot. Boil the sauce until well reduced and thickened; pour into a sauce bowl. Carve the meat into thick slices, arrange on a serving dish and garnish with radish flowers, turnip flowers and spring onions. Serve hot or cold, with the sauce.

Serves 6 to 8

SWEET AND SOUR PORK WITH CHINESE CABBAGE

350 g (12 oz) lean
  pork, cubed
salt and pepper
2 tablespoons dry
  sherry
1 egg, beaten
1–2 tablespoons
  cornflour
oil for deep-frying
SAUCE:
1 tablespoon oil
4 spring onions,
  chopped
2 cloves garlic,
  crushed
1 cm (½ inch) piece
  root ginger★, finely
  chopped
1 tablespoon cornflour
2 tablespoons cold
  water
1 green pepper,
  cored, seeded and
  finely chopped
4 tablespoons wine
  vinegar
2 tablespoons tomato
  purée
1 tablespoon soy
  sauce★
3 tablespoons clear
  honey
2 tablespoons sesame
  seed oil★
TO SERVE:
1 small head Chinese
  leaf★, roughly
  chopped
green pepper rings
red chilli flower (see
  page 155)

Put the pork into a bowl, sprinkle with salt and pepper and stir in the sherry. Leave to marinate for 20 minutes.

Stir in the beaten egg and cornflour and mix well to coat the meat. Heat the oil in a wok or deep-fryer. Add the pork and fry until browned on all sides. Drain on kitchen paper.

To make the sauce, heat the oil in a wok or frying pan, add the spring onions, garlic and ginger and stir-fry for 2 minutes. Blend the cornflour with the water and stir into the pan with the remaining ingredients. Bring to the boil and cook for 2 minutes.

Stir in the cooked pork and cook for 2 minutes.

To serve, arrange the Chinese leaf on a warmed serving dish and pile the sweet and sour pork on top. Garnish with pepper rings and a chilli flower.

Serves 4 to 6

LEFT: *Sweet and Sour Pork with Chinese Leaf; Braised Leg of Pork*
ABOVE, RIGHT: *Omelette with Meat Sauce*
BELOW, RIGHT: *Steamed Stuffed Aubergines*

OMELETTE WITH MEAT SAUCE

3 tablespoons oil
1 clove garlic, crushed
2 spring onions,
 finely chopped
2 celery sticks,
 chopped
1 boneless chicken
 breast, diced
125 g (4 oz) minced
 pork
2 teaspoons cornflour
1 tablespoon water
1 tablespoon dry
 sherry
2 tablespoons soy
 sauce★
OMELETTE:
6 eggs, beaten
salt and pepper
TO GARNISH:
spring onion flowers
 (see page 155)
celery leaves

Heat 1 tablespoon of the oil in a wok or frying pan, add the garlic, spring onions and celery and cook for 1 minute. Increase the heat, add the chicken and pork and cook for 2 minutes.

Blend the cornflour with the water. Stir into the sauce with the sherry and soy sauce and simmer, stirring occasionally, for 15 minutes.

Meanwhile, make the omelette. Season the eggs with salt and pepper to taste. Heat the remaining 2 tablespoons oil in a large frying pan, pour in the eggs and cook gently, drawing the cooked edges towards the centre with a fork, until set and browned on both sides.

Carefully transfer to a warmed serving dish. Spoon over the meat sauce and garnish with spring onions and celery leaves. Serve the omelette immediately.
Serves 4 to 6

STEAMED STUFFED AUBERGINES

1 tablespoon oil
2 cloves garlic,
 crushed
1 cm (½ inch) piece
 root ginger★, finely
 chopped
4 spring onions,
 chopped
2 red or green
 chillies★, seeded
 and chopped
250 g (8 oz) minced
 pork
2 tablespoons soy
 sauce★
2 tablespoons dry
 sherry
4 medium aubergines
50 g (2 oz) frozen
 peeled prawns,
 thawed
spring onion flowers
 to garnish (see
 page 155)

Heat the oil in a wok or deep frying pan, add the garlic, ginger and spring onions and stir-fry for 1 minute. Increase the heat, add the chillies and pork and cook for 2 minutes. Stir in the soy sauce and sherry and cook for 10 minutes.

Meanwhile, cut the aubergines in half lengthways, carefully scoop out the flesh and chop finely. Reserve the shells. Add the flesh to the pan and cook for 10 minutes. Stir in the prawns and cook for 1 minute.

Bring a large pan of water to the boil, add the aubergine shells and cook for 1 minute; remove from the pan and drain well. Spoon the stuffing mixture into the shells and place in an ovenproof dish. Cover with a lid or foil, place in a steamer and steam vigorously for 25 to 30 minutes.

Arrange on a warmed serving dish, garnish with spring onion flowers and serve immediately.
Serves 4 to 6

CRISPY BARBECUED PORK

1.5 kg (3 lb) lean
  belly pork, in one
  piece
salt
1 tablespoon soy
  sauce★
1 teaspoon 5-spice
  powder★
TO GARNISH:
radish rose (see page
  155)
turnip flowers (see
  page 155)
coriander leaves

Pour a kettleful of boiling water over the skin of the pork; drain and dry. Rub all the surfaces of the meat with salt and leave to dry for 45 minutes.

Score the skin of the pork in a diamond pattern. Pierce the meat with a skewer in several places. Rub the soy sauce and 5-spice powder into the pork. Cover and leave for 1 hour.

Place the pork, skin side up, in a roasting pan and cook in a preheated hot oven, 230°C (450°F), Gas Mark 8, for 20 minutes. Lower the heat to 200°C (400°F), Gas Mark 6, and cook for 50 to 55 minutes more, or until the pork is tender and the skin is crisp.

Garnish, cut into slices and serve.
Serves 6 to 8

RED-COOKED LAMB

1 kg (2 lb) lean
  lamb, cubed
4 cloves garlic, sliced
3 × 1 cm ($\frac{1}{2}$ inch)
  pieces root ginger★,
  finely chopped
1 teaspoon 5-spice
  powder★
6 tablespoons soy
  sauce★
3 tablespoons dry
  sherry
6 spring onions, each
  cut into 3 pieces
600 ml (1 pint) beef
  stock
50 g (2 oz) soft
  brown sugar
1 red pepper and
  1 green pepper,
  cored, seeded and
  diced

Put the lamb into a saucepan, sprinkle with the garlic and ginger and mix well. Add the 5-spice powder, soy sauce and sherry.

Sprinkle the spring onions over the lamb. Pour over the stock and stir in the brown sugar. Bring to the boil, cover and simmer for 1 to 1$\frac{1}{4}$ hours, until the meat is tender. Remove the lid and increase the heat to reduce the remaining stock to a thick sauce.

Spoon the red-cooked lamb and sauce on to a warmed serving dish. Sprinkle with the red and green peppers and serve immediately.
Serves 4 to 6

Crispy barbecued Pork; Red-Cooked Lamb

CHINESE LAMB BROCHETTES

1 teaspoon Szechwan peppercorns★
50 ml (2 fl oz) soy sauce★
2 tablespoons Chinese rice wine★ or dry sherry
3 cloves garlic, crushed
1 tablespoon finely chopped root ginger★
2 teaspoons sesame seed oil★
1 teaspoon 5- spice powder★
salt and black pepper
1 kg (2 lb) boneless lamb shoulder, trimmed and cut into 2.5 cm (1 inch) cubes
fresh coriander sprigs★ to garnish

Place the peppercorns in a small frying pan. Toast over a medium-high heat for 3 minutes, stirring frequently, until fragrant. Crush the peppercorns in a spice grinder or with a pestle and mortar.

Combine the peppercorns, soy sauce, rice wine, garlic, ginger, sesame seed oil, 5-spice powder, salt and pepper in a large bowl. Mix well. Add the lamb and toss well to coat. Cover and marinate at room temperature for at least 3 hours or chill overnight, turning the lamb cubes occasionally.

Remove the lamb from the marinade and reserve the marinade. Thread the lamb loosely on to 8 thin skewers.

Place the skewers 10 cm (4 inches) below a preheated grill. Grill, turning occasionally and basting with the reserved marinade for 8 minutes for medium-rare lamb. Serve immediately, garnished with the coriander sprigs.
Serves 6

PINE CONE CHICKEN PATTIES

3 × 125 g (4 oz) boneless chicken breasts, skinned and ground
½ beaten egg
2 tablespoons plain flour
1 teaspoon finely grated root ginger★
salt
TO FINISH:
75 g (3 oz) plain flour
350 ml (12 fl oz) water
3 tablespoons soy sauce★
2 tablespoons caster sugar
1 tablespoon sake★ or dry sherry

Combine all the ingredients for the patties in a large bowl and blend well. Divide the mixture into 8 portions. Lightly coat your hands with some of the flour and form the chicken portions into patties. Coat each patty with some of the remaining flour. Dip a table knife into the flour and score the top of each one diagonally in a crisscross pattern. Set aside.

In a large frying pan, bring the remaining ingredients to the boil over a medium-high heat. Add the patties, scored side up. Swirl the cooking liquid to cover the tops of the patties. Reduce the heat and simmer for 3 to 4 minutes. Turn the patties over and cook for a further 5 to 6 minutes. Turn again, then increase the heat to high, swirling the pan to glaze the patties. Cook for 2 minutes. Spoon some of the cooking liquid over the tops and serve on a heated platter.
Serves 4

┌─────────────────────────────────┐
SERVING CHINESE FOOD

A Chinese meal is rather like a buffet. Platters are used for each dish and everyone is expected to eat from all of the platters. Small rice bowls on plates are provided as a stop between platter and mouth.

The dishes which comprise a Chinese meal are chosen to contrast texture, colours and flavours. If a pale dish is presented, a brightly coloured one will also be served. A dish consisting of soft ingredients will be accompanied by another with crispy ingredients, while spicy dishes will be off-set by more bland ones.

A properly planned Chinese meal consists of one meat dish, one fowl dish and one fish dish accompanied by vegetables and rice or noodle dishes. For those new to Chinese cooking, a soup, two or three main courses, accompanied by rice, fruit and tea would be a good start.
└─────────────────────────────────┘

CORIANDER PORK WITH GARLIC AND PEPPER

1 bunch fresh coriander★ with roots, well cleaned
2 tablespoons crushed garlic
2 tablespoons each salt and black pepper
2 teaspoons caster sugar
120 ml (4 fl oz) oil
1 kg (2 lb) pork tenderloin, cut into 5 mm (¼ inch) slices and pounded to a 3 mm (⅛ inch) thickness

Finely chop enough coriander roots to fill 2 tablespoons and reserve a few sprigs for garnish. Combine the measured coriander root, garlic, salt, pepper, sugar and 50 ml (2 fl oz) of the oil in a small bowl to form a paste. Rub an equal amount on each side of the pork slices. Place the pork slices in a shallow dish, cover and stand at room temperature for 1 hour.

Heat the remaining oil in a large frying pan over a medium-high heat. Add the pork and cook for 3 to 4 minutes on each side until golden brown. Garnish and serve.
Serves 4

KOFTA CURRY

3 onions, sliced
2 cloves garlic
2 green chillies★
3.5 cm (1½ inch) piece
  root ginger★
25 g (1 oz) each
  coriander★ and
  mint leaves
2 teaspoons salt
500 g (1 lb) minced
  beef
4 tablespoons oil
1 teaspoon each chilli
  powder★ and
  ground cumin★
1 tablespoon ground
  coriander★
1 tablespoon water
6 curry leaves★
25 g (1 oz) tomato
  purée, diluted in
  300 ml (½ pint)
  water
mint leaves★ to
  garnish

Put 1 onion, 1 clove garlic, 2 chillies, 1 cm (½ inch) piece ginger, the herbs and half the salt into a food processor or electric blender and work to a paste.

Mix with the minced beef, roll into walnut-sized balls and fry lightly in 3 tablespoons of the oil. Drain on kitchen paper and set aside.

Heat the remaining oil in the pan, add the remaining onions and fry until golden. Crush the remaining garlic and chop the remaining ginger. Add to the pan with the chilli powder, cumin, ground coriander and the water. Fry, stirring, for 2 minutes. Add the curry leaves and fry for 30 seconds, then stir in the tomato purée and remaining salt. Simmer for 10 minutes. Slip the meat balls into the pan and simmer for 30 minutes. Garnish with mint to serve.
Serves 4

MASSALA FRY

500 g (1 lb) braising
  steak, cubed
4 tablespoons oil
300 ml (½ pint) hot
  water
SPICE PASTE:
25 g (1 oz)
  tamarind★
300 ml (½ pint) hot
  water
6 small dried red
  chillies★
1 teaspoon cumin
  seeds★
1 clove garlic
2.5 cm (1 inch) piece
  root ginger★,
  chopped
4 cardamom pods★,
  shelled
2 teaspoons turmeric★
1 teaspoon ground
  cloves
2 teaspoons ground
  cinnamon★
½ teaspoon salt

Make the spice paste: soak the tamarind in the water for 5–10 minutes, strain, squeezing out as much water as possible. Discard the tamarind pulp. Put the chillies, cumin seeds, garlic, ginger, cardamom pods and tamarind water into a food processor or electric blender and work to a smooth paste. Mix in the turmeric, cloves, cinnamon and salt.

Roll the cubed meat in the spice paste, cover and leave for 2 to 3 hours.

Heat the oil in a frying pan with a lid, add the meat and spices and fry for 10 minutes, stirring. Add the water, stir well, cover and simmer for 30 to 45 minutes, or until the meat is tender and most of the liquid has evaporated.

Transfer to a warmed serving dish.
Serves 4

KOFTA

In India, the Kofta or meat ball is a popular way of cooking mince. Everybody has a favourite recipe. In this case the Kofta are finished in a curry sauce. They can also be fried and served 'dry' with dhal or spiced vegetables.

Braising steak is best for Massala Fry. This is a tasty, dryish curry which goes well with Nān or Chapati (see page 144). Any left over is good in a sandwich.

Kofta Curry; Masala Fry

MONGOLIAN LAMB HOT POT

1 kg (2 lb) piece
    frozen lamb fillet
50 g (2 oz)
    transparent
    noodles★
1 large head Chinese
    leaf★
500 g (1 lb) spinach
2 cakes tofu★, thinly
    sliced
3 × 411 g (14½ oz)
    cans consommé

SAUCES:
6 spring onions,
    chopped
2 tablespoons
    shredded root
    ginger★
6 tablespoons sesame
    seed paste★
3 tablespoons sesame
    seed oil★
6 tablespoons soy
    sauce★
4 tablespoons chilli
    sauce★
4 tablespoons
    chopped coriander
    leaves★ (optional)

Allow the lamb to defrost slightly, but while it is still partially frozen, cut into paper-thin slices, arrange on a serving dish and allow to thaw.

Soak the noodles in hot water for 10 minutes; drain thoroughly.

Place the Chinese leaves and spinach in a basket or dish. Arrange the tofu and noodles on another dish.

Combine the spring onions and ginger in a sauce dish. Mix the sesame seed paste and oil in another sauce bowl. Put the soy sauce and chilli sauce in individual sauce bowls. If liked, serve chopped coriander in a separate bowl.

Heat the consommé in a fondue pot or similar dish at the table.

To serve, each person first mixes his own sauce in a small dish. Using chopsticks, fondue forks or long skewers, he dips a slice of meat into the hot consommé to cook, then dips it into his prepared sauce before eating.

When all the meat has been eaten the vegetables, tofu and noodles are added to the pot and cooked for about 5 to 10 minutes. Serve this soup at the end of the meal.

Serves 4 to 6

Mongolian Lamb Hot Pot

CHILLI FRY

4 tablespoons oil
1 large onion, finely
　chopped
½ teaspoon ground
　coriander★
½ teaspoon turmeric★
2.5 cm (1 inch) piece
　root ginger★, finely
　chopped
1 chilli★, chopped
500 g (1 lb) frying
　steak, cut into
　strips about 2.5 ×
　1 cm (1 × ½ inch)
1 green or red pepper,
　cored, seeded and
　roughly chopped
2 tomatoes, quartered
juice of 1 lemon
salt

Heat the oil in a lidded frying pan,
add the onion and fry until soft. Add
the coriander, turmeric, ginger and
chilli and fry over low heat for 5
minutes; if the mixture becomes dry,
add 1 tablespoon water.

Add the steak, increase the heat and
cook, stirring, until browned all over.
Add the chopped pepper, cover and
simmer gently for 5 to 10 minutes,
until the meat is tender. Add the
tomatoes, lemon juice and salt to taste
and cook, uncovered, for 2 to 3
minutes. This dish should be rather
dry.
Serves 4

ALOO 'CHOPS'

3 tablespoons oil
1 large onion, finely
　chopped
1 cm (½ inch) piece
　root ginger★, finely
　chopped
1 teaspoon ground
　coriander★
250 g (8 oz) minced
　beef
1 tablespoon raisins
salt
1 tablespoon finely
　chopped coriander
　leaves★
1 kg (2 lb) potatoes,
　boiled and mashed
　with a little milk
　and salt
flour for coating
oil for shallow-frying

Heat the oil in a frying pan, add the
onion and ginger and fry until golden.
Add the ground coriander and minced
beef and fry until brown. Add the
raisins and salt to taste and simmer for
about 20 minutes, until the meat is
cooked. Spoon out any fat in the pan.
Stir in the chopped coriander and
leave to cool.

Divide the mashed potato into 8
portions. With well floured hands,
flatten a portion on one palm, put 3
teaspoons of the meat mixture in the
centre and fold the potato over it.
Form gently into a round patty shape.

Dip the 'chops' lightly in flour and
shallow fry a few at a time in hot oil,
until crisp and golden, turning
carefully to brown the underside.
Serves 4

Chilli Fry; Aloo Chops

VEGETABLE KHEEMA

4 tablespoons oil
2 onions, chopped
2 teaspoons ground
    coriander★
½ teaspoon ground
    cumin★
½ teaspoon ground
    turmeric★
2.5 cm (1 inch) piece
    root ginger★, finely
    chopped
1 chilli★, finely
    chopped
1 heaped teaspoon
    garam masala★
500 g (1 lb) minced
    beef
250 g (8 oz) small
    potatoes, quartered
salt
500 g (1 lb) shelled
    peas

Heat the oil in a lidded frying pan, add the onions and cook until soft. Add the spices and fry for 5 minutes over low heat; add 1 tablespoon water if the mixture starts to burn. Stir in the minced beef and cook over high heat until very well browned.

Lower the heat and add the potatoes and salt to taste. Cover and cook gently for 5 minutes, then add the peas. Continue cooking until the potatoes and peas are tender. Serve hot.
Serves 4

KOFTA IN YOGURT

500 g (1 lb) minced
    beef
75 g (3 oz) fresh
    breadcrumbs
2 green chillies★,
    finely chopped
1 onion, finely
    chopped
2.5 cm (1 inch) piece
    root ginger★, finely
    chopped
2 teaspoons ground
    coriander★
salt
1 egg, lightly beaten
oil for frying
500 g (1 lb) natural
    yogurt
2 tablespoons chopped
    coriander leaves★

Mix the minced beef, breadcrumbs, chillies, onion, ginger, ground coriander, salt to taste and egg together and shape the mixture into walnut-sized balls.

Heat the oil in a large pan, add the meat balls and fry until well browned and cooked through. Drain carefully.

Pour the yogurt into a serving bowl and add the meat balls while still hot. Sprinkle with the chopped coriander and serve warm.
Serves 4

Vegetable Kheema; Kofta in Yogurt

BEEF CURRY WITH POTATOES

4 tablespoons oil
2 onions, finely
  chopped
2 cloves garlic,
  chopped
1 teaspoon chilli
  powder★
1 tablespoon ground
  cumin★
1½ tablespoons
  ground coriander★
2.5 cm (1 inch) piece
  root ginger★, finely
  chopped
750 g (1½ lb)
  stewing steak,
  cubed
2 tablespoons tomato
  purée
salt
350 g (12 oz) new
  potatoes, scraped
  and halved if large
4 green chillies★

Heat the oil in a large pan, add the onions and fry until lightly coloured. Add the garlic, chilli powder, cumin, coriander and ginger and cook gently for 5 minutes, stirring occasionally; if the mixture becomes dry, add 2 tablespoons water.

Add the beef and cook, stirring, until browned all over. Add the tomato purée, salt to taste and just enough water to cover the meat; stir very well. Bring to the boil, cover and simmer for about 1 hour or until the meat is almost tender. Add the potatoes and whole chillies and simmer until the potatoes are cooked.
Serves 4

STUFFED PEPPERS

5 tablespoons oil
1 onion, finely
  chopped
2 teaspoons ground
  coriander★
1 teaspoon ground
  cumin★
½ teaspoon chilli
  powder★
350 g (12 oz) minced
  beef
3 tablespoons long-
  grain rice
salt
4 large green or red
  peppers, sliced
  lengthways, cored
  and seeded
1 × 397 g (14 oz)
  can tomatoes

Heat 3 tablespoons of the oil in a saucepan, add the onion and fry until golden. Add the spices and cook for 2 minutes. Add the minced beef and fry, stirring, until browned. Add the rice and salt to taste and cook for 2 minutes. Remove from the heat and leave to cool.

Fill the pepper shells with the meat mixture.

Heat the remaining oil in a pan just large enough to hold the peppers. Place the peppers in the pan. Pour a little of the tomato juice into each pepper and the remaining juice and tomatoes into the pan, seasoning with salt to taste. Bring to simmering point, cover and cook for about 25 minutes, until the rice is tender.
Serves 4

ABOVE: *Stuffed Peppers*
RIGHT: *Beef Curry with Potatoes*

BEEF BUFFAD

3 tablespoons oil
2 onions, sliced
2 cloves garlic, finely
    chopped
3 green chillies★,
    chopped
3.5 cm (1½ inch)
    piece root ginger★,
    chopped
750 g (1½ lb) braising
    steak, cubed
½ teaspoon chilli
    powder★
1 teaspoon turmeric★
1 teaspoon pepper
1 teaspoon ground
    cumin★
1 tablespoon ground
    coriander★
½ teaspoon ground
    cinnamon★
½ teaspoon ground
    cloves
300 ml (½ pint)
    coconut milk or 75 g
    (3 oz) creamed
    coconut melted in
    250 ml (8 fl oz)
    warm water★
salt
85 ml (3 fl oz) wine
    vinegar
50 ml (2 fl oz) water

Heat the oil in a large saucepan, add the onions and fry until they are just beginning to brown, then add the garlic, chillies and ginger. Fry for 1 minute, then add the beef and remaining spices. Stir well and cook for 5 minutes, stirring occasionally.

Add the coconut milk, which should just cover the meat; if it does not, add a little water. Add salt to taste. Bring to simmering point, cover and cook for about 1½ hours, until the meat is almost tender.

Add the vinegar and water and continue cooking for about 30 minutes, until the meat is tender and the gravy thick.

Serves 4

SWEET AND SOUR
BEEF STEW

1 kg (2 lb) boneless
    stewing beef, cut
    into 5 cm (2 inch)
    cubes
1 large onion, thinly
    sliced
4 green chillies★,
    seeded and thinly
    sliced
2 thin slices root
    ginger★, crushed
2 large cloves garlic,
    crushed
2 tablespoons oil
1 teaspoon laos
    powder★
475 ml (16 fl oz) beef
    stock or water
120 ml (4 fl oz)
    ketjap manis★
4 tablespoons red wine
    vinegar
2 teaspoons sugar
salt

Combine the meat, onion, chillies, ginger, garlic, oil and laos powder in a large saucepan. Place over a medium-high heat and cook for 5 to 10 minutes, stirring occasionally, until the meat has browned on all sides.

Stir in the remaining ingredients and bring to the boil, stirring frequently. Lower the heat and stirring occasionally, simmer for 1 hour or until the meat is tender and the sauce is reduced to a thick glaze.

Transfer the stew to a heated serving dish and serve with rice.
Serves 4 to 6

LEFT: *Beef Buffad*   RIGHT: *Sweet and Sour Beef Stew*

LAMB GULE KAMBING

4 tablespoons oil
750 g (1½ lb) boned
    leg of lamb, cut in
    thin strips
900 ml (1½ pints) thin
    coconut milk★
juice of 1 lemon
6 curry leaves★
coriander leaves★ to
    garnish (optional)
SPICE PASTE:
3 small onions,
    quartered
3 cloves garlic
2.5 cm (1 inch) piece
    root ginger★,
    chopped
4 kemiri nuts★ or
    15 g (½ oz)
    blanched almonds
1 teaspoon turmeric★
1 teaspoon powdered
    lemon grass★ or
    grated lemon rind
½–1 teaspoon small
    dried red chillies★
1 teaspoon each
    ground cinnamon★,
    cloves and
    cardamom★
1 tablespoon ground
    coriander★
½ teaspoon ground
    cumin★
1 teaspoon laos★
    (optional)
1 teaspoon sugar
1 teaspoon salt

Make the spice paste: put all the ingredients into a food processor or electric blender and work until smooth.

Heat the oil in a large saucepan and fry the spice paste for 5 minutes, stirring. Add the meat and fry until brown, then add the coconut milk, lemon juice and curry leaves.

Bring to simmering point and cook, uncovered, for 25 to 30 minutes or until the lamb is tender, stirring frequently. Serve hot, garnished with coriander if wished.
Serves 4

Beef Rendang; Lamb Gule Kambing

BEEF RENDANG

50 g (2 oz)
    tamarind★
150 ml (¼ pint) hot
    water
900 ml (1½ pints)
    thick coconut milk★
1 teaspoon sugar
1 teaspoon salt
750 g (1½ lb) rump
    steak, cubed
4 curry leaves★
SPICE PASTE:
2 teaspoons chilli
    powder★
4 small onions,
    chopped
4 cloves garlic
5 cm (2 inch) piece
    root ginger★,
    chopped
1 teaspoon turmeric★
1 tablespoon ground
    coriander★
1 teaspoon ground
    cumin★
1 teaspoon lemon
    grass★

Soak the tamarind in the hot water for 5–10 minutes, strain, squeezing out as much water as possible. Discard the tamarind. Make the spice paste: put all the ingredients into a food processor or electric blender and work until smooth.

Put the spice paste in a large saucepan. Stir in the coconut milk, tamarind water, sugar and salt. When well mixed, add the beef and curry leaves and bring to the boil. Lower the heat to moderate and cook uncovered, stirring frequently, for about 30 minutes or until the sauce is thick.

Reduce the heat to low and continue cooking for about 1 to 1½ hours, until the curry is dry and deep brown. Stir frequently and be very careful not to let it burn. Serve hot, garnished with lime twists if liked.
Serves 4

RENDANG

Rendang is a famous Indonesian dry beef curry. Blistering hot in its native Sumatra – something you can alter by reducing the number of chillies – it is a dish which requires careful cooking, particularly in the final stages when the meat must turn a dark brown without burning. This curry improves with keeping, so make it a day before required.

The lamb curry also comes from Indonesia.

NARGIS KEBAB

KEBAB:
250 g (8 oz) minced
  beef or lamb
2 cloves garlic,
  crushed
2.5 cm (1 inch) piece
  root ginger★, grated
½ teaspoon ground
  coriander★
½ teaspoon ground
  cumin★
½–1 teaspoon chilli
  powder★
¼ teaspoon ground
  cloves
1 tablespoon cornflour
salt
1 egg yolk
4 small hard-boiled
  eggs
oil for shallow-frying
CURRY SAUCE:
4 tablespoons oil
5 cm (2 inch) piece
  cinnamon stick★
6 cloves
6 cardamom★
1 onion, finely
  chopped
2 cloves garlic,
  crushed
2.5 cm (1 inch) piece
  root ginger★, grated
2 teaspoons ground
  coriander★
1 teaspoon ground
  cumin★
½–1 teaspoon chilli
  powder★
4 tablespoons natural
  yogurt
1 × 397 g (14 oz)
  can tomatoes
2 tablespoons
  chopped coriander
  leaves★

Mix together the meat, garlic, spices, cornflour and salt to taste. Bind with the egg yolk and divide the mixture into 4 equal parts.

With well floured hands, flatten each portion into a round, place a hard-boiled egg in the centre and work the meat round to cover. Roll into a ball.

Heat the oil in a pan and shallow-fry the kebabs until they are brown all over. Lift out and set aside while making the sauce.

Heat the oil in a saucepan, add the cinnamon, cloves and cardamom and fry for a few seconds. Add the onion, garlic and ginger and fry until golden brown. Add the coriander, cumin and chilli powder and fry for 1 minute. Add the yogurt, a spoonful at a time, stirring until it is absorbed before adding the next spoonful.

Break up the tomatoes with a fork, add them with their juice and simmer for 1 minute. Add the kebabs to the sauce, season with salt to taste and cook, uncovered, for 25 minutes until the sauce is thick. Stir in the chopped coriander to serve.
Serves 4

KHEEMA DO PYAZA

500 g (1 lb) onions
4 tablespoons oil
2.5 cm (1 inch) piece
  root ginger★,
  chopped
1 clove garlic, finely
  chopped
2 green chillies★,
  finely chopped
1 teaspoon turmeric★
1 teaspoon ground
  coriander★
1 teaspoon ground
  cumin★
750 g (1½ lb)
  minced lamb
1 × 150 g (5 oz)
  carton natural
  yogurt
1 × 227 g (8 oz) can
  tomatoes
salt
sprigs of fresh thyme
  to garnish
  (optional)

Finely chop 350 g (12 oz) of the onions. Heat 2 tablespoons of the oil in a pan, add the chopped onion and fry until golden. Add the ginger, garlic, chillies and spices and fry for 2 minutes. Add the minced lamb and cook, stirring to break up, until well browned.

Stir in the yogurt, spoon by spoon, until it is absorbed, then add the tomatoes with their juice, and salt to taste. Bring to the boil, stir well, cover and simmer for 20 minutes or until the meat is cooked.

Thinly slice the remaining 150 g (4 oz) of the onions, then fry them in the remaining oil until brown and crisp.

Transfer the meat mixture to a warmed serving dish. Sprinkle with the fried onions and garnish with thyme, if using.
Serves 4

Nargis Kebab; Kheema do Pyaza

Thai Beef Curry; Chilli Pork and Prawns

THAI BEEF CURRY

750 ml (1¼ pints)
  thick coconut milk★
750 g (1½ lb) lean
  stewing steak,
  cubed
salt
2 chillies★, finely
  sliced
2 tablespoons fish
  sauce★ or soy
  sauce★
3 lime leaves
  (optional)
SPICE PASTE:
4 cloves garlic
2 small onions,
  quartered
3–6 small dried red
  chillies★
1 teaspoon powdered
  lemon grass★ or
  grated lemon rind
1 teaspoon laos★
  (optional)
1 cm (½ inch) piece
  root ginger★
1 tablespoon ground
  coriander★
1 teaspoon ground
  cumin★
1 teaspoon turmeric★

Bring 600 ml (1 pint) of the coconut milk to simmering point in a saucepan. Add the beef and salt to taste, cover and simmer for 1 to 1½ hours or until the meat is tender. Lift out the beef and set aside.

Meanwhile make the spice paste: put all the ingredients into a food processor or electric blender and work to a smooth paste.

Pour the remaining coconut milk into a second saucepan. Stir in the spice paste and cook, stirring, for 15 minutes or until the mixture is dry and well fried. Gradually pour in the coconut milk from the first pan and stir as it comes to simmering point. Add the beef, chillies, fish or soy sauce and lime leaves, if using. Cook for 10 to 15 minutes or until the sauce is thick.

Transfer to a warmed serving dish.

Serves 4

CHILLI PORK AND PRAWNS

300 ml (½ pint) thick
  coconut milk★
250 g (8 oz) raw
  peeled prawns,
  finely chopped
250 g (8 oz) pork
  fillet, finely
  chopped
2 red chillies★, finely
  chopped
1 teaspoon salt
1 teaspoon sugar
½ teaspoon black
  pepper

Pour the coconut milk into a saucepan and bring to simmering point. Mix the prawns and pork together and stir into the coconut milk.

Add the chillies, salt, sugar and pepper and simmer gently for 15 to 20 minutes.

Transfer to a warmed serving dish.

Serves 4

THAI RICE COOKING

For the Thais, plain boiled rice is the basis of all meals. 'Plain' is the right description as they tend to salt the rice very lightly, because the other dishes are so highly seasoned, particularly with their favourite flavouring, *nam pla* or fish sauce.

Thai curries – like these – are fiery, much hotter than the Indian curries from which they derive. They use the small, shiny, ferocious chillies which are available here – use them at your peril!

SPICED MEAT CURRY

500 g (1 lb) stewing
  beef, lamb or pork,
  cubed
500 g (1 lb) onions,
  finely chopped
2.5 cm (1 inch) piece
  cinnamon stick★
6 cloves
1 tablespoon ground
  coriander★
1 teaspoon ground
  cumin★
½ teaspoon turmeric★
1 teaspoon chilli
  powder★
2.5 cm (1 inch) piece
  root ginger★, finely
  chopped
1 tablespoon tomato
  purée
3 tablespoons oil
salt
250 g (8 oz) small
  new potatoes
  (optional)

Put all the ingredients except the potatoes into a saucepan, seasoning with salt to taste. Stir well. The mixture should be moist; add an extra tablespoon of oil if necessary. Cover the pan tightly and leave overnight in the refrigerator.

Cook over a moderately high heat until the mixture starts to fry briskly. Stir well, then lower the heat and simmer for about 1½ hours or until the meat is tender.

Add the potatoes, if using, about 20 minutes before the end of the cooking time.
Serves 4

Pork Vindaloo; Hurry Curry

PORK VINDALOO

1–2 teaspoons chilli
  powder★
1 teaspoon turmeric★
2 teaspoons ground
  cumin★
2 teaspoons ground
  mustard★
2 tablespoons ground
  coriander★
3.5 cm (1½ inch)
  piece root ginger★,
  finely chopped
salt
150 ml (¼ pint)
  vinegar
1 large onion, finely
  chopped
2 cloves garlic,
  crushed
750 g (1½ lb) pork
  fillet, cubed
4 tablespoons oil

Mix the spices, and salt to taste with the vinegar. Put the onion, garlic and pork into a bowl, pour over the vinegar mixture, cover and leave in the refrigerator overnight.

Heat the oil in a large saucepan, add the pork mixture, bring to simmering point, cover and cook for about 45 minutes or until the pork is tender.
Serves 4

MASALA CHOPS

1 teaspoon ground
    cumin★
2 teaspoons ground
    coriander★
¼ teaspoon chilli
    powder★
1 clove garlic, crushed
salt
lemon juice to mix
4 pork chops

Mix the spices, garlic, and salt to taste into a paste with lemon juice. Slash the pork chops on both sides. Rub the paste into the meat and leave for 30 minutes. Cook under a preheated moderate grill for 5 or 6 minutes on each side.
Serves 4

RAAN

2.25 kg (5 lb) leg of
    lamb, skin and fat
    removed
2 × 150 g (5 oz)
    cartons natural
    yogurt
150 g (5 oz) whole,
    unpeeled almonds
4 tablespoons brown
    sugar
1 teaspoon saffron
    threads★
3 tablespoons
    boiling water
SPICE PASTE:
50 g (2 oz) root
    ginger★, chopped
6 cloves garlic
rind of 1 lemon
juice of 2 lemons
2 teaspoons cumin
    seeds★
6 cardamom★, peeled
1 teaspoon ground
    cloves
1 teaspoon turmeric★
1½ teaspoons chilli
    powder★
1 tablespoon salt

Prick the lamb all over with a fork and make about 12 deep cuts.

Make the spice paste: blend the ginger, garlic, lemon rind and juice, spices and salt in an electric blender or food processor. Spread over the lamb and leave to stand for 1 hour in a flameproof casserole.

Blend 4 tablespoons of yogurt with the almonds and 2 tablespoons of sugar. Stir in the remaining yogurt and pour over the lamb. Cover and leave for 48 hours in the refrigerator.

Let the meat return to room temperature. Sprinkle over the remaining sugar and cook, uncovered, in a preheated hot oven, 220°C (425°F), Gas Mark 7, for 30 minutes. Cover, lower the temperature to 160°C (325°F), Gas Mark 3, and cook for 3 hours, basting occasionally. Meanwhile, soak the saffron in the water for 15 minutes. Strain and sprinkle it over the meat and cook for a further 30 minutes.

Remove the meat from the pan, wrap it in foil and keep warm. Skim off the fat from the casserole and boil the sauce until thick. Place the meat on a dish and pour over the sauce. Carve in thick slices to serve.
Serves 6

Masala Chops; Raan

STUFFED CABBAGE LEAVES

1 cabbage
5 tablespoons oil
1 onion, chopped
1 cm ($\frac{1}{2}$ inch) piece
    root ginger★,
    chopped
1 teaspoon turmeric★
500 g (1 lb) lean
    minced lamb
75 g (3 oz) long-
    grain rice
2 tomatoes, skinned
    and chopped
grated rind and juice
    of 2 lemons
2 teaspoons sugar
salt and pepper
150 ml ($\frac{1}{4}$ pint)
    water

Hollow out the stem end of the cabbage with a sharp knife. Place in a large pan, cover with water and bring to the boil. Remove from the heat, cover and leave for 15 minutes. Drain.

Fry the onion in 2 tablespoons of the oil until soft. Add the spices and fry gently for 1 minute. Add the lamb and fry briefly until brown. Cool slightly, then mix with the remaining ingredients, minus the water.

Carefully remove 12 inner leaves of the cabbage. Divide the meat mixture between the 12 leaves, gently squeezing out and reserving any liquid. Shape each leaf into a packet.

Heat the remaining oil in a large lidded frying pan. Add the cabbage rolls in one layer; heat through. Pour on the reserved liquid and water. Cover and simmer for about 30 minutes. If the liquid has not evaporated, increase heat and cook uncovered for a few minutes. Lower heat, turn the rolls, cover and cook for 5 minutes.
Serves 4 to 6

BHUNA GHOSHT

750 g (1$\frac{1}{2}$ lb) pork
    fillets, slit
    lengthways and
    quartered
2 tablespoons
    coriander seeds★,
    roughly pounded
1 teaspoon pepper
1 tablespoon paprika
salt
4 tablespoons oil
TO GARNISH:
2 tablespoons finely
    chopped coriander★
lemon wedges

Prick the pork fillets all over with a fork. Mix together the coriander, pepper, paprika, and salt to taste and rub into the meat on both sides. Leave to stand for 1 hour.

Heat the oil in a pan, add the meat and fry quickly on both sides to seal. Lower the heat and fry gently for 5 minutes or until cooked through, stirring and turning to prevent burning.

Sprinkle with the coriander and serve with lemon.
Serves 4

PORK KEBAB

4 cloves garlic,
    chopped
10 cardamom★,
    peeled
1 teaspoon cumin
    seeds★
juice of 3 lemons
1 teaspoon chilli
    powder★
1 teaspoon garam
    masala★
1 tablespoon oil
1 teaspoon salt
750 g (1$\frac{1}{2}$ lb) pork
    fillet, cubed

Put the garlic, cardamom, cumin and lemon juice into an electric blender or food processor and work to a paste. Add the chilli powder, garam masala, oil and salt and mix well. Pour over the meat, stirring well so that the cubes are thoroughly covered. Cover and leave in the refrigerator for 6 hours. Rub 4 skewers with oil, thread the meat on them and cook under a preheated moderate grill for 10 minutes, until cooked through, turning the skewers several times.
Serves 4

Bhuna Ghosht; Stuffed Cabbage Leaves; Pork Kebab

ROGHAN GHOSHT

4 tablespoons oil
2 onions, finely
  chopped
750 g (1½ lb) boned
  leg of lamb, cubed
2 × 150 g (5 oz)
  cartons natural
  yogurt
2 cloves garlic
2.5 cm (1 inch) piece
  root ginger★
2 green chillies★
1 tablespoon
  coriander seeds★
1 teaspoon cumin
  seeds★
1 teaspoon chopped
  mint leaves
1 teaspoon chopped
  coriander leaves★
6 cardamom★
6 cloves
2.5 cm (1 inch) piece
  cinnamon stick★
salt
125 g (4 oz) flaked
  almonds

Heat 2 tablespoons of the oil in a pan, add one onion and fry until golden. Add the lamb and 175 g (6 oz) of the yogurt, stir well, cover and simmer for 20 minutes.

Place the garlic, ginger, chillies, coriander seeds, cumin, mint, coriander and 2 to 3 tablespoons yogurt in an electric blender or food processor and work to a paste.

Heat the remaining oil in a large saucepan, add the cardamom, cloves and cinnamon and fry for 1 minute, stirring. Add the second onion, prepared paste and fry for 5 minutes, stirring constantly.

Add the lamb and yogurt mixture, and salt to taste, stir well and bring to simmering point. Cover and cook for 30 minutes. Add the almonds and cook for a further 15 minutes, until the meat is tender.

Serves 4

LAMB CURRY WITH YOGURT

4 tablespoons oil
3 onions, chopped
6 cardamom★
5 cm (2 inch) piece
  cinnamon stick★
1½ tablespoons
  ground coriander★
2 tablespoons ground
  cumin★
¼ teaspoon turmeric★
¼ teaspoon ground
  cloves
1–2 teaspoons chilli
  powder★
½ teaspoon grated
  nutmeg
2 tablespoons water
1 tablespoon paprika
2 × 150 g (5 oz)
  cartons natural
  yogurt
750 g (1½ lb) boned
  leg of lamb, cubed
1 large tomato,
  skinned
  and chopped
salt

Heat the oil in a large saucepan, add the onions, cardamom and cinnamon and fry until the onions turn golden. Stir in the coriander, cumin, turmeric, cloves, chilli powder and nutmeg. Fry until dry, then add the water and cook, stirring, for 5 minutes, adding a little more water if necessary.

Add the paprika and slowly stir in the yogurt. Add the lamb, tomato, and salt to taste and mix well. Bring to simmering point, cover and cook for 1 hour or until the meat is tender.

Serves 4

Roghan Ghosht; Lamb Curry with Yogurt

DRY LAMB CURRY

3 tablespoons oil
250 g (8 oz) onions,
　finely chopped
6 cloves
6 cardamom★
2.5 cm (1 inch) piece
　cinnamon stick★
2 green chillies★,
　finely chopped
750 g (1½ lb) boned
　leg of lamb, cut
　into strips
2 teaspoons ground
　coriander★
1 teaspoon ground
　cumin★
2 × 150 g (5 oz)
　cartons natural
　yogurt
2 tablespoons finely
　chopped coriander
　leaves★
3 curry leaves★
salt
1 teaspoon garam
　masala★

Heat the oil in a pan, add the onions and fry until soft. Add the cloves, cardamom and cinnamon and fry for 1 minute, then add the chillies and lamb. Fry for a further 10 minutes, turning the lamb to brown on all sides. Add the remaining ingredients, except the garam masala, seasoning with salt to taste. Stir well, bring to simmering point and cook, uncovered, for 40 minutes, until the meat is tender and the liquid evaporated. Stir in the garam masala and serve.
Serves 4

ABOVE: *Dry Lamb Curry*   RIGHT: *Lamb Korma*

LAMB KORMA

5 tablespoons oil
6 cardamom★
6 cloves
6 peppercorns
2.5 cm (1 inch) piece
　cinnamon stick★
750 g (1½ lb) boned
　leg of lamb, cubed
6 small onions,
　chopped
2 cloves garlic, chopped
5 cm (2 inch) piece
　root ginger★,
　chopped
2 tablespoons ground
　coriander★
2 teaspoons ground
　cumin★
1 teaspoon chilli
　powder★
salt
1 × 150 g (5 oz)
　carton natural
　yogurt
1 teaspoon garam
　masala★
2 tablespoons chopped
　coriander leaves★

Heat 4 tablespoons of the oil in a pan, add the cardamom, cloves, peppercorns and cinnamon and fry for 1 minute.

Add a few pieces of lamb at a time and fry well to brown all over; transfer to a dish. Remove the whole spices and discard.

Add the remaining oil to the pan and fry the onions, garlic and ginger for 5 minutes, then add the coriander, cumin, chilli powder, and salt to taste and cook for 5 minutes, stirring to avoid burning. Gradually stir in the yogurt until it is all absorbed.

Return the meat to the pan with any liquid collected in the dish and add sufficient water just to cover the meat. Bring to simmering point, cover and cook for about 1 hour or until the meat is tender.

Sprinkle on the garam masala and cook, stirring, for 1 minute. Top with chopped coriander before serving.
Serves 4

LAMB CURRY WITH COCONUT

4 tablespoons oil
2 onions, chopped
4 curry leaves★
750 g (1½ lb) boned
   leg of lamb, cubed
1 × 227 g (8 oz) can
   tomatoes
salt
2 tablespoons finely
   chopped coriander
   leaves★
SPICE PASTE:
grated flesh of ½
   fresh coconut★
4 dried red chillies★
1 teaspoon cumin
   seeds★
1 tablespoon
   coriander seeds★
1 tablespoon poppy
   seeds
1 teaspoon
   peppercorns
2.5 cm (½ inch) piece
   root ginger★,
   chopped
2 cloves garlic
1 teaspoon turmeric★
2 tablespoons lemon
   juice

Make the spice paste: heat the coconut, chillies, cumin, coriander seeds and poppy seeds in a dry frying pan for about 1 minute. Put into an electric blender or food processor with the peppercorns, ginger, garlic, turmeric and lemon juice and blend to a paste.

Heat the oil in a pan, add the onions and fry until soft, then add the curry leaves and the prepared paste and fry for 5 minutes. Add the lamb and cook, stirring, for 5 minutes, then add the tomatoes with their juice and salt to taste. Bring to simmering point, cover and cook for about 1 hour, until tender.

Sprinkle with chopped coriander to serve.

Serves 4

NOTE: If fresh coconut is not available, blend the other spices and lemon juice as above and add 50 g (2 oz) creamed coconut★ to the onions with the blended spices.

LAMB KEBAB

2 × 150 g (5 oz)
   cartons natural
   yogurt
1 tablespoon ground
   coriander★
½ teaspoon chilli
   powder★
1 tablespoon oil
salt
750 g (1½ lb) boned
   leg of lamb, cubed
4 onions
2 red peppers
4 tomatoes
2 tablespoons finely
   chopped coriander
   leaves★

Put the yogurt, coriander, chilli, oil, and salt to taste in a large bowl and stir to combine. Add the meat, mix well, cover and leave in the refrigerator overnight.

Cut the onions in quarters and separate the layers. Core and seed the peppers and cut into squares and cut the tomatoes in half.

Thread the onion, lamb and red pepper alternately on 8 skewers, beginning and ending each kebab with a tomato half. Cook under a preheated hot grill for about 10 minutes, turning frequently and basting with any remaining marinade as necessary. Sprinkle with the chopped coriander to serve.

Serves 4

SERVING INDIAN FOOD

The average middle-class Indian main meal consists of two or three vegetable dishes, including perhaps one pulse dish. If the household is not vegetarian, fish or meat may be included. Rice and bread are the standard accompaniments, along with poppadoms, yogurt, pickles, chutneys, sliced onions and chopped mint. All the food is put on the table at the same time, usually on *thalis* – large round metal trays with separate bowls. The bowls are filled with the various dishes and rice is placed in the centre of the *thali*. Chutneys, pickles and other side dishes are also included on the *thali*. In Western kitchens, the main dishes may be placed on large serving platters in the centre of the table, with side dishes arranged around.

Lamb Kebab

TANDOORI TURKEY BREASTS

4 boneless turkey
breasts

MARINADE:

1 teaspoon chilli
powder★

1 small piece ginger
root★, very finely
chopped

2 cloves garlic,
crushed

1 teaspoon each
ground coriander★
and cumin★

2 teaspoons paprika

salt and pepper

300 g (10 oz) natural
yogurt

1 tablespoon lemon
juice

TO GARNISH:

shredded lettuce

onion rings

mint sprigs

lemon twists

Make the marinade: put the chilli powder, ginger, garlic, coriander, cumin and paprika into a large bowl, with salt and pepper to taste. Stir in the yogurt and lemon juice.

Place the turkey breasts in a shallow dish and spoon over the marinade. Cover and leave in the refrigerator overnight.

Remove the turkey from the marinade. Cook under a preheated moderate grill for 10 to 12 minutes on each side, basting frequently with the marinade, until the turkey is cooked through.

Arrange the lettuce on a plate, place the turkey on top and garnish with onion rings, mint sprigs and lemon twists. Serve immediately.

Serves 4

CORIANDER LAMB

2 cloves garlic, thinly
sliced

½ teaspoon chilli
powder★

2 teaspoons ground
ginger★

1 teaspoon ground
coriander★

2 tablespoons chopped
coriander leaves★

1 × 150 g (5 oz)
carton natural
yogurt

salt and pepper

4 lamb chump chops

TO GARNISH:

lime or lemon wedges

coriander leaves★

Put the garlic, chilli powder, ginger, ground coriander, coriander leaves and yogurt in a bowl, with salt and pepper to taste; mix well.

Place the chops in a shallow dish, spoon over the yogurt mixture, cover and leave to marinate for 2 hours, turning occasionally.

Remove from the marinade. Cook under a preheated moderately hot grill for 8 to 10 minutes on each side, until cooked through and browned, basting frequently with the marinade.

Serve hot, garnished with lime or lemon wedges and coriander.

Serves 4

Tandoori Turkey Breasts; Coriander Lamb

CHINESE LAMB TITBITS WITH DIPPING SAUCE

DIPPING SAUCE:
85 ml (3 fl oz) soy
    sauce★
2 tablespoons Chinese
    rice wine★
2 tablespoons
    Worcestershire
    sauce
2 tablespoons caster
    sugar
1 tablespoon finely
    chopped fresh
    coriander★
2 teaspoons sesame
    seed oil★
2 teaspoons grated
    root ginger★
1 teaspoon Chinese
    hot pepper oil★
2 cloves garlic,
    crushed
1 spring onion, green
    part only, finely
    chopped
LAMB TITBITS:
4.5 litres (8 pints)
    water
1 kg (2 lb) lamb
    shoulder, trimmed
    and cut through the
    bones into bite-
    sized pieces
4 spring onions,
    coarsely chopped
4 thin slices root
    ginger★, crushed
2 tablespoons Chinese
    rice wine★
2 tablespoons soy
    sauce★
7.5 cm (3 inch)
    cinnamon stick★
1 teaspoon Szechwan
    peppercorns★
2 whole star anise★
salt

To make the dipping sauce, combine all the ingredients in a small bowl and stir until the sugar has dissolved. Divide the sauce into 6 small serving dishes, cover and set aside.

Place 5½ pints of the water in a wok or large saucepan and bring quickly to the boil. Add the lamb and cook for 1 minute. Drain in a colander, then refresh under cold running water, shaking well to remove excess water. Clean the pan.

Place the lamb, the remaining water, spring onions, ginger, rice wine, soy sauce, cinnamon, peppercorns, star anise and salt to taste in the rinsed pan. Bring the mixture just to the boil over a medium-high heat then reduce the heat immediately and simmer for 30 minutes until the lamb is tender. Using a skimmer, transfer the lamb to a heated serving dish. Serve with the dipping sauce.
Serves 6

APRICOT AND LAMB CURRY

4 onions, 2 quartered
    and 2 finely
    chopped
2 cloves garlic
½–1 teaspoon small
    dried red chillies★
50 g (2 oz) blanched
    almonds
1 tablespoon ground
    coriander★
3 tablespoons oil
5 cm (2 inch)
    cinnamon stick★
6 cardamom pods★
8 cloves
750 g (1½ lb) boned
    leg of lamb, cubed
2 × 150 g (5 oz)
    cartons natural
    yogurt
250 g (8 oz) dried
    apricots, soaked
    overnight
salt
1 tablespoon chopped
    mint leaves

Put the quartered onions, garlic, chillies, almonds and coriander in a food processor or electric blender and work to a smooth paste.

Heat the oil in a saucepan and fry the cinnamon, cardamom and cloves for a few seconds. As soon as they begin to change colour, remove with a slotted spoon and discard.

Add the remaining onions to the pan and fry until soft. Add the prepared paste and fry for 3 to 4 minutes. Add the lamb and fry, stirring, for 5 minutes. Stir in the yogurt a spoonful at a time, then add the drained apricots and salt to taste. Simmer, partly covered, for 40 minutes or until the lamb is tender, stirring occasionally and adding a little water if the sauce starts to stick. Stir in the mint and serve immediately.
Serves 4

PALAK MURG

3 tablespoons oil
2 onions, chopped
2 cloves garlic,
    crushed
2.5 cm (1 inch) piece
    root ginger★,
    chopped
2 teaspoons ground
    coriander★
1 teaspoon chilli
    powder★
salt
750 g (1½ lb)
    chicken legs and
    thighs, skinned
750 g (1½ lb) spinach
2–3 tablespoons milk

Heat the oil in a large saucepan, add the onions and fry until golden. Add the garlic, ginger, coriander, chilli powder, and salt to taste and fry gently for 2 minutes, stirring.

Add the chicken and fry on all sides until browned. Add the spinach, stir well, cover and simmer for 35 minutes, until the chicken is tender.

If the mixture becomes too dry during cooking, add the milk. If there is too much liquid left at the end, uncover and cook for a few minutes until evaporated.
Serves 4

INDONESIAN SPICY CHICKEN

8 chicken pieces,
    skinned
juice of 1 lemon
3 tablespoons oil
300 ml (½ pint) water
SPICE PASTE:
4 tablespoons
    desiccated coconut,
    soaked in 4
    tablespoons hot
    water
2–4 red chillies★,
    chopped
4 small onions,
    quartered
2 cloves garlic
4 kemiri★ or brazil
    nuts
1 teaspoon laos★
    (optional)
1 cm (½ inch) piece
    root ginger★
1 teaspoon powdered
    lemon grass★ or
    grated lemon rind
1 teaspoon blachan★
    or shrimp paste
1 teaspoon sugar
1 teaspoon salt

Rub the chicken pieces all over with the lemon juice and set aside for 20 minutes.

Put all the ingredients for the spice paste in a food processor or electric blender and work until smooth. Heat the oil in a large frying pan and fry the paste, stirring, for 5 minutes.

Add the chicken pieces and fry for 5 minutes. Stir in the water and cook, uncovered, for 30 minutes or until the chicken is tender and the sauce thick.

Transfer to a warmed serving dish.
Serves 4

Indonesian Spicy Chicken; Chicken Korma

CHICKEN KORMA

2 tablespoons oil
2 onions, thinly sliced
1 clove garlic
1 cm (½ inch) piece
    root ginger★,
    chopped
1 tablespoon ground
    coriander★
½–1 teaspoon chilli
    powder★
2 teaspoons poppy
    seeds
1 teaspoon ground
    cumin★
1½ × 150 g (5 oz)
    cartons natural
    yogurt
4 chicken breasts,
    skinned
1 teaspoon salt
coriander leaves★ to
    garnish (optional)

Heat the oil in a pan, add 1 onion and fry until browned. Remove with a slotted spoon, drain on kitchen paper, then put with the garlic, ginger, coriander, chilli powder, poppy seeds, cumin and 1 tablespoon of the yogurt into an electric blender or food processor and work to a paste.

Fry the remaining onion in the oil until golden. Add the spice paste and fry for 2 minutes, stirring occasionally. Add the chicken and fry over high heat for 3 minutes.

Stir in the yogurt a spoonful at a time, waiting for one to be absorbed before adding the next. Add the salt. Lower the heat, cover and simmer for 20 minutes, or until the chicken is tender; if the curry seems to be drying out, stir in 2 or 3 tablespoons water.

Transfer to a warmed serving dish and garnish with coriander if wished.
Serves 4

ACCOMPANIMENTS

Two quick and easy chicken dishes. Serve the Indonesian Spicy Chicken with fried bananas and a selection of sambals.

Chicken Korma is a tasty blend of yogurt and spices. Lean pork can be used instead of chicken, but cooking times will need to be adjusted. Serve with Dhal Sag (see page 106) and boiled rice.

JAPANESE 'ODDS AND ENDS' POT

250 g (8 oz) boneless
    chicken pieces,
    skinned and cut
    into strips
250 g (8 oz) boneless
    lean pork, very
    thinly sliced
250 g (8 oz) large
    raw prawns, peeled
    and deveined, tails
    left intact
15 cm (6 inch) piece
    of kamaboko★,
    thinly sliced
250 g (8 oz) Chinese
    leaves★, cut into 5
    × 2.5 cm (2 × 1
    inch) pieces
125 g (4 oz) young
    spinach leaves,
    stalks removed
12 small button
    mushrooms
4 spring onions, cut
    diagonally into 5
    cm (2 inch) pieces
1 carrot, sliced thinly
    diagonally
250 g (8 oz) udon
    noodles★
250 g (8 oz) soba
    noodles★
2.25 litres (4 pints)
    chicken stock
120 ml (4 fl oz) soy
    sauce★
2 tablespoons sake★ or
    dry sherry
salt
shichimi★ to serve

Arrange the meats, fish and vegetables
attractively on three separate platters,
cover and set aside. Place the udon and
soba noodles on a plate and set aside.

Combine the chicken stock, soy
sauce, sake and salt to taste in a large
saucepan over a moderate heat. Bring
to the boil, then remove from the
heat.

Transfer the stock mixture to a
fondue pot or flameproof casserole.
Place a portable heater in the centre of
the dining table, and put the stockpot
on the ring. Allow the stock to come
to a simmer. Meanwhile, surround the
stockpot with the prepared platters of
meats, fish and vegetables.

Each guest adds a selection from the
platters to the simmering stockpot and
eats their titbits, sprinkled with
shichimi, when it is ready. Chopsticks
or fondue forks can be used. The
stronger-flavoured foods are usually
added near the end.

The noodles are added to the
simmering stock when all the food has
been eaten. When the noodles are
tender, distribute soup bowls to the
guests and let them serve themselves.
Serves 4

RIGHT: *Japanese 'Odds and Ends' Pot*
FAR RIGHT: *Spicy Grilled Chicken*

INDONESIAN FRIED CHICKEN

1 × 1.25 kg (2¼ lb)
　chicken, cut into
　serving pieces
salt and black pepper
4 tablespoons oil
1 medium onion, very
　finely chopped
1 clove garlic, crushed
1 teaspoon finely
　grated root ginger★
½ teaspoon ground
　coriander★
¼ teaspoon ground
　cardamom★
600 ml (1 pint)
　chicken stock
600 ml (1 pint) thick
　coconut milk★

Season the chicken pieces with the salt and pepper. Heat 3 tablespoons of the oil in a large saucepan or flameproof casserole over a moderate heat. Add the chicken and cook for 10 minutes, turning frequently, until browned. Drain on kitchen paper and set aside.

Discard the fat and wipe the pan clean. Add the remaining oil and place over a medium-high heat. Add the onion, garlic and spices, and cook for 5 minutes, stirring frequently. Stir in the stock and bring to the boil. Blend in the coconut milk and cook, stirring constantly, for 10 minutes. Return the chicken to the pan and reduce the heat. Cover and simmer for 30–40 minutes, stirring occasionally.

Serves 4

CHICKEN MOLEE

3 tablespoons oil
4 chicken breasts,
　skinned and boned,
　cut into 3 pieces
6 cardamom★
6 cloves
5 cm (2 inch) piece
　cinnamon stick★
1 large onion, finely
　sliced
2 cloves garlic
3.5 cm (1½ inch)
　piece root ginger★,
　chopped
3 green chillies★,
　seeded
juice of 1 lemon
1 teaspoon turmeric★
50 g (2 oz) creamed
　coconut★
150 ml (¼ pint) hot
　water
salt

Heat the oil in a pan, add the chicken and fry quickly all over. Remove with a slotted spoon and set aside.

Add a little more oil to the pan if necessary and fry the cardamom, cloves and cinnamon for 1 minute. Add the onion and fry until soft.

Place the garlic, ginger, chillies and lemon juice in an electric blender or food processor and work to a smooth paste. Add to the pan with the turmeric and cook for 5 minutes.

Melt the coconut in the hot water and add to the pan with salt to taste. Simmer for 2 minutes, then add the chicken pieces and any juices. Simmer for 15 to 20 minutes, until tender.

Serves 4

SPICY GRILLED CHICKEN

250 g (8 oz) red
　peppers, cored,
　seeded and chopped
6 cloves garlic
1½ teaspoon blachan★
　or shrimp paste
1 teaspoon ground
　dried lemon grass★
½ teaspoon chilli
　powder★
salt and black pepper
1 × 1.5 kg (3¼ lb)
　chicken, cut into
　serving pieces
25 ml (1 fl oz) oil
50 ml (2 fl oz)
　chicken stock
3 tablespoons lime
　juice

Put the peppers, garlic, blachan, lemon grass, chilli powder and salt into a food processor or electric blender and liquidize to a thin paste. Transfer to a bowl, cover and set aside.

Season the chicken with salt and pepper. Place the chicken, skin side down, 10 cm (4 inches) below a preheated grill. Cook for 15 minutes, then turn the pieces over and grill for 5 minutes, until the breasts are done. Remove he breasts and keep warm while grilling the remaining chicken pieces for 5 to 10 minutes until cooked through.

Heat the oil in a wok or large frying pan over a high heat. Carefully add the red pepper paste and stir-fry the mixture for 5 minutes. Blend in the stock and lime juice, then bring the mixture to the boil. Add the chicken, turning over the pieces to coat with the sauce. Simmer for 5 to 10 minutes, stirring constantly, or until the chicken is heated through. Transfer the mixture to a heated serving platter and serve immediately.

Serves 4

KASHMIRI CHICKEN

125 g (4 oz) butter
3 large onions, finely
　sliced
10 peppercorns
10 cardamom★
5 cm (2 inch) piece
　cinnamon stick★
5 cm (2 inch) piece
　root ginger★,
　chopped
2 cloves garlic, finely
　chopped
1 teaspoon chilli
　powder★
2 teaspoons paprika
salt
1.5 kg (3 lb) chicken
　pieces, skinned
250 g (8 oz) natural
　yogurt

Melt the butter in a deep, lidded frying pan. Add the onions, peppercorns, cardamom and cinnamon and fry until the onions are golden. Add the ginger, garlic, chilli powder, paprika and salt to taste and fry for 2 minutes, stirring occasionally. Add the chicken pieces and fry until browned. Gradually add the yogurt, stirring constantly. Cover and cook gently for about 30 minutes.
Serves 6

CHICKEN CURRY

2 cloves garlic,
　chopped
5 cm (2 inch) piece
　root ginger★,
　chopped
1 teaspoon turmeric★
2 teaspoons cumin
　seeds★, ground
1 teaspoon chilli
　powder★
1 teaspoon pepper
3 tablespoons finely
　chopped coriander
　leaves★
1 × 500 g (1 lb)
　carton natural
　yogurt
salt
1 kg (2 lb) chicken
　pieces, skinned
4 tablespoons oil
2 onions, chopped

Put the garlic, ginger, turmeric, cumin, chilli, pepper, coriander, yogurt and salt to taste into a large bowl. Mix well, add the chicken and leave for 4 hours, turning occasionally.

　Heat the oil in a pan, add the onions and fry until golden. Add the chicken and the marinade. Bring to simmering point, cover and cook for about 30 minutes, until the chicken is tender.
Serves 4

Kashmiri Chicken; Chicken Curry

MURGH MUSSALAM

2 onions
2 cloves garlic
5 cm (2 inch) piece
    root ginger★
1 teaspoon poppy
    seeds
8 peppercorns
2 × 150 g (5 oz)
    cartons natural
    yogurt
1 teaspoon garam
    masala★
salt
1 × 1.5 kg (3 lb)
    oven-ready chicken
125 g (4 oz) long-
    grain rice, soaked
    in cold water for
    1 hour
3 tablespoons
    concentrated butter
    or ghee★
½ teaspoon chilli
    powder★
50 g (2 oz) sultanas
50 g (2 oz) slivered
    almonds
350 ml (12 fl oz)
    water

Put the onions, garlic, ginger, poppy seeds, peppercorns and half the yogurt into an electric blender or food processor and work to a paste. Stir in the garam masala, add salt to taste.

Prick the chicken all over with a fork and rub in the blended mixture. Leave for 1 hour. Drain the rice.

Heat 1 tablespoon of the butter in a pan, add the rice and fry for 3 minutes, stirring constantly. Add the chilli powder, sultanas, almonds and salt to taste and stir well. Pour in 175 ml (6 fl oz) of the water, cover and simmer for about 10 minutes, until the rice is almost tender; cool.

When the rice mixture is cold, use it to stuff the chicken; sew up both ends. Heat the remaining butter in a pan and add the chicken, on its side. Pour in any marinade and the remaining water. Bring to simmering point, cover and cook for 1 hour, turning over halfway through cooking time.

Add the remaining yogurt, a spoonful at a time, stirring until it is all absorbed. Add more salt if necessary. Cook for a further 15 minutes, until the chicken is tender. Serve immediately.
Serves 4

TANDOORI CHICKEN

½–1 teaspoon chilli
    powder★
1 teaspoon pepper
1 teaspoon salt
2 tablespoons lemon
    juice
1 × 1.5 kg (3 lb)
    oven-ready
    chicken, skinned
50 g (2 oz) butter,
    melted
SPICE PASTE:
4 tablespoons natural
    yogurt
3 cloves garlic
5 cm (2 inch) piece
    root ginger★
2 small dried red
    chillies★
1 tablespoon
    coriander seeds★
2 teaspoons cumin
    seeds★

Mix the chilli powder, pepper, salt and lemon juice together. Slash the chicken all over and rub the mixture into the cuts. Set aside for 1 hour.

Make the spice paste: put the yogurt, garlic, ginger, chillies, coriander and cumin into an electric blender or food processor and work to a paste. Spread it all over the chicken. Cover and leave in the refrigerator overnight. Return to room temperature before cooking.

Place on a rack in a roasting pan and pour over half the butter. Cook in a preheated moderately hot oven, 200°C (400°F), Gas Mark 6, for 1 hour or until tender. Baste occasionally and pour on the remaining butter halfway through cooking time.
Serves 4

ABOVE: *Tandoori Chicken*
RIGHT: *Murgh Mussalam*

WOK DISHES

The wok has dominated the Chinese kitchen for centuries and without it, many of the most popular Chinese dishes would not exist. However, it is only comparatively recently that this all-purpose cooking utensil has become available in this country.

Choose a wok made from carbon steel rather than stainless steel or aluminium which tend to scorch. Gas is the best source of heat for cooking with a wok; electric hobs do not give such good results as the heat is not spread in the same way. Electric woks are not very satisfactory as they do not heat up to a sufficiently high temperature and tend to be too shallow. Non-stick woks are readily available and are preferred by some people, while others believe the flavour of the food is different. Iron woks, which are commonly used in South-East Asia, are also available.

The wok is best known for the 'stir-frying' method of cooking – a technique which involves frying foods over a very high heat while moving them about the pan the whole time. A small amount of oil is poured into the wok and heated to a high temperature, and the food is added and stirred vigorously at a very high heat for just a few minutes.

As well as stir-frying, the wok, with its high sloping sides, can also be used for deep-frying, steaming and braising. There are several points to remember about wok cookery. Always heat the wok before you add the oil to help maintain a high temperature. Stir constantly while cooking, using a flipping motion to transfer the food from the bottom of the wok to the top. Cook vegetables only until they are crisp-tender to retain all the nutrients.

QUICK-FRIED SQUID WITH CRAB SAUCE

500 g (1 lb) cleaned
  squid, fresh or if
  frozen thawed
1 tablespoon oil
2 × 1 cm (½ inch)
  pieces root ginger★,
  finely chopped
3 spring onions,
  finely chopped
1 × 177 g (6 oz) can
  crabmeat
1 × 65 g (2¼ oz)
  can tomato purée
1 teaspoon sugar
1 tablespoon light
  soy sauce★
4 tablespoons chicken
  stock
1 tablespoon dry
  sherry
2 teaspoons cornflour
1 tablespoon water
chopped spring onion
  to garnish

Cut the squid into 2.5 cm (1 inch)
pieces.

Heat the oil in a wok or deep frying
pan, add the ginger and spring onions
and stir-fry for 1 minute. Add the
squid and cook for 2 minutes. Add the
remaining ingredients, except the
cornflour and water, and mix well.
Cook for 2 minutes, stirring.

Blend the cornflour to a smooth
paste with the water. Stir into the pan
and cook, stirring, until thickened.

Spoon into a warmed serving dish,
garnish with spring onion and serve
immediately.
Serves 4 to 6

QUICK-FRIED CRAB IN AROMATIC OIL

1 large freshly cooked
  crab or 2 × 177 g (6
  oz) cans crabmeat
2 tablespoons oil
1 clove garlic, crushed
2 × 1 cm (½ inch)
  pieces root ginger★,
  finely chopped
4 spring onions,
  chopped
1 leek, thinly sliced
salt
1 egg, beaten
150 ml (¼ pint) fish
  or chicken stock
2 tablespoons dry
  sherry
2 teaspoons
  cornflour
1 tablespoon water
2 teaspoons sesame
  seed oil★
lemon wedges to
  garnish

If using freshly cooked crab, break off
the legs and crack the claws of the
crab. Using a chopper, crack the shell
into 4 or 5 pieces. Remove all the
meat and cut into pieces, discarding
the black sac and intestinal thread.

Heat the oil in a wok or frying pan,
add the garlic, ginger and spring
onions and stir-fry for 1 minute. Add
the crab and stir-fry for 5 minutes
over a high heat. Add the leek and salt
to taste.

Lower the heat and pour in the egg
in a thin stream. Add the stock and
sherry and cook for 1 minute. Blend
the cornflour with the water and add
to the pan with the sesame oil; cook,
stirring, until thickened.

Turn on to a warmed serving dish
and serve immediately, garnished with
lemon wedges.
Serves 4 to 6

THAI FRIED NOODLES

1 kg (2 lb) boneless chicken breasts, skinned and cut into 5 mm ($\frac{1}{4}$ inch) slices

4 tablespoons dry sherry

6 dried Chinese mushrooms★

350 g (12 oz) rice stick noodles★

6 tablespoons oil

25 g (1 oz) fresh basil

8 cloves garlic, thinly sliced

6 small onions, thinly sliced

4 red chillies★, seeded and finely chopped

1 teaspoon blachan★ or shrimp paste

salt

175 g (6 oz) peeled prawns

3 tablespoons tomato purée

2 tablespoons sugar

1 tablespoon nam pla★

25 g (1 oz) bean sprouts★

TO GARNISH:

2 tablespoons roasted peanuts, coarsely chopped

$\frac{1}{2}$ teaspoon dried red pepper flakes★

Toss the chicken with the sherry in a medium bowl. Cover and marinate for 30 minutes. Soak the mushrooms in warm water for 15 minutes and the noodles in hot water for 15 minutes. Squeeze the mushrooms dry and discard the hard stalks, then thinly slice the mushroom caps. Drain the noodles.

Heat 2 tablespoons of the oil in a small frying pan, add half the basil and stir-fry briefly until crisp. Drain on kitchen paper, then set aside for a garnish.

Heat 3 tablespoons of the oil in the frying pan over a moderate heat. Add the garlic and onions, then fry until crisp. Using a slotted spoon, remove from the oil and set aside for a garnish. Remove the oil to a large heatproof bowl, add the noodles and toss gently to coat. Set aside.

Combine the chillies, blachan and salt to taste in a mortar and pound until smooth. Heat the remaining oil in a wok or large frying pan over a high heat. Add the chilli mixture and stir-fry for 1 minute. Add the chicken mixture and mushrooms. Stir-fry for 3 minutes. Add the prawns and cook just until heated through. Blend in the tomato purée, sugar and nam pla. Add the bean sprouts and the remaining basil. Stir-fry for 2 minutes. Add the noodles in 3 batches, tossing gently after each addition until thoroughly coated and heated through.

Transfer the mixture to a heated serving platter. Sprinkle with the fried basil, garlic and onions, peanuts and pepper flakes. Serve immediately.
Serves 4

LEFT: *Quick-Fried Squid with Crab Sauce; Quick-Fried Crab in Aromatic Oil*
RIGHT: *Thai Fried Noodles*

CHINESE VEGETABLES

1 tablespoon oil
4 spring onions,
  chopped
250 g (8 oz) mange
  tout
250 g (8 oz)
  asparagus, cut into
  small pieces
125 g (4 oz) canned
  water chestnuts★,
  drained and sliced
1 tablespoon light soy
  sauce★
1–2 tablespoons dry
  sherry
pinch of salt
½ teaspoon sugar
1 teaspoon sesame
  seed oil★

Heat the oil in a wok, add the spring onions and stir-fry for 3 seconds. Add the mange tout, asparagus and water chestnuts, toss well in the oil and cook for 1 minute. Add the remaining ingredients and continue stir-frying for 3 minutes.

Transfer to a warmed serving dish and serve immediately.
Serves 4

STIR-FRIED MUSHROOMS

50 g (2 oz) small
  Chinese dried
  mushrooms★
1 tablespoon oil
1 teaspoon finely
  chopped root
  ginger★
2 spring onions, finely
  chopped
1 clove garlic, crushed
250 g (8 oz) button
  mushrooms
1 × 227 g (8 oz) can
  straw mushrooms★,
  drained
1 teaspoon chilli bean
  sauce★ or chilli
  powder★
2 teaspoons dry sherry
  or rice wine
  2 teaspoons dark
  soy sauce★
1 tablespoon chicken
  stock
pinch of sugar
pinch of salt
1 teaspoon sesame
  seed oil★
coriander leaves★ to
  garnish

Soak the dried mushrooms in warm water for 15 minutes. Drain and squeeze dry, discard the hard stalk. Heat the oil in a wok or frying pan, add the ginger, spring onions and garlic and stir-fry for 5 seconds. Stir in the dried and button mushrooms and cook, stirring, for 5 minutes. Stir in the remaining ingredients, mixing thoroughly to ensure that all the mushrooms are coated in the sauce. Continue to stir-fry for 5 minutes, until the mushrooms are cooked through and have absorbed all the flavourings.

Transfer to a warmed serving dish, garnish with coriander leaves and serve immediately.
Serves 4 to 6

Chinese Vegetables; Stir-Fried Mushrooms

RICE WINE

Rice wine is a popular Chinese drink made from a blend of glutinous rice, millet and spring water. Its unique flavour is attributed to the special type of yeast used. The finest variety is that of Shaoxing, in the Zhejiang province in Eastern China. This wine is stored for as long as 40 years in underground cellars.

Rice wine is available from Chinese and Oriental supermarkets, but dry sherry – which has been used instead throughout this book – is an excellent substitute.

DICED TURKEY WITH CELERY

4 Chinese dried
  mushrooms★
350 g (12 oz)
  boneless turkey
  breast, skinned and
  diced
salt
1 egg white
1 tablespoon cornflour
4 tablespoons oil
2 cloves garlic, sliced
2 slices root ginger★,
  finely chopped
2 leeks, diagonally
  sliced
1 small head celery,
  diagonally sliced
1 red pepper, cored,
  seeded and sliced
3 tablespoons light soy
  sauce★
2 tablespoons dry
  sherry
celery leaves to
  garnish

Soak the mushrooms in warm water for 15 minutes. Squeeze dry and discard the hard stalks, then slice the mushroom caps.

Season the diced turkey with salt, dip in the egg white, then coat with cornflour. Heat the oil in a wok or frying pan. Add the turkey and stir-fry for 1 minute, until golden brown. Remove with a slotted spoon and drain on kitchen paper.

Increase the heat, add the garlic, ginger, leeks and celery and stir-fry for 1 minute. Return the turkey to the pan, add the red pepper and stir-fry for 30 seconds. Stir in the soy sauce and sherry and cook for a further 30 seconds. Spoon into a warmed serving dish, garnish with celery leaves and serve immediately.
Serves 4

Diced Turkey with Celery; Turkey Parcels

TURKEY PARCELS

Turkey Parcels are a variation of the traditional paper-wrapped chicken, where the food is wrapped in greaseproof paper and fried or steamed. The parcels are served wrapped and diners unwrap them with their chopsticks.

TURKEY PARCELS

1 tablespoon soy
  sauce★
1 tablespoon dry
  sherry
1 tablespoon sesame
  seed oil★
500 g (1 lb) turkey
  breast, cut into 16
  equal pieces
4 spring onions, each
  cut into 4 pieces
2 × 2.5 cm (1 inch)
  pieces root ginger★,
  shredded
½ red pepper, cored,
  seeded and shredded
1 celery stick,
  shredded
4 tablespoons oil

Mix the soy sauce, sherry and sesame seed oil together, add the turkey and toss well to coat. Leave to marinate for 15 to 20 minutes.

Cut out 16 pieces of foil large enough to enclose the pieces of turkey generously. Brush the foil with oil, place a piece of turkey in the centre of each one and top with a piece of spring onion, ginger, pepper and celery. Fold the foil over to enclose the turkey and seal the edges well.

Heat the oil in a wok or frying pan, add the foil parcels and fry for about 2 minutes each side. Remove from the pan and leave to drain.

Reheat the oil to very hot and return the turkey parcels to the pan for 1 minute. Drain well and serve immediately in the foil parcels.
Serves 4

SHANGHAI CHICKEN

50 g (2 oz) egg
    noodles
salt
2 tablespoons oil
5 cm (2 inch) piece
    root ginger★,
    shredded
2-3 cloves garlic,
    sliced
500 g (1 lb) boneless
    chicken breasts,
    very thinly sliced
1 carrot, cut into
    flowers (see page
    155)
3 spring onions, finely
    sliced
2 celery sticks, thinly
    sliced
1 × 241 g (8 oz)
    can bamboo
    shoots★, drained
    and sliced
1 green pepper, cored,
    seeded and shredded
175 g (6 oz) bean
    sprouts★
4 spring onion flowers
    (see page 155) to
    garnish
GLAZE:
1 tablespoon
    cornflour
1 tablespoon soy
    sauce★
6 tablespoons dry
    sherry
2 tablespoons stock
pinch of chilli
    powder★

Put the noodles in a jug and cover
with boiling, salted water. Cover and
leave for at least 8 minutes.

Mix together the ingredients for the
glaze, adding salt to taste.

Heat the oil in a wok or large
frying pan. Add the ginger and garlic
and stir-fry over high heat for about 1
minute. Add the chicken and stir-fry
for a further minute. Add the carrot,
spring onions, celery, bamboo shoots
and green pepper and stir-fry for 30
seconds. Drain the noodles, add to the
pan with the bean sprouts and stir-fry
for 30 seconds.

Add the glaze, turn off the heat and
toss until the ingredients are well
coated. Garnish with the spring onion
brushes and serve at once.
Serves 4

JAVANESE FRIED CHICKEN

1 teaspoon coriander
    seeds★
2 salted macadamia
    nuts★ or almonds
1 small onion,
    chopped
2 green chillies★,
    seeded
½ teaspoon turmeric★
½ teaspoon laos
    powder★
250 ml (8 fl oz)
    coconut milk★
1 stalk lemon grass★,
    finely sliced
1 teaspoon sugar
salt
1 × 1.25 kg (2½ lb)
    chicken, cut into
    serving pieces
120 ml (4 fl oz) oil

Place the coriander seeds and nuts in a
food processor or electric blender and
grind to a coarse powder. Add the
onion, chillies, turmeric, laos powder
and liquidize to a paste. With the
motor running, add the coconut milk
and liquidize until smooth. Pour the
mixture into a shallow dish and stir in
the lemon grass, sugar and salt. Add
the chicken pieces, turning to coat
with the mixture. Cover and marinate
at room temperature for 2 to 3 hours,
turning the chicken occasionally.

Transfer the chicken mixture to a
wok or deep saucepan. Place the wok
over a medium-high heat and bring
the mixture to the boil. Reduce the
heat and simmer gently for 45 minutes
until the chicken is tender and the
liquid has evaporated.

Remove the wok from the heat and
lift out the chicken pieces. Clean the
wok, then add the oil. Place the wok
over a medium-high heat and let the
oil get hot. Add the chicken pieces and
fry for 10 minutes, turning
occasionally, until golden brown.
Serves 4

CHICKEN

Chicken is a common ingredient in Oriental cooking, and
today's chickens are descended from the wild red jungle fowl
which was domesticated around 2000 BC in India and used
initially as a sacred bird in religious ceremonies. From India, it
travelled westwards through China and the Pacific Islands and
eastwards to Eastern Europe around 1500 BC. Strangeley, the
chicken bypassed the Mediterranean – the common transit
point of most Eastern food – and only arrived in Egypt
around 1350 BC.

DICED CHICKEN WITH CHILLIES

2 tablespoons oil
1 clove garlic, sliced
350 g (12 oz)
    boneless
    chicken breast,
    diced
1 red pepper, cored,
    seeded and diced
2 green chillies★,
    seeded and sliced
50 g (2 oz) bean
    sprouts★
2 tablespoons soy
    sauce★
2 tablespoons chilli
    sauce★
coriander leaves★ to
    garnish

Heat the oil in a wok or frying pan, add the garlic and fry for 1 minute. Add the chicken and stir-fry for 1 minute. Add the pepper and chillies and cook for a further minute. Stir in the bean sprouts, soy sauce and chilli sauce and cook for 2 minutes.

Turn into a warmed serving dish, garnish with coriander and serve immediately.
Serves 4

CHICKEN IN SESAME SAUCE

500 g (1 lb) boneless
    chicken breast, cut
    into cubes
1 tablespoon oil
125 g (4 oz)
    unsalted cashew
    nuts
75 g (3 oz) canned
    straw mushrooms★,
    drained and halved
MARINADE:
3 spring onions,
    chopped
3 tablespoons soy
    sauce★
2 tablespoons each
    hot pepper oil★
    and sesame seed
    oil★
1 tablespoon sesame
    seed paste★
1 teaspoon ground
    Szechuan
    peppercorns★

Put the marinade ingredients into a bowl. Add the chicken cubes, turning to coat thoroughly. Leave to marinate for 30 minutes.

Meanwhile, heat the oil in a wok or frying pan, add the cashew nuts and fry until golden brown. Drain on kitchen paper.

Add the chicken and marinade to the pan and stir-fry for 2 minutes. Add the mushrooms to the pan. Cook for a further minute. Pile the mixture on to a warmed serving dish and sprinkle with the nuts. Serve immediately.
Serves 4 to 6

Diced Chicken with Chillies; Chicken in Sesame Sauce

INDONESIAN FRIED NOODLES

3 tablespoons oil
1 clove garlic, crushed
1 cm ($\frac{1}{2}$ inch) piece
　root ginger★, finely
　chopped
175 g (6 oz) boneless
　chicken breast,
　diced
175 g (6 oz) large
　raw prawns,
　peeled, deveined
　and coarsely
　chopped
4 large Chinese
　leaves★, ribs
　removed, then
　shredded
2 medium carrots, cut
　into matchstick
　pieces
1 large celery stick,
　sliced thinly
　diagonally
250 g (8 oz) cooked
　thin Chinese egg
　noodles★
salt and black pepper
125 ml (4 fl oz)
　boiling chicken
　stock
2 tablespoons soy
　sauce★
TO GARNISH:
1 medium onion,
　thinly sliced and
　fried until brown
　and crisp
2 red chilli peppers★,
　thinly sliced or
　chilli pepper
　flowers (see page
　155)

Heat the oil in a wok or large frying pan over a medium-high heat. Add the garlic and ginger, then stir-fry for 30 seconds. Add the chicken and prawns, then stir-fry for 2 to 3 minutes until the chicken is opaque. Add the Chinese leaves, carrots and celery, then stir-fry for 3 minutes. Add the noodles, salt and pepper. Stir-fry until the noodles are well coated. Pour in the stock and soy sauce and cook for 1 minute.

To serve, transfer the noodle mixture to a heated serving platter, then garnish with the onion slices and chillies.

Serves 4

NASI GORENG

4 medium onions,
　chopped
2 large cloves garlic,
　chopped
2.5 cm (1 inch) piece
　root ginger★,
　chopped
2 red chillies★,
　coarsely chopped
1 teaspoon blachan★
　or shrimp paste
85 ml (3 fl oz) oil
3 eggs, lightly beaten
100 g (4 oz) large
　raw prawns, peeled
　and deveined
225 g (8 oz) cooked
　chicken, diced
500 g (1 lb) cold,
　cooked long-grain
　rice
2 tablespoons soy
　sauce★
2 tablespoons lemon
　juice
1 teaspoon demerara
　sugar
salt and black pepper
50 g (2 oz) ham, cut
　into thin strips
TO SERVE:
50 g (2 oz) salted
　peanuts, coarsely
　chopped
2 tomatoes, thinly
　sliced
1 small onion, thinly
　sliced

Place the onions, garlic, ginger, chillies and blachan in a food processor or electric blender; liquidize to a purée then set aside.

Heat 2 tablespoons of the oil in a medium frying pan, add the eggs and allow to set like a thin pancake. Cook until golden and solid; do not stir. Remove from the pan and cut into thin strips. Set aside and keep warm.

Heat the remaining oil in a wok or large frying pan over a medium-high heat. Add the onion mixture and cook for 5 to 10 minutes, stirring constantly, until golden brown. Add the prawns and stir-fry until pink. Stir in the remaining ingredients, except for the ham and egg strips. Cook, stirring constantly, until the mixture is heated through and the rice is coated.

Transfer the rice mixture to a heated platter and garnish with the ham and egg strips. Serve immediately, handing the peanuts, tomato and onion slices separately.

Serves 4

(Picture, page 84)

SPICY CHICKEN AND PEANUTS

125 g (4 oz) unsalted
  peanuts
2 tablespoons oil
1 dried red chilli★
350 g (12 oz)
  boneless chicken
  breasts, skinned and
  cut into 2.5 cm (1
  inch) cubes
2 tablespoons dry
  sherry
1 tablespoon dark soy
  sauce★
pinch of sugar
1 clove garlic, crushed
2 spring onions,
  chopped
2.5 cm (1 inch) piece
  root ginger★, finely
  chopped
1 teaspoon wine
  vinegar
2 teaspoons sesame
  seed oil★
red chilli flowers (see
  page 155) to
  garnish

Immerse the peanuts in a bowl of boiling water for about 2 minutes. Drain well, remove the skins and place on kitchen paper to dry thoroughly.

Heat the oil in a wok or frying pan. Crumble in the chilli, add the chicken and peanuts and stir-fry for 1 minute; remove from the pan. Add the sherry, soy sauce, sugar, garlic, spring onions, ginger and vinegar to the pan. Bring to the boil, then simmer for 30 seconds. Return the chicken, chilli and peanuts to the pan and cook for 2 minutes. Sprinkle over the sesame seed oil.

Pile into a warmed serving dish, garnish with red chilli flowers and serve immediately.
Serves 4

CHINESE CHICKEN DISHES

The Cashew Chicken recipe originates from the southern region of China, and exemplifies the Chinese taste for contrasting textures.

Spicy Chicken and Peanuts is a classic Western Chinese dish, better known as Gongbao Chicken. Although there are many versions of this recipe, this is close to the original.

Both recipes use the best Chinese cooking principles: stir-frying to seal in the juices of the chicken, then stir-frying again with other ingredients to flavour it.

CASHEW CHICKEN

1 egg white
4 tablespoons dry
  sherry
2 teaspoons cornflour
350 g (12 oz)
  boneless chicken
  breasts, skinned and
  cut into 1 cm (½
  inch) cubes
3 tablespoons oil
4 spring onions,
  chopped
2 cloves garlic, thinly
  sliced
2.5 cm (1 inch) piece
  root ginger★, finely
  chopped
1 tablespoon light soy
  sauce★
125 g (4 oz) unsalted
  cashew nuts

Combine the egg white, half the sherry and the cornflour, add the chicken and toss well until evenly coated.

Heat the oil in a wok or frying pan, add the spring onions, garlic and ginger and stir-fry for 30 seconds. Add the chicken and cook for 2 minutes. Pour in the remaining sherry and the soy sauce and stir well. Add the cashew nuts and cook for a further 30 seconds. Serve immediately.
Serves 4

Spicy Chicken and Peanuts; Cashew Chicken

CHICKEN WITH SESAME SEED

1 egg white
½ teaspoon salt
2 teaspoons cornflour
350 g (12 oz) boneless chicken breasts, cut into 7.5 cm (3 inch) shreds
2 tablespoons sesame seeds★
2 tablespoons oil
1 tablespoon dark soy sauce★
1 tablespoon wine vinegar
½ teaspoon chilli bean sauce★
½ teaspoon sesame seed oil★
1 tablespoon dry sherry
½ teaspoon roasted Szechuan peppercorns★
4 spring onions, chopped

Combine the egg white, salt and cornflour, toss in the chicken and mix thoroughly. Leave to stand for 15 minutes.

Fry the sesame seeds in a wok or frying pan until they are golden brown. Remove from the pan and set aside.

Heat the oil in the pan, add the chicken and stir-fry briskly for 1 minute. Remove with a slotted spoon.

Add the soy sauce, vinegar, chilli bean sauce, sesame seed oil, sherry and peppercorns to the pan and bring to the boil. Add the chicken and spring onions and cook for 2 minutes. Sprinkle with the sesame seeds and serve immediately.
Serves 4

Chicken with Sesame Seeds; Stir-Fried Sesame Beef

STIR-FRIED SESAME BEEF

1 tablespoon light soy sauce★
1 tablespoon dark soy sauce★
1 tablespoon soft light brown sugar
1 teaspoon sesame seed oil★
1 tablespoon dry sherry
350 g (12 oz) rump steak, cut across the grain into thin slices
2 tablespoons sesame seeds★
2 tablespoons oil
1 clove garlic, thinly sliced
2 celery sticks, sliced diagonally
2 carrots, sliced diagonally
50 g (2 oz) button mushrooms, sliced

Combine the soy sauces, sugar, sesame seed oil and sherry. Toss in the meat and leave to marinate for 15 minutes.

Fry the sesame seeds in a wok or frying pan until they are golden brown. Remove from the pan and set aside.

Heat the oil in the pan, add the garlic, celery and carrots and stir-fry briskly for 1 minute; remove from the pan. Increase the heat, add the beef and stir-fry for about 3 minutes, until well browned. Return the vegetables to the pan, add the mushrooms and cook for a further 30 seconds.

Spoon into a warmed serving dish, sprinkle with the sesame seeds and serve immediately.
Serves 4

| SESAME SEEDS |

Sesame seeds are often used in Chinese cooking. They have a nutty and aromatic taste which enhances the flavour of both sweet and savoury dishes. Sesame seed oil and paste are derivatives of the seed and are often stirred into or sprinkled on to a dish just before serving to increase its aromatic flavour.

The seeds can be used raw or toasted. To toast them, fry in a dry wok until they jump and are golden brown.

FRIED LIVER SZECHUAN-STYLE

500 g (1 lb) lambs'
  liver, sliced
salt and pepper
2 tablespoons dry
  sherry
2 tablespoons oil
50 g (2 oz) canned
  bamboo shoots★,
  drained and sliced
3 spring onions,
  chopped
1 clove garlic, crushed
¼ cauliflower, broken
  into florets
2 carrots, sliced
  diagonally
2 tablespoons
  Szechuan pickled
  vegetables★
2 tablespoons soy
  sauce★

Season the liver with salt and pepper to taste. Mix in the sherry and leave to marinate for 15 minutes.

Heat the oil in a wok or deep frying pan, add the bamboo shoots, spring onions and garlic and stir-fry for 1 minute.

Add the cauliflower and carrots to the pan and cook, stirring, for 2 minutes. Add the liver and sherry and fry quickly until browned all over. Stir in the Szechuan vegetables and soy sauce and bring to the boil. Spoon into a warmed serving dish and serve immediately.

Serves 4 to 6

STIR-FRIED PORK AND MANGE TOUT

350 g (12 oz) lean
  pork, thinly sliced
2 tablespoons soy
  sauce★
2 tablespoons dry
  sherry
4 dried Chinese
  mushrooms★
1 tablespoon oil
250 g (8 oz)
  mange tout

Put the pork into a bowl with the soy sauce and sherry. Mix well to coat, then leave to marinate for 15 minutes.

Soak the dried mushrooms in warm water for 15 minutes. Squeeze dry and discard the hard stalks, then slice the mushroom caps.

Heat the oil in a wok or frying pan, add the meat and marinade. Stir-fry for 2 minutes, then add the mushrooms and cook for 1 minute. Add the mange tout and stir-fry for 2 minutes.

Spoon the mixture on to a warmed serving dish and serve immediately.

Serves 4 to 6

QUICK-FRIED BEEF IN OYSTER SAUCE

2 tablespoons oil
4 spring onions,
  chopped
2 cloves garlic, sliced
4 carrots, sliced
  diagonally
2 celery sticks, sliced
  diagonally
350 g (12 oz) rump
  or sirloin steak, cut
  into thin slices
salt
125 g (4 oz) bean
  sprouts★
1 tablespoon soy
  sauce★
2 tablespoons dry
  sherry
3 tablespoons oyster
  sauce★
TO GARNISH:
carrot flower (see
  page 155)
celery leaves

Heat the oil in a wok or frying pan, add the spring onions and garlic and fry quickly for about 30 seconds. Add the carrots and celery and stir-fry for 1 minute.

Sprinkle the steak slices with salt. Add to the pan and fry until browned on all sides. Stir in the bean sprouts, soy sauce, sherry and oyster sauce and cook for 2 minutes.

Spoon the mixture on to a warmed serving dish and garnish with the carrot flower and celery leaves to serve.

Serves 4 to 6

Quick-Fried Beef in Oyster Sauce

STIR-FRIED CHILLI BEEF

500 g (1 lb) rump
  steak, cut across
  the grain into thin
  slices
salt
2 tablespoons oil
2 dried red chillies★
2 cloves garlic, thinly
  sliced
1 cm (½ inch) piece
  root ginger★,
  shredded
4 spring onions,
  shredded
2 tablespoons dark soy
  sauce★
2 tablespoons light soy
  sauce★
2 tablespoons dry
  sherry
2 green chillies★,
  seeded and chopped

Season the steak slices well with salt.

Heat the oil in a wok or deep frying pan, add the red chillies and fry for 1 minute. Remove from the pan. Increase the heat, add the steak and stir-fry for 1 minute, until browned. Add the garlic, ginger and spring onions and cook for 30 seconds. Pour over the soy sauces and sherry, add the green chillies and cook for a further minute.

Transfer to a warmed serving dish and serve immediately.
Serves 4

CHILLI PORK SPARE RIBS

1 kg (2 lb) lean spare
  ribs, cut into 5 cm
  (2 inch) pieces
salt
2 tablespoons oil
2 dried red chillies★
1 cm (½ inch) piece
  root ginger★, finely
  chopped
1 clove garlic, thinly
  sliced
spring onion shreds to
  garnish
SAUCE:
4 tablespoons each
  clear honey and
  wine vinegar
2 tablespoons light soy
  sauce★
2 tablespoons dry
  sherry
1 × 142 g (5 oz) can
  tomato purée
1 teaspoon chilli
  powder★
2 cloves garlic,
  crushed

Mix all the sauce ingredients together and set aside.

Sprinkle the spare rib pieces with salt.

Heat the oil in a wok or deep frying pan, quickly fry the whole chillies and remove from the oil. Add the ginger and garlic and stir-fry for 30 seconds. Add the spare ribs and fry for 5 minutes, until golden brown. Lower the heat and cook for 10 minutes.

Add the sauce to the pan, cover with a lid or foil and simmer gently for 25 to 30 minutes, until the meat is tender, stirring occasionally.

Arrange the spare ribs on a warmed serving dish and garnish with the spring onion.
Serves 4 to 6

STIR-FRIED KIDNEY FLOWERS

15 g (½ oz) wooden
  ears★ (optional)
500 g (1 lb) pigs'
  kidney
4 tablespoons oil
75 g (3 oz) canned
  bamboo shoots★,
  drained and sliced
75 g (3 oz) canned
  water chestnuts★,
  drained and sliced
2 celery sticks, sliced
  diagonally
4 spring onions,
  sliced
2 cloves garlic, sliced
1 cm (½ inch) piece
  root ginger★,
  finely chopped
125 g (4 oz) frozen
  spinach, thawed
3 tablespoons soy
  sauce★
1 tablespoon wine
  vinegar

Soak the wooden ears in warm water
for 10 minutes, if using; drain.

Remove the thin white film and
any fat from the kidneys, cut each one
in half lengthways and discard the
white core. Score the surface of each
kidney in a diagonal criss-cross pattern,
then cut into 2 or 3 pieces.

Heat the oil in a wok or deep frying
pan, add the kidney and fry for 1
minute, stirring constantly; the kidneys
will curl up to form little flowers.
Remove from the pan and keep
warm. Add the wooden ears, if using,
bamboo shoots, water chestnuts,
celery, spring onions, garlic and ginger
and stir-fry for 2 minutes.

Return the kidney flowers to the
pan with the spinach. Stir in the soy
sauce and vinegar and cook for 1 to 2
minutes. Spoon on to a warmed
serving dish and serve immediately.
Serves 4 to 6

CARE OF YOUR WOK

Though there are electric and non-stick woks available on the
market, the following are tips for the care of the standard iron
wok.

Before you use an iron wok for the first time, you should
season it. Heat it over a high heat, then brush it lightly with
oil. Wipe it clean, then repeat the procedure twice to remove
all the dirt and impurities in the wok. Rinse well and dry
thoroughly. To keep your wok clean after use, fill it with hot
water and let it soak until all the particles of food can be easily
wiped off with a cloth. Do not scour with strong detergents
or abrasive cleaners as this will destroy the seasoning process.
Whenever you use an iron wok, you should dry it
thoroughly, otherwise the wok will develop rust patches. If it
does, scour the rust off, then brush the wok with oil.

SZECHUAN HOT SHREDDED BEEF

500 g (1 lb) rump or
  frying steak, cut
  into 5 cm (2 inch)
  long thin slices
2 tablespoons
  cornflour
salt
3 tablespoons oil
4 spring onions,
  chopped
2 celery sticks, sliced
  diagonally
4 carrots, sliced
  diagonally
2 tablespoons soy
  sauce★
1 tablespoon hoisin
  sauce★
1 tablespoon chilli
  sauce★
2 tablespoons dry
  sherry

Toss the steak in the cornflour and
season with salt to taste.

Heat the oil in a wok or deep frying
pan, add the spring onions and fry for
1 minute. Add the meat slices and
cook for 4 minutes, stirring, until the
meat is lightly browned. Add the
celery and carrots and cook for 2
minutes. Stir in the soy, hoisin and
chilli sauces and the sherry, bring to
the boil and cook for 1 minute.

Arrange on a warmed serving dish,
garnish with carrot flowers and celery
leaves and serve immediately.
Serves 4 to 6

LEFT: *Stir-Fried Chilli Beef; Chilli Pork Spare Ribs*
RIGHT: *Szechuan Hot Shredded Beef*

STIR-FRIED ORANGE BEEF

2 teaspoons sesame
　seed oil★
2 tablespoons dark soy
　sauce★
1 tablespoon dry
　sherry★
1 cm ($\frac{1}{2}$ inch) piece
　root ginger★, finely
　chopped
2 teaspoons cornflour
350 g (12 oz) rump
　steak cut across the
　grain into 5 cm (2
　inch) long slices
4 tablespoons oil
2 dried red chillies★,
　crumbled
shredded rind of 1
　orange
pinch of salt
$\frac{1}{2}$ teaspoon roasted
　Szechuan
　peppercorns★,
　finely ground
1 teaspoon soft light
　brown sugar
TO GARNISH:
orange slices
parsley sprigs

Combine half the sesame oil and soy sauce, the sherry, ginger and cornflour, add the meat and toss until well coated. Leave to marinate for 15 minutes; drain well.

Heat the oil in a wok or deep frying pan and quickly brown the meat on all sides for 2 minutes; drain on kitchen paper. Pour off all but 1 tablespoon oil from the pan. Heat the pan, add the chillies and stir-fry for 30 seconds. Return the meat to the pan, add the orange rind, salt, peppercorns, sugar and remaining soy sauce. Stir-fry for 4 minutes, sprinkle with the remaining sesame oil and serve immediately, garnished with the orange slices and parsley sprigs.
Serves 4

STIR-FRIED GARLIC LAMB

2 tablespoons dry
　sherry
2 tablespoons light soy
　sauce★
1 tablespoon dark soy
　sauce★
1 teaspoon sesame
　seed oil★
350 g (12 oz) lamb
　fillet, cut across the
　grain into thin
　slices
2 tablespoons oil
6 cloves garlic, thinly
　sliced
1 cm ($\frac{1}{2}$ inch) piece
　root ginger★ finely
　chopped
1 leek, thinly sliced
　diagonally
4 spring onions,
　chopped
spring onion flowers
　to garnish (see
　page 155)

Combine the sherry, soy sauces and sesame oil, add the lamb and toss until well coated. Leave to marinate for 15 minutes, then drain, reserving the marinade.

Heat the oil in a wok or deep frying pan, add the meat and about 2 teaspoons of the marinade and fry briskly for about 2 minutes, until well browned. Add the garlic, ginger, leek and spring onions, and fry for a further 3 minutes.

Transfer to a warmed serving plate, garnish with the spring onion flowers and serve immediately.
Serves 4

LEFT: *Stir-Fried Orange Beef; Stir-Fried Garlic Lamb*
RIGHT: *Stir-Fried Lamb with Noodles*

STIR-FRIED LAMB WITH NOODLES

125 g (4 oz)
  transparent
  noodles★
1 tablespoon oil
3 spring onions, finely
  chopped
1 cm (½ inch) piece
  root ginger★, finely
  chopped
2 cloves garlic, sliced
2 celery sticks,
  chopped
500 g (1 lb) very lean
  lamb, thinly sliced
1 red pepper, cored,
  seeded and sliced
2 tablespoons light
  soy sauce★
2 tablespoons dry
  sherry
150 ml (¼ pint)
  stock
2 teaspoons sesame
  seed oil★
TO GARNISH:
green chilli flowers
  (see page 155)
spring onion flowers
  (see page 155)

Soak the noodles in warm water for 10 minutes; drain.

Heat the oil in a wok or frying pan, add the spring onions, ginger and garlic and stir-fry for 1 minute. Add the celery and lamb and cook for 2 minutes. Add the red pepper, soy sauce and sherry and bring to the boil. Stir in the stock and noodles and simmer for 5 minutes. Sprinkle with the sesame seed oil.

Transfer to a warmed serving dish and garnish with chilli and spring onion flowers. Serve immediately.
Serves 4 to 6

TOFU AND MUSHROOMS

2 tablespoons oil
125 g (4 oz) lean
  pork, diced
4 spring onions,
  chopped
2 cloves garlic, sliced
1 green pepper, cored,
  seeded and diced
1 small cauliflower,
  broken into florets
125 g (4 oz) small
  flat mushrooms
1 tablespoon dry
  sherry
3 tablespoons crushed
  yellow bean
  sauce★
4 cakes tofu★, diced

Heat the oil in a wok or deep frying pan, add the pork, spring onions and garlic and stir-fry for 2 minutes. Add the green pepper, cauliflower and mushrooms and cook for 1 minute. Stir in the sherry and yellow bean sauce and cook for 2 minutes. Stir in the tofu and cook for a further minute.

Spoon into a warmed serving dish and serve immediately.
Serves 4 to 6

CHILLIES

Chillies are used extensively in Western China.

Fresh red chillies are milder than the green ones, because they become sweeter as they ripen. Dried red chillies are used to season the oil for stir-fried dishes. The seeds are often left in, which makes the dish very hot and spicy; they may be removed if a less hot dish is preferred.

Use fresh chillies with care, since they have a stinging action on the skin. Do not touch your face or rub your eyes when handling them, and wash your hands immediately afterwards.

Chilli paste is made from chilli, soya bean, salt, sugar and flour. It is worth buying, but chilli powder is a reasonable substitute.

BRAISED CHINESE LEAF

2 tablespoons oil
4 spring onions, chopped
1 large head Chinese leaf★, cut into 5 cm (2 inch) slices
250 g (8 oz) spinach, chopped
125 g (4 oz) spring greens, chopped
1 tablespoon light soy sauce★
2 teaspoons dry sherry
50 g (2 oz) peeled prawns

Heat the oil in a wok or deep frying pan, add the spring onions and stir-fry for 1 minute. Add the Chinese leaves, spinach and greens and stir over a medium heat for 2 minutes. Pour over the soy sauce and sherry and cook for 2 minutes. Add the prawns and cook for 1 minute.

Spoon into a warmed serving dish and serve immediately.
Serves 4 to 6

FRIED LETTUCE AND PRAWNS

3 tablespoons oil
3 spring onions, cut into 2.5 cm (1 inch) lengths
1 cm (½ inch) piece root ginger★, shredded
125 g (4 oz) frozen peeled prawns, thawed
1 large or 2 medium cos lettuce, separated into leaves
1 tablespoon dry sherry
salt

Heat the oil in a wok or deep frying pan, add the spring onions and stir-fry for 30 seconds until lightly browned. Add the ginger and prawns and cook for 1 minute. Add the lettuce with the sherry and salt to taste. Stir quickly for 1 to 2 minutes until the lettuce leaves are just limp.

Arrange on a warmed serving dish and serve immediately.
Serves 4 to 6

Braised Chinese Leaf; Fried Lettuce and Prawns

DRY-COOKED BAMBOO SHOOTS

2 tablespoons dried
  shrimps★
  (optional)
2 tablespoons oil
1 × 500 g (1 lb) can
  bamboo shoots★,
  drained
1 cm (½ inch) piece
  root ginger★, finely
  chopped
50 g (2 oz)
  Szechuan pickled
  vegetables★,
  chopped
2 teaspoons caster
  sugar
pinch of salt
150 ml (¼ pint)
  chicken stock
2 red peppers, cored,
  seeded and sliced
1 tablespoon sesame
  seed oil★

Soak the dried shrimps in warm water for 15 minutes, if using; drain.

Heat the oil in a wok or deep frying pan, add the bamboo shoots and stir-fry for 2 minutes until pale brown around the edges. Remove from the pan and drain on kitchen paper.

Add the ginger, shrimps, if using, and Szechuan pickles to the pan and cook for 1 minute. Stir in the sugar, salt and stock and bring to the boil. Return the bamboo shoots to the pan. Add the red peppers, mixing well, and cook for 2 minutes.

Transfer to a warmed serving dish and sprinkle over the sesame seed oil. Serve immediately.

Serves 4 to 6

Dry-Cooked Bamboo Shoots; Tofu Fry; Chinese Leaf & Mushrooms

TOFU FRY

4 cakes tofu★
4 tablespoons oil
1 clove garlic, sliced
2 small leeks, sliced
  diagonally
2 celery sticks, sliced
  diagonally
125 g (4 oz) button
  mushrooms, sliced
125 g (4 oz) lean
  pork, shredded
4 dried chillies★,
  crushed
1 tablespoon chilli
  paste★
1 tablespoon dry
  sherry

Cut each tofu into 3 thin slices, then cut each slice into 2 triangles.

Heat half the oil in a wok or deep frying pan, add the garlic, leeks and celery and fry quickly for 1 minute. Stir in the mushrooms and pork and cook for 2 minutes. Remove from the pan and keep warm.

Heat the remaining oil in the pan, add the tofu and fry for 2 minutes; drain on kitchen paper.

Return the vegetables, pork and tofu to the pan, stir in the dried chillies, chilli paste and sherry and cook for 1 minute.

Transfer to a warmed serving dish, discard the dried chillies and serve immediately.

Serves 4 to 6

CHINESE LEAF AND MUSHROOMS

8 dried Chinese
  mushrooms★
500 g (1 lb) Chinese
  leaves★
1 tablespoon oil
1 cm (½ inch) piece
  root ginger★,
  shredded
1 clove garlic, sliced
3 dried chillies★,
  seeded and sliced
1 green pepper, cored,
  seeded and sliced
1 tablespoon each
  wine vinegar and
  light soy sauce★
1 teaspoon sesame
  seed oil★

Soak the mushrooms in warm water for 15 minutes. Squeeze dry and remove the hard stalks. Tear the Chinese leaves into pieces.

Heat the oil in a wok or deep frying pan, add the ginger, garlic and chillies and stir-fry for 1 minute. Stir in the green pepper, mushroom caps and Chinese leaves and cook for 1 minute. Add the vinegar and soy sauce and mix well.

Pile into a warmed serving dish and sprinkle over the sesame seed oil. Serve immediately.

Serves 4 to 6

VEGETARIAN DISHES

One of the most appealing features of Eastern cuisine is the variety of vegetables and seasonings available, some familiar and others less so, which are combined in an ingenious fashion to bring out the best of their flavours.

The tradition of serving plain boiled vegetables with a pat of butter and a sprinkling of salt is put to shame by the methods used in this chapter. Vegetables come into their own in curries, lentil-based dishes and a bumper crop of braised and stir-fried dishes. For example, to tempt your taste buds we have Mushrooms in Oyster Sauce which consists of dried Chinese mushrooms, straw and button mushrooms stir-fried together in a fragrant sauce. The clever combination of different textures has turned the simplest of ingredients into gourmet fare.

Vegetarianism in various forms – usually for religious reasons – is an important influence in Oriental cookery. Hindus do not eat beef and some of them are completely vegetarian. Most Muslims do not eat pork. Buddhists and Taoists can be very strictly vegetarian and do not eat meat, poultry, fish or any of their by-products. These are not hard-and-fast rules and you will find exceptions throughout the Far East. In fact, some Buddhist monks have been known to indulge a taste for ham sandwiches, on the basis that they were not in the monastery at the time and therefore somehow exempt from the dietary rules!

Even if you aren't a vegetarian, do sample some of the dishes in this chapter. It's often said that if you try vegetarian dishes, you won't miss meat, so why not put this maxim to the test?

CABBAGE FOOGATH

2 tablespoons oil
1 large onion, finely
 minced
2.5 cm (1 inch) piece
 root ginger★, finely
 chopped
3 green chillies★,
 sliced
1 clove garlic, crushed
500 g (1 lb) green
 cabbage, shredded
25 g (1 oz) freshly
 grated coconut★
125 g (4 oz) peeled
 prawns

Heat the oil in a deep frying pan, add the onion, ginger, chillies and garlic and fry until beginning to colour. Stir in the cabbage and continue frying for 5 minutes. Add the coconut and cook, stirring, for 2 minutes. Add the prawns and simmer for 2 minutes.

Transfer to a warmed serving dish.
Serves 4

POTATO AND COURGETTE

3 tablespoons oil
1 large clove garlic,
 crushed
½ teaspoon chilli
 powder★
2 teaspoons ground
 coriander★
1 teaspoon ground
 cumin★
1 teaspoon salt
2 tablespoons water
500 g (1 lb)
 courgettes, sliced
250 g (8 oz) new
 potatoes, cut in half
1 tablespoon finely
 sliced red pepper to
 garnish

Heat the oil in a saucepan and fry the garlic for 30 seconds. Add the spices, salt and water, stir well and fry gently for 2 minutes. Add the vegetables, stir thoroughly, cover the pan and cook gently for 20 minutes or until the vegetables are cooked, stirring occasionally.

Garnish with the red pepper to serve.
Serves 4

Cabbage Foogath; Potato and Courgette

LENTILS IN YOGURT

250 g (8 oz) yellow
    lentils or mung
    dhal★, washed and
    drained
1 teaspoon turmeric★
1 teaspoon salt
1.2 litres (2 pints)
    water
    (approximately)
2 tablespoons oil
4 dried red chillies★
2 tablespoons black
    cumin seeds★
350 g (12 oz) natural
    yogurt

Put the lentils, turmeric and salt into a large pan and pour in the water. Partly cover the pan and simmer for 1 hour. If the mixture dries out, add more water – 150 ml ($\frac{1}{4}$ pint) at a time; the final result should be a fairly thick gruel.

Heat the oil in a pan, add the chillies and cumin and fry for 1 minute. Carefully pour in the yogurt and when bubbling add the lentils. Simmer for 2 minutes, stirring.

Transfer to a warmed serving dish. NOTE: The lentils tend to boil over when they first start cooking. Be very careful when adding the yogurt to the oil because it will almost certainly spit.
Serves 4

LENTIL COCONUT CURRY

40 g (1$\frac{1}{2}$ oz) butter
3 onions, finely
    chopped
2 cloves garlic, finely
    chopped
1 tablespoon grated
    root ginger★
2–4 green chillies★,
    finely chopped
1 teaspoon turmeric★
250 g (8 oz) yellow
    lentils or mung
    dhal★, washed and
    drained
1.2 litres (2 pints)
    water
salt
50 g (2 oz) creamed
    coconut★
juice of 1 lemon
finely sliced green
    chilli rings★

Melt the butter in a large saucepan, add the onions, garlic, ginger and chillies and fry gently, stirring, until soft.

Stir in the turmeric and immediately add the lentils. Fry, stirring, for 1 minute. Pour in the water, add salt to taste and bring to the boil, then partly cover the pan and simmer gently for 40 minutes.

Add the coconut and stir until dissolved, then stir in the lemon juice. Taste the curry, adding more salt if necessary, cover the pan and simmer for 10 minutes.

Transfer to a warmed serving dish and garnish with chilli rings before serving.
Serves 4

Lentils in Yogurt; Lentil Coconut Curry

DHAL SAG

250 g (8 oz) yellow
  lentils or mung
  dhal★, washed and
  drained
600 ml (1 pint) water
3 onions, 1 sliced and
  2 finely chopped
1 teaspoon chilli
  powder★
½ teaspoon turmeric★
salt
3 tablespoons oil
1 clove garlic
2 green chillies★,
  finely chopped
2 teaspoons finely
  grated root ginger★
1 teaspoon fennel
  seeds★
1 kg (2 lb) spinach,
  chopped

Put the lentils, water, sliced onion, chilli powder, turmeric and 1 teaspoon salt into a saucepan and bring to the boil, then partly cover the pan and simmer for 1 hour.

In another saucepan, heat the oil, add the chopped onions and garlic and fry until soft and golden. Stir in the chillies, ginger and fennel seeds and fry for 1 minute. Add the spinach and cook, stirring, for 10 minutes. Stir in the lentils and continue to cook for 5 to 10 minutes. Add more salt if necessary.

Transfer to a warmed serving dish.

Serves 4

CELERY SAMBAR

250 g (8 oz) pigeon
  peas, washed and
  drained
1 teaspoon salt
1 teaspoon turmeric★
1.2 litres (2 pints)
  water
¼ head celery, cut into
  5 cm (2 inch)
  lengths
50 g (2 oz)
  tamarind★
150 ml (¼ pint) hot
  water
2 tablespoons
  desiccated coconut
3 tablespoons boiling
  water
½–1 teaspoon small
  dried red chillies★
1 teaspoon ground
  cumin★
2 teaspoons ground
  coriander★
25 g (1 oz) butter
pinch of asafoetida★
1 teaspoon mustard
  seeds★

Put the pigeon peas, salt, turmeric, water and celery into a saucepan and bring to the boil. Boil rapidly for 10 minutes then partly cover the pan and simmer for 1 hour.

Soak the tamarind in the hot water for 30 minutes, strain, squeezing out as much water as possible. Discard the tamarind. Put the coconut and boiling water into a food processor or electric blender and work for 20 seconds. Add the chillies, cumin and coriander and work until smooth. Stir into the pigeon peas with the tamarind water and simmer for 15 minutes.

Heat the butter in a small frying pan, add the asafoetida and the mustard seeds. When the seeds begin to pop, tip the contents of the pan into the pigeon pea mixture. Serve hot.

Serves 4

Dhal Sag; Celery Sambar

INDIAN LENTIL DISHES

Dhâl Sag, from northern India, is served with Chapatis (see page 144). For an even more filling dish add 250 g (8 oz) cubed potatoes before the spinach. Serve with relishes, salads and chutneys.

Celery Sambar is a southern Indian dish. It is usually served with a small, thick pancake called *idli* made from ground rice and lentils, but this is difficult for the novice to make. Serve with boiled rice instead.

Lentils are eaten every day at every meal by most Indian people. For vegetarians they provide valuable protein and are particularly nutritious eaten with a grain, such as rice or wheat.

SRI LANKAN CURRY

2 onions, thinly sliced
2 cloves garlic, finely
    chopped
1 tablespoon grated
    root ginger★
4 green chillies★, 2
    finely chopped and
    2 slit
1 teaspoon powdered
    lemon grass★ or
    finely grated lemon
    rind
1 teaspoon turmeric★
salt
6 curry leaves★
600 ml (1 pint) thin
    coconut milk★
250 g (8 oz) each
    courgettes, potatoes,
    peppers and carrots,
    sliced
300 ml ($\frac{1}{2}$ pint) thick
    coconut milk★

Put the onions, garlic, ginger, chopped chillies, lemon grass or lemon rind, turmeric, salt to taste, curry leaves and thin coconut milk into a saucepan. Bring to simmering point and cook gently, uncovered, for 20 minutes.

Add the vegetables, slit chillies and thick coconut milk and cook for a further 20 minutes or until the vegetables are tender.

Transfer to a warmed serving dish.
Serves 4

Sri Lankan Curry; Avial Vegetable Curry

VEGETABLE CURRIES

As a large portion of the Indian sub-continent population is vegetarian, commonly for religious reasons, it is not surprising that there is a plethora of non-meat dish recipes available. Pulses are the most important part of this vegetarian diet.

To plan your own vegetarian curry menu, start with a bean, lentil, nut or egg-based main dish for the protein content. If it is a 'dry' curry (one with little or no sauce), accompany it by 'wet' (sauced) vegetable dishes. The reverse is true for a 'wet' main curry dish. The vegetable dishes should also be chosen with an eye for contrasting colours and textures. To round out the menu, many of the standard accompaniments to curries – Pilau Rice, Chapatis, raitas and pickles – are perfectly acceptable on a vegetarian diet. If you would like to add further interest to your curries, here are a few suggestions for garnishes. Try slivered toasted almonds, thinly sliced chilli peppers, sliced or sieved hard-boiled eggs, crispy-fried onion rings, finely chopped fresh coriander or parsley, grated fresh coconut or dessicated coconut.

AVIAL VEGETABLE CURRY

250 g (8 oz) sweet
    potato, cubed
250 g (8 oz)
    courgettes, sliced
250 g (8 oz) okra,
    topped and tailed
2 green cooking
    bananas
    (plantains), sliced
    (optional)
250 g (8 oz) celery,
    sliced
1 teaspoon chilli
    powder★
1 teaspoon turmeric★
1 teaspoon salt
3 tablespoons
    desiccated coconut
3 tablespoons hot
    water
300 g (10 oz) natural
    yogurt
2 green chillies★,
    finely chopped
6 curry leaves★

Put all the vegetables, bananas, chilli powder, turmeric and salt into a saucepan. Add just enough water to cover the bottom of the pan by 1 cm ($\frac{1}{2}$ inch) and simmer for 20 to 25 minutes or until the vegetables are tender; be careful not to let the pan dry out.

Soak the coconut in the hot water for 15 minutes, drain. Mix the yogurt, coconut and chillies together and pour into the pan. Add the curry leaves, bring to the boil, then simmer for 5 minutes. Serve immediately.
Serves 4

BRINJAL AND POTATO CURRY

350 g (12 oz)
  aubergine, cubed
2 teaspoons salt
3 tablespoons oil
1–2 teaspoons chilli
  powder★
1 teaspoon turmeric★
2 teaspoons ground
  cumin★
2 teaspoons ground
  coriander★
2.5 cm (1 inch) piece
  root ginger★, finely
  chopped
350 g (12 oz)
  potatoes, cubed
1 × 227 g (8 oz) can
  tomatoes, sieved
juice of 1 lemon
2 tablespoons chopped
  coriander leaves★
1 teaspoon garam
  masala★
lemon or lime slices to
  garnish (optional)

Sprinkle the aubergine with 1 teaspoon of the salt, place in a colander and set aside for 20 minutes.

Heat the oil in a saucepan, add the chilli powder, turmeric, cumin, ground coriander and ginger and fry for 2 minutes. Add the potatoes and drained aubergine and fry, stirring, for 2 minutes.

Add the tomatoes, lemon juice, chopped coriander and remaining salt, cover and simmer for 25 minutes or until the vegetables are tender. If the sauce dries out, add a little water to prevent burning. Just before serving, stir in the garam masala. Garnish with lemon or lime slices, if liked.

Serves 4

YOGURT CURRY

1 × 500 g (1 lb)
  carton natural
  yogurt
2 tablespoons gram
  flour★
2 tablespoons oil
½ teaspoon ground
  cumin★
½ teaspoon ground
  coriander★
2 cloves garlic,
  crushed
3–4 green chillies★,
  finely chopped
1 teaspoon turmeric★
salt
1 tablespoon chopped
  coriander leaves★
6 curry leaves★
coriander leaves

Mix the yogurt and gram flour together.

Heat the oil in a saucepan, add the cumin, ground coriander, garlic and chillies and fry for 1 minute. Stir in the turmeric, then immediately pour in the yogurt mixture. Add salt to taste and simmer, uncovered, for 10 minutes, stirring occasionally.

Add the chopped coriander and the curry leaves and continue cooking for a further 10 minutes.

Transfer to a warmed serving dish and garnish with coriander leaves to serve, if liked.

Serves 4

┌─────────────────────────────────┐
│ VEGETARIAN CURRY MENUS │
└─────────────────────────────────┘

Different versions of Yogurt Curry are made all over India. Delicious as it is, diced root vegetables or cauliflower florets can be added – cooking times may have to be adjusted. Ideal with a dry vegetable or meat curry and rice.

Brinjal and Potato Curry is an example of curries made with combinations of vegetables. Potato is a popular ingredient because it absorbs the spices and juices. Good with Puri (see page 136).

LEFT: *Yogurt Curry; Brinjal and Potato Curry*
RIGHT: *Spicy Turnips; Tomato and Coriander*

SPICY TURNIPS

about 3 tablespoons
  concentrated butter
  or ghee★
1 kg (2 lb) turnips,
  quartered
2 cloves garlic
2 green chillies★
2.5 cm (1 inch) piece
  root ginger★
1 teaspoon cumin
  seeds★
2 teaspoons coriander
  seeds★
2 tablespoons natural
  yogurt
1 teaspoon salt
150 ml (¼ pint) water
1 teaspoon sugar
1 teaspoon garam
  masala★

Heat the butter in a pan, add the turnips and fry lightly; set aside.

Put the garlic, chillies, ginger, cumin, coriander and yogurt into an electric blender or food processor and work to a paste. Add to the pan, adding more butter if necessary, and fry for 2 minutes.

Return the turnips to the pan, add the salt and stir well. Add the water and simmer, covered, for about 10 minutes, until almost tender. Uncover the pan, add the sugar and garam masala and cook briskly, stirring, until most of the liquid has evaporated.

Serves 4 to 6

TOMATO AND CORIANDER

3 tablespoons oil or
  concentrated butter
  or ghee★
2 onions, chopped
1 kg (2 lb) tomatoes,
  sliced
2.5 cm (1 inch) piece
  root ginger★,
  chopped
1 teaspoon ground
  cumin★
1 teaspoon ground
  coriander★
½ teaspoon chilli
  powder★
1 teaspoon salt
3 green chillies★
1 teaspoon sugar
50 g (2 oz) coriander
  leaves★, finely
  chopped

Heat the oil or butter in a pan, add the onions and fry until soft. Add the tomatoes, ginger, cumin, coriander, chilli powder, and salt and simmer, uncovered, until the mixture begins to thicken. Add the chillies and sugar and continue cooking for 5 to 10 minutes, until fairly thick. Stir in the coriander and serve.

Serves 4

PHUL GOBI WITH PEPPERS

3 tablespoons oil
1 onion, sliced
½ teaspoon turmeric★
1 cauliflower, broken
   into florets
salt
2 green chillies★,
   seeded
1 green, 1 yellow and
   1 red pepper,
   cored, seeded and
   cut into strips

Heat the oil in a pan, add the onion and fry until soft. Add the turmeric and cook for 1 minute. Add the cauliflower and salt to taste, stir well, cover and cook gently for about 10 minutes, until the cauliflower is almost cooked.

Add the chillies and peppers, stir and cook for a further 5 minutes or until tender.
Serves 4

ALOO MATTAR

5 tablespoons oil
1 onion, chopped
2.5 cm (1 inch) piece
   root ginger★,
   chopped
1 green chilli★, finely
   chopped
2 cloves garlic,
   crushed
1 teaspoon turmeric★
750 g (1½ lb)
   potatoes, cut into
   small cubes
salt
6–8 mint leaves
250 g (8 oz) shelled
   or frozen peas

Heat the oil in a pan, add the onion and fry until soft and translucent. Add the ginger, chilli, garlic and turmeric, stir well and cook for 5 minutes. Add the potatoes and salt to taste, stir well, cover and cook for 5 minutes.

Add the mint and fresh peas, stir well and cook for 20 minutes, until tender. If using frozen peas, add them after the potatoes have cooked for 15 minutes and cook for 3 minutes only.
Serves 4 to 6

LEFT: *Phul Gobi with Peppers; Aloo Mattar; Gobi Ki Foogath*
RIGHT: *Masoor Dhal*

GOBI KI FOOGATH

3 tablespoons oil
1 onion, finely sliced
2 cloves garlic,
  crushed
3 green chillies★,
  seeded and finely
  chopped
2.5 cm (1 inch) piece
  root ginger★, finely
  chopped
500 g (1 lb) white
  cabbage, finely
  sliced
salt

Heat the oil in a large pan, add the onion and fry until just soft. Add the garlic, chillies and ginger and cook for 1 minute. Add the cabbage, with the water clinging to the leaves after washing, and salt to taste. Stir well, cover and cook, stirring occasionally, for about 15 minutes; the cabbage should still be slightly crunchy. If liquid gathers, uncover the pan for the last 5 minutes to allow it to evaporate.
Serves 4

VEGETABLE BIRYANI

500 g (1 lb) Basmati
  rice, washed,
  soaked and drained
  (see Plain Boiled
  Rice, page 126)
salt
3 tablespoons oil
5 cm (2 inch)
  cinnamon stick★
6 cardamom pods★
6 cloves
2 onions, sliced
2 cloves garlic, finely
  sliced
2 green chillies★,
  finely sliced
1 tablespoon grated
  root ginger★
1 kg (2 lb) mixed
  vegetables, cut into
  pieces
1 × 397 g (14 oz) can
  tomatoes
1 tablespoon chopped
  coriander leaves★
  (optional)

Parboil the rice in plenty of boiling salted water for 3 minutes, then drain.

Heat the oil in a large saucepan and fry the cinnamon, cardamom and cloves for a few seconds. Add the onions, garlic, chillies and ginger and fry until soft and golden. Add the vegetables and fry for 2 to 3 minutes. Add the tomatoes, with their juice, and salt to taste. Cover and simmer for 20 minutes or until the vegetables are tender.

Layer the vegetables and rice in a casserole, beginning and ending with vegetables. Cover tightly and cook in a preheated moderate oven, 180°C (350°F), Gas Mark 4, for 25 to 30 minutes or until the rice is tender. Sprinkle with the chopped coriander leaves, if using, to serve.
Serves 4 to 6

MASOOR DHAL

4 tablespoons oil
6 cloves
6 cardamom★
2.5 cm (1 inch) piece
  cinnamon stick★
1 onion, chopped
2.5 cm (1 inch) piece
  root ginger★,
  chopped
1 green chilli★, finely
  chopped
1 clove garlic, chopped
½ teaspoon garam
  masala★
250 g (8 oz) orange
  lentils or masoor
  dhal★
salt
juice of 1 lemon

Heat the oil in a pan, add the cloves, cardamom and cinnamon and fry until they start to swell. Add the onion and fry until translucent. Add ginger, chilli, garlic and garam masala and cook for about 5 minutes.

Add the lentils, stir thoroughly and fry for 1 minute. Add salt to taste and enough water to come about 3 cm (1¼ inches) above the level of the lentils. Bring to the boil, cover and simmer for about 20 minutes, until really thick and tender.

Sprinkle with the lemon juice, stir and serve immediately.
Serves 4

COURGETTES, PEAS AND CORIANDER

4 tablespoons oil
2 onions, sliced
2 cloves garlic, finely
  chopped
2 green chillies★,
  chopped
2.5 cm (1 inch) piece
  root ginger★,
  chopped
4 tablespoons finely
  chopped coriander
  leaves★
salt
500 g (1 lb)
  courgettes, cut into
  5 mm ($\frac{1}{4}$ inch)
  slices
250 g (8 oz) shelled
  peas

Heat the oil in a pan, add the onions and fry until soft. Add the garlic, chillies, ginger, coriander and salt to taste and cook for 5 minutes, stirring occasionally. Add the courgettes and peas, stir well, cover and cook for 30 minutes, or until the peas are tender. If necessary, boil quickly to evaporate any liquid before serving.
Serves 4

ALOO SAG

6 tablespoons oil
1 onion, chopped
2.5 cm (1 inch) piece
  root ginger★,
  chopped
2 green chillies★,
  finely chopped
1 teaspoon turmeric★
2 cloves garlic, finely
  chopped
500 g (1 lb) potatoes,
  cut into small
  pieces
salt
2 × 227 g (8 oz)
  packets frozen
  spinach leaf,
  thawed

Heat the oil in a lidded frying pan, add the onion and cook until soft. Add the spices and garlic and cook for 5 minutes. Add the potatoes, and salt to taste, stir well, cover and cook for 10 minutes.

Squeeze out any liquid from the spinach and chop. Add to the potatoes and cook for about 5 minutes, until both vegetables are tender.
Serves 4

SPROUTING MUNG BEANS

250 g (8 oz) whole
  mung beans, rinsed
3–4 tablespoons oil
1 onion, thinly sliced
2 green chillies★,
  seeded and chopped
2.5 cm (1 inch) piece
  root ginger★, cut
  into fine matchstick
  pieces
1 teaspoon fennel
  seeds★
salt
300 ml ($\frac{1}{2}$ pint)
  water

A day in advance, put the beans in a bowl and barely cover them with warm water. Cover the bowl with cling film and leave in a warm dark place. Do not let the beans dry out; add a little extra water if necessary. The beans will have sprouted by the next day. Rinse and drain them.

Heat the oil in a saucepan. Add the onion and fry, stirring, for 3 minutes. Stir in the chillies, ginger, and fennel seeds and cook, stirring, until the onions have softened a little.

Add the beans, salt to taste and the water. Bring to simmering point, cover and cook gently, stirring occasionally, for 25 to 30 minutes or until the beans are soft and there is no liquid left.
Serves 4

Aloo Sag; Sprouting Mung Beans; Courgettes, Peas and Coriander

TAMATAR ALOO

2 tablespoons oil
½ teaspoon mustard
   seeds★
250 g (8 oz)
   potatoes, cut into
   small cubes
1 teaspoon turmeric★
1 teaspoon chilli
   powder★
2 teaspoons paprika
juice of 1 lemon
1 teaspoon sugar
salt
250 g (8 oz)
   tomatoes,
   quartered
2 tablespoons finely
   chopped coriander
   leaves★ to garnish

Heat the oil in a pan, add the mustard
seeds and fry until they pop – just a
few seconds. Add the potatoes and fry
for about 5 minutes. Add the spices,
lemon juice, sugar and salt to taste, stir
well and cook for 5 minutes.

Add the tomatoes, stir well, then
simmer for 5 to 10 minutes until the
potatoes are tender.

Sprinkle with coriander to serve.
Serves 4

DHAI ALOO

4 tablespoons oil
1 onion, chopped
2.5 cm (1 inch) piece
   root ginger★, finely
   chopped
1 tablespoon ground
   coriander★
2 green chillies★,
   finely chopped
750 g (1½ lb) small
   new potatoes
1 × 227 g (8 oz) can
   tomatoes
100 g (3½ oz) raisins
salt
2 × 150 g (5 oz)
   cartons natural
   yogurt
2 tablespoons chopped
   coriander leaves★ to
   garnish

Heat the oil in a large pan, add the
onion and ginger and fry until soft.
Stir in the ground coriander and
chillies and fry for 2 minutes. Add the
potatoes, stir well, cover and cook
very gently for 5 minutes, stirring
occasionally so they colour evenly.

Add the tomatoes with their juice,
raisins and salt to taste and stir well.
Increase the heat a little and cook,
uncovered. As the liquid evaporates,
add half the yogurt, a tablespoon at a
time. When the potatoes have cooked
for 20 minutes and are just about
ready, add the remaining yogurt, a
tablespoon at a time, lower the heat
and cook for 2 minutes. Sprinkle with
coriander to serve.
Serves 4 to 6

Tamatar Aloo; Dhai Aloo

Bharta; Dhai Bhindi

BHARTA

500 g (1 lb)
  aubergines
2 tablespoons oil
1 large onion, finely
  chopped
1 clove garlic, crushed
1 green chilli★, seeded
  and chopped
1 tablespoon ground
  coriander★
1 tablespoon finely
  chopped coriander
  leaves★
salt
1 tablespoon lemon
  juice

Cook the aubergines in a preheated moderate oven, 180°C (350°F), Gas Mark 4, for 30 minutes or until soft. Cool slightly, then slit open, scoop out all the flesh and beat it with a fork.

Heat the oil in a pan, add the onion, garlic and chilli and fry until the onion is soft but not coloured. Add the ground and fresh coriander and salt to taste. Add the aubergine pulp, stir well and fry, uncovered, for 2 minutes, then cover and simmer very gently for 5 minutes. Sprinkle with lemon juice and serve.

Serves 4

DHAI BHINDI

250 g (8 oz) okra
2 tablespoons oil
2.5 cm (1 inch) piece
  root ginger★,
  chopped
1 teaspoon turmeric★
salt
2–3 tablespoons water
2 × 150 g (5 oz)
  cartons natural
  yogurt
½ teaspoon chilli
  powder★
2 tablespoons grated
  coconut★
1 tablespoon finely
  chopped coriander
  leaves★

Cut the tops off the okra and halve them lengthways. Heat the oil in a pan, add the okra and fry for 5 minutes. Add the ginger, turmeric, and salt to taste, stir well, add the water, cover and cook for 10 minutes, until the okra is tender.

Mix the remaining ingredients together; add to the pan, stir well and serve.

Serves 4

POTATO
WITH MUSTARD SEED

4 tablespoons oil
1 teaspoon mustard
  seeds★
1 teaspoon turmeric★
1–2 green chillies★,
  chopped
500 g (1 lb) potatoes,
  boiled and diced
juice of 1 lemon
salt

Heat the oil in a frying pan and add the mustard seeds. When they begin to pop, stir in the turmeric and chillies and cook for a few seconds. Add the potatoes and stir well to mix. Pour in the lemon juice and add salt to taste. Stir well and heat through.

Serves 4

ORIENTAL NOODLE SALAD

DRESSING:
125 g (4 oz) smooth
    peanut butter
85 ml (3 fl oz)
    vegetable stock
50 ml (2 fl oz) soy
    sauce★
4 tablespoons sesame
    seed oil★
2 tablespoons red wine
    vinegar
1 tablespoon crushed
    fresh garlic
1 tablespoon finely
    grated root ginger★
1 teaspoon hot pepper
    oil★
50 ml (2 fl oz) thick
    coconut milk★ or
    double cream
SALAD:
3.5 litres (6 pints)
    water
1 tablespoon oil
salt
300 g (10 oz) thin
    Chinese egg
    noodles★
125 g(4 oz) bean
    sprouts★
2 tablespoons sesame
    seed oil★
1 × 425 g (15 oz) can
    whole baby
    sweetcorn★, drained
125 g (4 oz) carrots,
    sliced thinly
    diagonally
125 g (4 oz)
    cucumber, sliced
    thinly diagonally
25 g (1 oz) spring
    onions, sliced thinly
    diagonally

(Picture, page 102)

Kabli Channa

To make the dressing: combine all the ingredients, except the coconut milk, in a food processor or an electric blender and liquidize until smooth. With the motor running, add the coconut milk in a thin stream. Liquidize until smooth. Transfer the dressing to a sauceboat. Cover and set aside.

Bring the water, oil and salt to the boil in a large saucepan over a high heat. Add the noodles and cook until just firm. Drain in a colander, then rinse under cold running water until cool. Drain again. Transfer the noodles to a large bowl. Add the bean sprouts and sesame seed oil and toss well to combine. Set aside.

Arrange the baby sweetcorn, carrots and cucumber attractively round the edge of a large oval platter. Mound the noodle mixture carefully in the centre and sprinkle the spring onions carefully round the edge of the noodles. Serve immediately, handing the dressing separately.

Serves 4

KABLI CHANNA

250 g (8 oz) chick
    peas or Bengal
    gram★
750 ml (1¼ pints)
    water
1 teaspoon salt
2 tablespoons
    concentrated butter★
    or oil
1 onion, chopped
2.5 cm (1 inch) piece
    cinnamon stick★
4 cloves
2 cloves garlic,
    crushed
2.5 cm (1 inch) piece
    root ginger★,
    chopped
2 green chillies★,
    finely chopped
2 teaspoons ground
    coriander★
150 g (5 oz)
    tomatoes, chopped
1 teaspoon garam
    masala★
1 tablespoon chopped
    coriander leaves★

Wash the gram and soak in the water overnight. Add the salt and simmer until tender. Drain, reserving the water, and set aside.

Heat the butter or oil in a pan, add the onion and fry until golden. Add the cinnamon and cloves and fry for a few seconds, then add the garlic, ginger, chillies and ground coriander and fry for 5 minutes. Add the tomatoes and fry until most of the liquid has evaporated.

Add the gram and cook gently for 5 minutes, then add the reserved water and simmer for 20 to 25 minutes. Add the garam masala and stir well. Sprinkle with the chopped coriander and serve immediately.

Serves 4

MUSHROOMS
IN OYSTER SAUCE

50 g (2 oz) small
 dried Chinese
 mushrooms★
2 tablespoons oil
4 spring onions,
 chopped
150 ml (¼ pint)
 stock
1 × 227 g (8 oz) can
 straw mushrooms★,
 drained
125 g (4 oz) button
 mushrooms
3 tablespoons oyster
 sauce★
1 tablespoon dry
 sherry

Soak the dried mushrooms in warm
water for 15 minutes. Drain, squeeze
dry and discard the hard stalks.

Heat the oil in a wok or frying pan,
add the spring onions and stir-fry for
30 seconds. Add the mushroom caps
and pour over the stock. Simmer for
15 to 20 minutes, until the mushrooms
are tender.

Add the straw mushrooms and
button mushrooms and cook for 1
minute. Pour over the oyster sauce and
sherry, stir well and cook for 2
minutes.

Pile into a warmed serving dish and
serve immediately.
Serves 4 to 6

CHINESE LEAF
AND MUSHROOMS

8 dried Chinese
 mushrooms★
1 tablespoon oil
1 cm (½ inch) piece
 root ginger★,
 shredded
1 clove garlic, sliced
3 chillies★, seeded and
 sliced
1 green pepper, cored,
 seeded and sliced
500 g (1 lb) Chinese
 leaves★, torn into
 pieces
1 tablespoon wine
 vinegar
1 tablespoon light soy
 sauce★
1 teaspoon sesame
 seed oil★·

Soak the mushrooms in warm water
for 15 minutes. Squeeze dry and
remove the hard stalks.

Heat the oil in a wok or deep frying
pan, add the ginger, garlic and chillies
and stir-fry for 1 minute. Stir in the
green pepper, mushroom caps and
Chinese leaves and cook for 1 minute.
Add the vinegar and soy sauce and
mix well.

Pile into a warmed serving dish and
sprinkle over the sesame seed oil. Serve
immediately.
Serves 4 to 6

STIR-FRIED
SUMMER VEGETABLES

2 tablespoons oil
2 spring onions,
 sliced
1 cm (½ inch) piece
 root ginger★, sliced
2 cloves garlic, sliced
2 chillies★, seeded and
 chopped
50 g (2 oz) button
 mushrooms
125 g (4 oz) baby
 carrots
125 g (4 oz)
 mange tout
125 g (4 oz) French
 beans
50 g (2 oz) bean
 sprouts★
1 red pepper, cored
 seeded and sliced
2 celery sticks,
 sliced
few cauliflower
 florets
4 tablespoons light
 soy sauce★
2 tablespoons dry
 sherry
1 teaspoon sesame
 seed oil★

Heat the oil in a wok or deep frying
pan, add the spring onions, ginger and
garlic and stir-fry for about 30
seconds. Add the chillies and all the
vegetables. Toss well and cook,
stirring, for 2 minutes. Stir in the soy
sauce and sherry and cook for 2
minutes.

Sprinkle over the sesame seed oil,
pile into a warmed serving dish and
serve immediately.
Serves 4 to 6

VEGETABLES IN CHINESE COOKING

In Chinese cooking, vegetables are most often quickly stir-
fried to retain their colour and nutritional value. Dried and
pickled – as well as fresh – vegetables are used, as are
numerous varieties of soybean-based products, ranging from
fresh and dried bean curd skin to various soy flavourings. The
Chinese are very fond of the cabbage family, frequently using
mustard greens or different varieties of cabbages as part of
their repertoire. Baby corn, bamboo shoots, water chestnuts,
fresh bean sprouts, lotus root and mange tout are also
commonly used.

BRAISED AUBERGINES

oil for shallow-frying

4 spring onions, sliced

4 cloves garlic, sliced

1 cm (½ inch) piece root ginger★, shredded

2 large aubergines, cut into 5 cm (2 inch) strips

2 tablespoons soy sauce★

2 tablespoons dry sherry

2 teaspoons chilli sauce★

chopped red and green chillies★ to garnish

Heat 2 tablespoons oil in a wok or deep frying pan. Add the spring onions, garlic and ginger and stir-fry for about 30 seconds. Remove from the pan and set aside. Increase the heat, add the aubergine strips and fry until browned, adding more oil to the pan as necessary. Remove from the pan and drain on kitchen paper.

Pour off the oil from the pan. Return the spring onions, garlic, ginger and aubergine strips to the pan. Pour over the soy sauce, sherry and chilli sauce, stir well and cook for 2 minutes.

Spoon into a warmed serving dish, sprinkle with chillies and serve immediately.

Serves 4 to 6

BRAISED BAMBOO SHOOTS

6 Chinese dried mushrooms★

2 tablespoons oil

1 cm (½ inch) piece root ginger★, shredded

2 cloves garlic, sliced

6 spring onions, sliced

2 green chillies★, seeded and chopped

1 × 500 g (1 lb) can bamboo shoots★, drained and sliced

2 tablespoons light soy sauce★

2 tablespoons dry sherry

125 g (4 oz) cooked lean ham, shredded

Soak the mushrooms in warm water for 15 minutes. Squeeze dry, discard the hard stalks and slice the mushroom caps.

Heat the oil in a wok or deep frying pan, add the ginger, garlic, spring onions and chillies and stir-fry for 1 minute. Stir in the remaining ingredients, mixing well, and cook for 3 minutes.

Pile into a warmed serving dish and serve immediately.

Serves 4 to 6

Braised Aubergines; Braised Bamboo Shoots

INDIAN VEGETABLE MEDLEY

3 tablespoons oil
1 teaspoon fennel
    seeds★
2 onions, sliced
1 teaspoon each
    ground coriander★
    and ground cumin★
1 teaspoon chilli
    powder★
2 teaspoons finely
    chopped root
    ginger★
2 cloves garlic,
    crushed
1 small aubergine,
    thinly sliced
1 potato, cubed
1 green pepper, cored,
    seeded and sliced
2 courgettes, sliced
1 × 397 g (14 oz) can
    tomatoes
2 green chillies★,
    chopped, including
    seeds
salt
50 g (2 oz) frozen
    peas

Heat the oil in a large wok or frying pan, stir in the fennel seeds and cook for 1 minute, stirring constantly. Add the onions and cook for 5 minutes, until pale brown. Lower the heat, add the coriander, cumin and chilli powder and cook, stirring, for 1 minute. Add the ginger, garlic, aubergine and potato, mix well and cook for 15 minutes. Add the green pepper, courgettes, tomatoes with their juice, chillies and salt to taste. Bring slowly to the boil, then simmer for 10 minutes, stirring occasionally.

Stir in the peas and cook for 3 minutes, until the vegetables are tender and the liquid absorbed.

Transfer to a warmed serving dish and serve immediately.
Serves 4 to 6

CORIANDER TOMATOES

3 tablespoons oil
2 onions, finely
    chopped
1 teaspoon ground
    coriander★
1 teaspoon ground
    cumin★
½ teaspoon chilli
    powder★
2 teaspoons finely
    chopped root
    ginger★
1–2 cloves garlic,
    crushed
1 kg (2 lb) tomatoes,
    sliced
2 green chillies★,
    finely chopped,
    seeded if liked
½–1 teaspoon salt
1–2 tablespoons
    chopped coriander
    leaves★
coriander leaves to
    garnish★

Heat a large wok or frying pan, add the oil and place over a moderate heat. Add the onions and cook for about 5 minutes, until golden brown, stirring occasionally.

Lower the heat, stir in the coriander and the cumin and chilli powder and cook for 2 minutes, stirring. Add the ginger, garlic, tomatoes and chillies; stir well to coat the tomatoes in the spices. Lower the heat and cook for 5 to 7 minutes, until fairly thick. Season with salt and cook for a further minute.

Spoon into a warmed serving dish and sprinkle with the chopped coriander. Serve immediately, garnished with coriander leaves.
Serves 4

Indian Vegetable Medley; Coriander Tomatoes

STIR-FRIED SPICED CUCUMBER

1½ cucumbers
2 teaspoons salt
1 tablespoon oil
¼ teaspoon chilli bean
    sauce★ or chilli
    powder★
6 cloves garlic,
    crushed
1½ tablespoons black
    beans★, coarsely
    chopped
5 tablespoons chicken
    stock, preferably
    homemade
1 teaspoon sesame
    seed oil★
cucumber slices to
    garnish

Peel the cucumbers, slice in half lengthways, remove the seeds with a teaspoon, then cut into 2.5 cm (1 inch) cubes. Sprinkle with salt and leave to drain in a colander for about 20 minutes. Rinse in cold water, drain well and dry thoroughly on kitchen paper.

Heat a wok or frying pan until it is hot, add the oil and when it is almost smoking, add the chilli bean sauce or powder, garlic and black beans and stir-fry for about 30 seconds. Add the cucumber and toss well for about 3 seconds to coat in the spices. Add the stock and continue stir-frying over a high heat for 3 to 4 minutes, until almost all the liquid has evaporated and the cucumber is tender.

Transfer to a warmed serving dish. Sprinkle with the sesame seed oil, garnish with slices of raw cucumber and serve immediately.
Serves 4

DEEP-FRIED GREEN BEANS

600 ml (1 pint) oil for
    deep-frying
500 g (1 lb) French
    beans
3 cloves garlic,
    crushed
1 tablespoon chopped
    root ginger★
4 spring onions,
    chopped
4 dried red chillies★
1 tablespoon whole
    yellow bean sauce★
1 tablespoon dry
    sherry
1 tablespoon dark soy
    sauce★
pinch of sugar
1 tablespoon stock

Heat the oil in a wok or deep-fat fryer until a single bean dropped into the oil sizzles. Deep-fry half the beans for about 3 to 4 minutes, until they are slightly wrinkled; remove and drain well. Repeat with the remaining beans.

Transfer about 1 tablespoon of the oil to a wok or frying pan and heat. Add the garlic, ginger and spring onions and stir-fry for 5 seconds. Add the chillies and cook for a further 30 seconds, until they turn black. Remove the chillies, then add the remaining ingredients and stir-fry for a few seconds. Stir in the drained beans and stir-fry for 2 minutes, until they are hot and coated in the sauce.

Transfer to a warmed serving dish and serve immediately.
Serves 4

Stir-Fried Spiced Cucumber; Deep-Fried Green Beans

WESTERN CHINA

The western region of China is the area from which these two recipes originate. Called the 'Land of Abundance', it is virtually surrounded by mountains and includes the provinces of Szechuan and Hunan. It is the most heavily populated and one of the most fertile regions of China, with the Yangtze River running across it. The crops include rice, sugar-cane, maize, beans and tobacco.

CHINESE LEAF AND PEPPER SALAD

1 leek, finely sliced
1 head of Chinese
  leaf★, shredded
1 green pepper,
  cored, seeded and
  finely sliced
6 tablespoons Herb
  Dressing (see page
  155)

Separate the leek slices into rings and mix with the Chinese leaves in a bowl. Add the green pepper and dressing and toss thoroughly. Transfer to a salad bowl and serve immediately.
Serves 6 to 8

BEAN SPROUT AND CRESS SALAD

125 g (4 oz) Chinese
  leaves★
125 g (4 oz) bean
  sprouts★ or alfalfa★
2 cartons salad cress
6 spring onions,
  sliced
6 tablespoons
  Vinaigrette
  Dressing (see page
  155)

Slice the Chinese leaves thinly and place in a salad bowl. Add the bean sprouts to the bowl with the cress and spring onions; mix well.

Pour over the dressing and toss well just before serving.
Serves 4 to 6

ONION AND CHILLI SALAD

A hot onion side dish which makes a tasty accompaniment to a curry or cold meats.

5 tablespoons cider
  vinegar
3 tablespoons water
1 green chilli★, seeded
  and chopped
salt and pepper
2 Spanish onions,
  thinly sliced

Mix together the vinegar, water, chilli, and salt and pepper to taste.

Put the onions into a shallow serving dish and pour over the dressing. Leave to stand for 1 hour, stirring occasionally.
Serves 6

LENTIL SALAD

250 g (8 oz) green
  lentils
salt and pepper
6 tablespoons Soy
  Sauce Dressing★
  (see page 155)
4 tomatoes, skinned
  and chopped
1 small onion,
  chopped
125 g (4 oz) bean
  sprouts★
2 celery sticks, sliced
1 tablespoon chopped
  summer savory

Cover the lentils with boiling water and leave to soak for 20 minutes. Drain, place in a pan and cover with cold water. Bring to the boil, add a little salt, then cover and simmer for 20 minutes, until softened. Drain well and transfer to a bowl. Pour over the dressing and mix well while still warm. Leave to cool.

Add the remaining ingredients, seasoning with the salt and pepper to taste, toss thoroughly and transfer to a serving dish.
Serves 6 to 8

TRI-COLOURED VEGETABLES

25 ml (1 fl oz)
  chicken stock
2 tablespoons oyster
  sauce★
1 tablespoon soy
  sauce★
1 tablespoon mirin★
  or dry sherry
2 teaspoons cornflour
2 tablespoons oil
625 g (1¼ lb) broccoli,
  broken into florets
25 ml (1 fl oz) water
1 × 425 g (15 oz) can
  whole baby
  sweetcorn, drained
250 g (8 oz) small
  button mushrooms,
  halved
1 tablespoon sesame
  seed oil★
1 tablespoon toasted
  sesame seeds★ to
  garnish

Place the stock, oyster sauce, soy sauce, mirin and cornflour in a small bowl and whisk until smooth. Cover and set aside.

Heat the oil in a wok or large frying pan over a moderate heat. Add the broccoli and cook for 2 minutes, stirring frequently. Pour in the water, cover and steam for 1 minute. Add the sweetcorn and mushrooms, then stir-fry for 2 minutes. Stir the stock mixture to recombine, then pour into the vegetables. Cover and cook for 1 minute. Stir the sesame seed oil into the vegetable mixture, then transfer to a heated serving dish.

Garnish with the sesame seeds, then serve immediately.
Serves 4

(Picture, page 102)

STIR-FRIED GARLIC SPINACH

1kg (2 lb) spinach
2 tablespoons oil
4 spring onions, chopped
1 teaspoon light soy sauce★
pinch of sugar
pinch of salt
2 cloves garlic, crushed
1 teaspoon toasted sesame seeds★

Wash the spinach thoroughly and remove all the stems. Drain thoroughly.

Heat the oil in a large wok or frying pan, add the spring onions and fry for 30 seconds. Add the spinach and stir-fry for about 2 minutes, until the leaves are coated in the oil and have wilted. Add the soy sauce, sugar, salt and garlic and continue stir-frying for 3 minutes. Pour off any excess liquid.

Transfer to a warmed serving dish and sprinkle with the sesame seeds to serve.

Serves 4

STIR-FRIED GINGER BROCCOLI

500 g (1 lb) broccoli
salt
2 tablespoons oil
1 clove garlic, thinly sliced (optional)
2.5 cm (1 inch) piece root ginger★, finely shredded
½–1 teaspoon sesame seed★ oil

Separate the broccoli heads into small florets, and peel and diagonally slice the stems. Blanch in boiling salted water for 30 seconds, drain well and cool rapidly under cold running water; drain thoroughly.

Heat the oil in a large wok or frying pan, add the garlic and ginger and stir-fry for 2 to 3 seconds. Add the blanched broccoli and cook for 2 minutes. Sprinkle over the sesame seed oil and stir-fry for a further 30 seconds.

Spoon into a warmed serving dish and serve immediately.

Serves 4

Stir-Fried Garlic Spinach; Stir-Fried Ginger Broccoli

RICE, NOODLES AND DUMPLINGS

Rice is the staff of life for more than half the world's population. In fact, it can form the major portion of many people's daily diet in parts of the East.

There are many different types of rice. Among them are the prized long-grain Basmati rice from the foothills of the Himalayas, the glutinous or sticky rice especially favoured by the Japanese and short-grain rice, which is generally used for desserts. Included in this chapter are the Indian specialities of Biryani and Pilau Rice, a taste of Indonesia with its Coconut Rice and the stunning Lotus Leaf Rice from China.

Though Orientals eat some bread, their wheat is more often made into noodles in a variety of shapes. Noodles are also made from ground mung beans, rice flour, sweet potatoes, dried peas and buckwheat. Our recipes for Dan Dan Noodles, Mixed Seafood Stick Noodles and Crispy Fried Noodles should tempt your taste buds to experiment in this much neglected field of Oriental cookery.

Dumplings, too, have long played a part in Chinese cuisine. However, these are not giant floury-tasting balls but small titbits, delicately shaped and filled. Eating Chinese Dim Sum, translated as 'delights of the heart' for breakfast is a national pastime. Trolleys piled high with a steaming assortment of savoury and sweet dumplings are wheeled past the customers who only have to point at their choice – a good example of Chinese fast food. Try the Fried Steamed Dumplings to get a taste of this amiable custom.

Biryani

> ### BIRYANI
>
> Biryani is a north Indian dish of lamb and rice that is Mogul in origin. It may be served as an entire meal with just a bowl of yogurt or yogurt salad (with cucumber or banana sliced into it) as an accompaniment.
>
> This dish requires a good-quality Basmati rice; other rice will not give either the flavour or aroma required of a good Biryani. For the same reasons, use saffron threads rather than the powder.

BIRYANI

8 tablespoons concentrated butter or ghee★
10 cm (4 inch) piece cinnamon stick★
8 cardamom pods★
12 cloves
4 cloves garlic, crushed
3.5 cm (1½ inch) piece root ginger★, chopped
1 teaspoon fennel seeds★
½ teaspoon chilli powder★
1 kg (2 lb) boned leg of lamb, cubed
2 × 150 g (5 oz) cartons natural yogurt
150 ml (¼ pint) water
2 teaspoons salt
½ teaspoon saffron threads★
3 tablespoons boiling water
500 g (1 lb) Basmati rice, washed, soaked and drained (see Plain Boiled Rice, page 126)

TO GARNISH:
2 tablespoons concentrated butter or ghee★
1 large onion, sliced
4 tablespoons flaked almonds
4 tablespoons sultanas

Heat 6 tablespoons of the butter in a large saucepan. Add the cinnamon, cardamom and cloves and fry for a few seconds, stirring. When the spices let out a strong aroma, stir in the garlic, ginger, fennel seeds and chilli powder. Fry for 5 minutes, stirring constantly.

Add the lamb and fry well on all sides. Stir in the yogurt a tablespoon at a time, allowing each spoonful to be absorbed before adding the next. Add the water and half the salt, cover and simmer for 40 minutes or until the lamb is tender.

Meanwhile, soak the saffron in the boiling water for 15 minutes, then strain. Discard the saffron.

Fill another large pan two-thirds full with water and bring to the boil. Add the rice and remaining salt, boil for 3 minutes, then drain.

Put the remaining butter in a large casserole, cover the base with rice and sprinkle with the saffron water. Cover with a layer of lamb. Repeat the layers, finishing with rice. Pour in any liquid from the lamb, cover closely with a foil-lined lid and cook in a preheated moderately hot oven, 190°C (375°F), Gas Mark 5, for 25 to 30 minutes or until the rice is tender.

Meanwhile, prepare the garnish. Heat the butter in a small frying pan, add the onion and fry until golden. Remove from the pan and set aside. Add the almonds and sultanas to the pan and fry until the almonds are lightly coloured and the sultanas plump.

Transfer the biryani to a warmed serving dish and sprinkle with the onion, almonds and sultanas to serve.
Serves 4 to 6

PRAWN AND SPINACH RICE

500 g (1 lb) Basmati rice, washed, soaked and drained (see Plain Boiled Rice, page 126)

salt

½ teaspoon turmeric★

50 g (2 oz) butter

3 tablespoons oil

2 onions, sliced

3 cloves garlic, finely chopped

1 tablespoon grated root ginger★

1–2 teaspoons chilli powder★

2 teaspoons ground coriander★

1 kg (2 lb) spinach, chopped

500 g (1 lb) peeled prawns

Fill a large saucepan two-thirds full with water and bring to the boil. Add the rice, 1 teaspoon salt and the turmeric. Boil for 3 minutes, then drain. Stir in the butter.

Heat the oil in a large saucepan, add the onions, garlic and ginger and fry until golden. Stir in the chilli powder, coriander and 1 teaspoon salt and fry for a few seconds. Add the spinach and cook, stirring, until soft. Stir in the prawns.

Layer the spinach and prawns with the buttered rice in a casserole, beginning and ending with spinach. Cover tightly and cook in a preheated moderate oven, 180°C (350°F), Gas Mark 4, for 30 minutes. Serve hot.

Serves 4

CHICKEN AND CARROT RICE

1 teaspoon chilli powder★

salt

3 chicken supremes, cut into strips

75 g (3 oz) butter

2 cloves garlic, finely chopped

1 onion, sliced

50 g (2 oz) split almonds

50 g (2 oz) raisins

1 teaspoon turmeric★

350 g (12 oz) Basmati rice, washed, soaked and drained (see Plain Boiled Rice, page 126)

500 g (1 lb) carrots, grated

450 ml (¾ pint) chicken stock

Mix the chilli powder and ½ teaspoon salt on a plate and lightly dip the chicken pieces in the mixture.

Heat 25 g (1 oz) of the butter in a frying pan, add the chicken pieces and garlic and fry, turning them over constantly, for 2 minutes. Reduce the heat to low, cover and cook for 10 minutes or until the chicken is tender.

Meanwhile, heat the remaining butter in a large saucepan, add the onion, almonds and raisins and fry until golden. Stir in the turmeric, then the rice and fry, stirring, for 1 to 2 minutes. Add salt to taste then stir in the carrots, chicken pieces and stock. Bring to the boil, cover tightly, reduce the heat to very low and simmer for 20 minutes or until the rice is cooked and all the liquid absorbed.

Transfer to a warmed serving dish.

Serves 4

BROWN RICE

Brown rice can be used in the Prawn and Spinach Rice above as an alternative to Plain Boiled Rice. The result will be totally different, but delicious. Cook completely before layering it with the other ingredients.

To cook brown rice, wash it and put it in a saucepan with double the quantity of water. Bring to the boil, reduce the heat to a bare simmer and cover the pan tightly with a lid. The water should be absorbed and the rice tender 45 minutes after it has been brought to the boil.

Saffron Rice; Coconut Rice

PLAIN BOILED RICE

350 g (12 oz) long-
  grain rice
450 ml (¾ pint) water
salt
coriander leaves★ to
  garnish (optional)

Wash the rice thoroughly under cold running water, then soak in cold water for 30 minutes; drain.

Put the rice into a pan with the measured water and salt, bring to the boil, cover and simmer gently for 20 minutes, until the rice is tender and the liquid absorbed. If cooking on an electric hob, the heat can be turned off once the rice has come to the boil.

Transfer the rice to a warmed serving dish and garnish with coriander leaves, if using. Serve as an accompaniment to curries and other spicy dishes.

NOTE: The best rice for Indian meals is Basmati, although Patna rice can also be used. There are many different methods of cooking rice, but one of the most important things to remember is to wash the rice before cooking. This helps to prevent the grains of rice from sticking together during cooking.
Serves 4

COCONUT RICE

450 ml (¾ pint) thin
  coconut milk★
½ teaspoon turmeric★
350 g (12 oz)
  Basmati rice,
  washed, soaked and
  drained (see Plain
  Boiled Rice, above,
  right)
8 small onions,
  roughly chopped
20 peppercorns
1 teaspoon salt
finely chopped spring
  onions (optional) to
  garnish

Put the coconut milk in a saucepan, stir in the turmeric, then add the rice. Bring to the boil, then cover and simmer gently for about 10 minutes. Add the onions, peppercorns and salt and continue cooking gently for another 10 minutes or until the rice is tender. Be careful not to let the rice burn.

Transfer to a warmed serving dish and garnish with spring onion, if using.
Serves 4

SAFFRON RICE

1 teaspoon saffron
  threads★
2 tablespoons boiling
  water
50 g (2 oz)
  concentrated butter
  or ghee★
5 cm (2 inch)
  cinnamon stick★
6 cardamom pods★
6 cloves
1 onion, sliced
350 g (12 oz)
  Basmati rice,
  washed, soaked and
  drained (see Plain
  Boiled Rice, above)
450 ml (¾ pint) water
salt

Soak the saffron in the boiling water for 15 minutes, strain.

Melt the butter in a large saucepan and fry the spices for a few seconds. Add the onion and fry, stirring, until golden. Add the rice and fry for 2 to 3 minutes.

Add the saffron and the water, salt the water, stir and bring to the boil. Cover and cook gently for 20 minutes or until the rice is tender and the liquid is absorbed.
Serves 4

TOMATO RICE

3 tablespoons oil
1 onion, sliced
1 clove garlic, crushed
2.5 cm (1 inch) piece
  root ginger★,
  chopped
250 g (8 oz) long-
  grain rice, washed,
  soaked and drained
  (see Plain Boiled
  Rice, page 126)
1 × 539 g (1 lb 3 oz)
  can tomatoes
salt
2 tablespoons finely
  chopped coriander
  leaves★

Tomato Rice; Kitcheri

Heat the oil in a large pan, add the onion and fry until golden. Add the garlic and ginger and fry for 2 minutes. Add the rice, stir well and fry for 2 minutes.

Break up the tomatoes in their juice and add to the rice with salt to taste. Bring to the boil, then cover and simmer for 15 to 20 minutes, until tender.

Transfer to a warmed serving dish and sprinkle with the coriander.
Serves 4

KITCHERI

175 g (6 oz) long-
  grain rice
175 g (6 oz) red
  lentils or masoor
  dhal★
50 g (2 oz) butter
1 onion
1 clove garlic,
  chopped
5 cm (2 inch) piece
  cinnamon stick★
5 cardamom pods★
5 cloves
10 peppercorns
450 ml (¾ pint)
  boiling water
salt
fried onion rings to
  garnish (optional)

Wash the combined rice and lentils under running cold water, then leave to soak in fresh cold water for 30 minutes.

Melt the butter in a large pan. Add the onion to the pan with the garlic, cinnamon, cardamom, cloves and peppercorns. Fry gently until the onion is soft.

Add the drained rice and lentils to the pan and fry gently, stirring, for 2 minutes. Add the water, and salt to taste and boil for 2 minutes. Cover tightly and simmer for about 20 minutes, until the water is absorbed.

Transfer the rice mixture to a warmed serving dish to serve. Garnish with onion rings, if wished.
Serves 4

CHICKEN PILAU

5 tablespoons
  concentrated butter
  or ghee★
5 cm (2 inch) piece
  cinnamon stick★
8 cloves
6 cardamom pods★
2 cloves garlic,
  crushed
½–1 teaspoon chilli
  powder★
1 tablespoon fennel
  seeds★
1 × 1.5 kg (3½ lb)
  oven-ready chicken,
  skinned and cut
  into pieces
5 tablespoons natural
  yogurt
350 g (12 oz)
  Basmati rice,
  washed, soaked and
  drained (see Plain
  Boiled Rice, page
  126)
1 teaspoon powdered
  saffron★
1½ teaspoons salt
about 600 ml (1 pint)
  chicken stock
TO GARNISH:
4 tablespoons
  concentrated butter
  or ghee★
2 large onions, sliced

Melt the butter in a large flameproof casserole. Add the cinnamon, cloves and cardamom and fry for 30 seconds. Stir in the garlic, chilli and fennel and fry for 30 seconds.

Add the chicken and fry, turning, for 5 minutes. Add the yogurt a spoonful at a time, stirring until absorbed before adding the next spoonful. Cover and simmer for 25 minutes or until tender.

Add the rice, saffron and salt. Fry, stirring, until the rice is well mixed and glistening. Add enough stock to cover the rice by 5 mm (¼ inch) and bring to the boil. Reduce the heat to very low, cover tightly and cook for 20 minutes or until the rice is cooked and the liquid absorbed.

Melt the butter in a small pan, add the onions and fry until golden. Transfer the pilau to a warmed dish, and garnish with the fried onions.

Serves 6

PRAWN PILAU

6 tablespoons
  concentrated butter
  or ghee★
1 tablespoon
  coriander seeds★,
  crushed
½ teaspoon turmeric★
1 small pineapple,
  cubed, or 1 × 227 g
  (8 oz) can
  pineapple cubes,
  drained
227 g (8 oz) frozen
  prawns, thawed
350 g (12 oz)
  Basmati rice,
  washed, soaked and
  drained (see Plain
  Boiled Rice, page
  126)
1 teaspoon salt
about 600 ml (1 pint)
  fish or chicken
  stock
TO GARNISH:
2 tablespoons
  concentrated butter
  or ghee★
2 tablespoons
  sultanas
2 tablespoons cashew
  nuts
2 hard-boiled eggs,
  quartered
2 tablespoons
  chopped coriander
  leaves★

Melt the butter in a large saucepan, add the coriander seeds and fry for 30 seconds. Add the turmeric and stir for a few seconds, then add the pineapple and fry, stirring, for 30 seconds. Add the prawns, rice and salt. (If using a stock cube, omit the salt.) Fry, stirring, for 1 minute, then pour in enough stock to cover the rice by 5 mm (¼ inch). Bring to the boil, cover tightly and cook very gently for 25 minutes or until the rice is cooked and the liquid absorbed.

Meanwhile, prepare the garnish. Heat the butter in a small pan, add the sultanas and cashews and fry for 1 to 2 minutes, until the sultanas are plump and the nuts lightly coloured.

Transfer the rice to a warmed serving dish and gently fork in the sultanas and nuts. Arrange the egg around the edge and sprinkle the coriander on top.

Serves 6

PILAUS

Pilau rice – also known as pilaff, puloa, pulao or pillo – originated in the Middle East. It can be anything from a simple spiced rice dish to an extravaganza full of meats and vegetables. Garnishes for pilaus include chopped hard-boiled eggs, chopped almonds, chopped pistachio nuts, deep-fried onion rings, deep-fried nuts, sultanas or, in the case of Navrattan Rice, an impressive orange, green and white rice dish, edible silver or gold foil.

Pilau rice can be made earlier in the day, then reheated in the oven. Cover your dish with a tightly fitting lid or aluminium foil and place in a 180°C (350°F), Gas Mark 4 preheated oven for 30 minutes.

Fried Rice; Pilau Rice

FRIED RICE

4 tablespoons oil
250 g (8 oz) long-grain rice
3 cloves garlic, thinly sliced
2 teaspoons chopped root ginger★
6 spring onions, chopped
about 300 ml (½ pint) boiling chicken stock, preferably homemade
125 g (4 oz) button mushrooms, sliced
50 g (2 oz) cooked ham, diced
50 g (2 oz) peeled prawns
2 tablespoons light soy sauce★
50 g (2 oz) frozen peas
1 tablespoon finely chopped coriander leaves★

Heat the oil in a wok or frying pan, add the rice and cook for about 5 minutes, until pale golden. Add the garlic, ginger and spring onions and stir well. Pour over sufficient boiling chicken stock just to cover the rice, bring to the boil, then cover and simmer for 10 minutes, stirring occasionally.

Fold in the mushrooms and cook for 2 minutes. Add the remaining ingredients and mix well. Cook for a further 5 minutes, stirring occasionally.

Pile into a warmed serving dish and serve immediately.

Serves 4 to 6

PILAU RICE

½ teaspoon saffron threads★
3 tablespoons boiling water
6 tablespoons oil
5 cm (2 inch) piece cinnamon stick★
6 cardamom pods★
4 cloves
3 onions, sliced
2 cloves garlic, crushed
2 teaspoons finely chopped root ginger★
250 g (8 oz) Basmati rice
600 ml (1 pint) beef stock, preferably homemade
1 teaspoon salt
TO GARNISH:
lime wedges
toasted flaked almonds

Soak the saffron in the water for 15 minutes.

Heat the oil in a wok or frying pan, add the cinnamon, cardamom pods and cloves and fry for a few seconds. Add the onions and fry for 10 minutes, until golden. Add the garlic, ginger and rice and fry for 5 minutes, stirring occasionally.

Add the stock and salt, bring to the boil, then simmer, uncovered, for 10 minutes. Stir in the saffron threads and soaking liquid, increase the heat and cook for 2 minutes, until the rice is tender and the liquid absorbed.

Transfer to a warmed serving dish, garnish with wedges of lime, and sprinkle with almonds.

Serves 4

LOTUS LEAF RICE

8 lotus leaves★
1 tablespoon oil
1 clove garlic, crushed
3 spring onions,
    chopped
125 g (4 oz) button
    mushrooms, sliced
50 g (2 oz) cooked
    ham, diced
125 g (4 oz) cooked
    chicken, diced
few green peas
50 g (2 oz) canned
    bamboo shoots★,
    drained and
    chopped
175 g (6 oz) long-
    grain rice, cooked
2 tablespoons soy
    sauce★
2 tablespoons dry
    sherry

Soak the lotus leaves in warm water for 30 minutes. Drain thoroughly.

Heat the oil in a wok or deep frying pan, add the garlic and spring onions and stir-fry for 1 minute. Add the remaining ingredients, except the lotus leaves, and cook for 2 minutes.

Cut each lotus leaf into 2 or 3 pieces and divide the mixture between them, spooning into the centre. Fold the leaf, enclosing the filling, to form a parcel and secure with string or raffia. Place in a steamer and steam vigorously for 15 to 20 minutes.

Pile the parcels into a warmed serving dish and serve immediately; each diner opens his own parcels.
Serves 4 to 6
NOTE: If lotus leaves are unavailable use vine leaves instead. You will need one vine leaf for each parcel.

DAN-DAN NOODLES

500 g (1 lb) noodles
salt
2 tablespoons sesame
    seed paste★
4 tablespoons water
6 spring onions,
    chopped
2 cloves garlic,
    crushed
1 cm (½ inch) piece
    root ginger★, finely
    chopped
1 tablespoon soy
    sauce★
2 teaspoons red wine
    vinegar
900 ml (1½ pints)
    beef or chicken
    stock
2 teaspoons hot
    pepper oil★
    (optional)

Cook the noodles in boiling salted water according to packet instructions, until just tender. Drain and keep hot.

Blend the sesame seed paste with the water and put into a pan, together with the remaining ingredients, except the stock and pepper oil. Cook over moderate heat, stirring frequently, for about 5 minutes.

Meanwhile, bring the stock to the boil and simmer for 2 minutes.

Divide the noodles and hot sauce between 4 individual soup bowls. Spoon over the hot stock and top with the hot pepper oil, if using. Serve immediately.
Serves 4

STEAMED RICE

1.5 litres (2½ pints) water
salt
225 g (8 oz) long-grain rice

Pour the water into a large saucepan, add the salt and bring to the boil. Stir in the rice, then simmer for 10 minutes.

Drain the rice in a metal colander. Place the colander over a saucepan of boiling water and cover with a tea towel and a tightly fitting lid. Steam for 15 minutes until the rice is fluffy and dry. Transfer the rice to a heated serving dish and serve immediately.
Serves 4

VEGETABLE RICE

2 tablespoons oil
2 leeks, sliced
1 cm (½ inch) piece root ginger★, finely chopped
1 clove garlic, thinly sliced
250 g (8 oz) long-grain rice
salt
250 g (8 oz) spring greens, shredded

Heat the oil in a wok or deep frying pan, add the leeks, ginger and garlic and fry quickly for 30 seconds. Add the rice, stirring to coat each grain with the oil mixture. Add sufficient boiling water just to cover the rice. Season to taste with salt. Bring to the boil, cover and simmer for 5 minutes. Add the greens, bring back to the boil and simmer for 7 to 9 minutes until the rice is just tender.

Drain and serve the vegetable rice immediately.
Serves 4 to 6

LONG-GRAIN RICE

In India, 275–350 g (11–12 oz) raw rice are normally served per person. People in the West, however, find it difficult to ingest such large amounts, so 75–125 g (3–4 oz) raw rice per person would be more reasonable.

You may think there are only a few types of rice – long-grain, short-grain and glutinous. There are, in fact, 7,000 different varieties of the grass, *oryza sativa*.

In China, rice was once used as wages. A young apprentice would have received one bag of rice per month, weighing on average 33 lbs. The rice would have been used as money, or given to family and relatives as room and board fees. The importance of rice in the Chinese diet has created many customs and sayings. Children are taught to eat the last grain of rice in their bowls. If they do not, each grain left uneaten will become a pock-mark on their face. It is considered bad luck to upset a rice bowl. 'Breaking one's rice bowl' means you have quit your job.

LEFT: *Lotus Leaf Rice; Dan-Dan Noodles*
RIGHT: *Vegetable Rice*

MIXED SEAFOOD STICK NOODLES

4 dried Chinese
  mushrooms★
500 g (1 lb) rice stick
  noodles★
salt
2 tablespoons oil
4 spring onions,
  chopped
2 cloves garlic, sliced
1 cm (½ inch) piece
  root ginger★, finely
  chopped
50 g (2 oz) frozen
  peeled prawns,
  thawed
125 g (4 oz) fresh or
  frozen squid,
  sliced (optional)
1 × 225 g (7.5 oz)
  can clams, drained
2 tablespoons dry
  sherry
1 tablespoon soy
  sauce★

Soak the mushrooms in warm water for 15 minutes. Squeeze well, discard the stalks, then slice the mushroom caps.

Cook the rice stick noodles in boiling salted water for 7 to 8 minutes until just tender. Drain and rinse in cold water. Keep on one side.

Heat the oil in a wok or deep frying pan, add the spring onions, garlic and ginger and stir-fry for 30 seconds. Stir in the mushrooms, prawns and squid, if using, then cook for 2 minutes. Stir in the remaining ingredients, then carefully stir in the noodles and heat through.

Pile the mixture into a warmed serving dish and serve immediately.
Serves 4 to 6

NOODLES TOSSED WITH MEAT AND VEGETABLES

2 tablespoons oil
2 green chillies★,
  seeded and thinly
  sliced
1 clove garlic, thinly
  sliced
350 g (12 oz)
  minced pork
2 carrots, cut into
  matchstick pieces
3 celery sticks, cut
  into matchstick
  pieces
½ cucumber, cut into
  matchstick pieces
4 spring onions,
  sliced
1 small green pepper,
  cored, seeded and
  sliced
1 tablespoon soy
  sauce★
2 tablespoons sweet
  red bean paste★
1 tablespoon dry
  sherry
350 g (12 oz)
  noodles, cooked

Heat the oil in a wok or deep frying pan, add the chillies and garlic and fry quickly for about 30 seconds. Add the pork and cook for 2 minutes. Increase the heat, add the vegetables and cook for 1 minute. Stir in the soy sauce, bean paste, sherry and noodles. Stir well to mix and heat through.

Pile into a warmed serving dish and serve immediately.
Serves 4 to 6

FRIED STEAMED DUMPLINGS

500 g (1 lb) self-raising flour
pinch of salt
200–250 ml (⅓ pint – 8 fl oz) water
oil for deep-frying
FILLING:
350 g (12 oz) minced pork
1 tablespoon soy sauce★
1 tablespoon dry sherry
2 teaspoons sesame seed oil★
2 spring onions, finely chopped
1 cm (½ inch) piece root ginger★, finely chopped
125 g (4 oz) canned bamboo shoots★, drained and chopped
TO GARNISH:
radish flowers (see page 155)
spring onions

Sift the flour and salt into a mixing bowl. Add sufficient water to mix to a firm dough. Divide in half and knead each piece on a floured surface. Form each piece into a roll, 5 cm (2 inches) in diameter. Slice both rolls into 14 equal pieces. Roll out each piece into a 7.5 cm (3 inch) circle.

Mix all the filling ingredients together and divide the filling evenly between the rounds, placing it in the centre. Gather the sides of the dough up around the filling to meet at the top, then firmly twist the top of the dough to close tightly.

Arrange the dumplings on a moist piece of muslin in a steamer and steam vigorously for 20 minutes; drain.

Heat the oil in a wok or deep-fryer, add the dumplings and fry for 5 to 6 minutes until golden brown all over. Drain on kitchen paper.

Serve immediately, garnished with radish flowers and spring onions.

Serves 4 to 6

(Picture, page 122)

DIM SUM

Chinese dumplings, or dim sum, may be savoury (stuffed with meat or seafood) or sweet (filled with pastes or preserves). You can order dim sum from the menu in some Chinese restaurants but traditionally, women push trolleys stacked high with wooden steamers filled with dim sum through the restaurant, stopping at each table. Each steamer normally contains two to four dumplings. Some of the more common savoury dim sum choices include Steamed Prawn Dumplings, Steamed Beef Dumplings, Chickens' Feet in Black Bean Sauce, Glutinous Rice-Stuffed Lotus Leaves and Bean Curd Rolls. Deep-fried items also appear on dim sum menus and include Yam Croquettes, Spring Rolls, Deep-Fried Won Tons and Paper-Wrapped Prawns. For sweet dim sum, look for Sweet Bean Paste-Filled Buns or Egg Tarts.

LEFT: *Mixed Seafood Stick Noodles; Noodles Tossed with Meat and Vegetables*
RIGHT: *Curried Prawn Ring*

CURRIED PRAWN RING

350 g (12 oz) long-grain rice
salt
few saffron threads★
1 tablespoon sunflower oil
1 tablespoon curry powder
8 spring onions, chopped
1 red pepper, cored, seeded and chopped
50 g (2 oz) pine nuts
75 g (3 oz) sultanas
250 g (8 oz) peeled prawns
DRESSING:
4 tablespoons olive oil
2 tablespoons white wine vinegar
1 teaspoon dry mustard
1 teaspoon sugar
2 tablespoons chopped coriander leaves★
TO GARNISH:
orange wedges
celery leaves

Cook the rice in boiling salted water, with the saffron added, for about 20 minutes, until the rice is tender and the liquid absorbed.

Meanwhile, place the dressing ingredients in a screw-top jar and shake well to blend.

Drain the rice, place in a bowl and stir in the dressing while still warm. Set aside to cool slightly.

Heat the oil in a pan, add the curry powder, spring onions, red pepper, pine nuts and sultanas and cook, stirring, for 1½ minutes. Add to the rice and leave until completely cold.

Stir in the prawns, then spoon the mixture into a lightly oiled 1.5 litre (2½ pint) ring mould, pressing down well. Chill until required.

To serve, invert the ring on to a serving plate and garnish with orange wedges and celery leaves.

Serves 4 to 6

BREADS AND ACCOMPANIMENTS

It is a common misconception that rice is the only form of starch available in the Far East. In the northern wheat-growing areas of India and Pakistan, various forms of 'roti' or bread are also eaten. Most of them are unleavened breads made from wholemeal flour and they are usually round and flat in shape. They may be cooked on a griddle, in a tandoor or clay oven or they can be fried. Puris, nans, chapatis and parathas are among the more familiar Indian breads and feature in the following pages.

Bread also has a small place in the Chinese diet, particularly in the north. Their unleavened breads include Mandarin Pancakes which, with their soft texture and hint of sesame oil, make a perfect foil to the richness of Peking Duck.

When you go to an Oriental restaurant, you will usually be offered a selection of chutneys and pickles to go with your meal. It is thought that a dish without accompaniments is like an oil painting without a frame. The selection of dishes in this chapter also includes chutneys, spicy vegetable and fruit salads and pickles – designed to sweeten, spice and extend the flavours of the meal.

Oriental dishes, particularly those from India, Pakistan, Malaysia and Indonesia frequently include cooling yogurt-based raitas and fiery relishes or sambals such as Sambal Oelek or Sambal Bajak. If you do not know how hot your guests like their curries, it is best to serve a mild curry. Offer a few sambals to those who enjoy a mouth-numbing sensation and prepare a raita for those who may find even your mild curry too hot.

Puri; Nān

NĀN

15 g (½ oz) fresh
 yeast
¼ teaspoon sugar
2 tablespoons warm
 water
500 g (1 lb) self-
 raising flour
1 teaspoon salt
150 ml (¼ pint) tepid
 milk
1 × 150 g (5 oz)
 carton natural
 yogurt (at room
 temperature)
2 tablespoons melted
 butter or oil
TO FINISH:
2 3 tablespoons
 melted butter
1 tablespoon poppy or
 sesame seeds★

Put the yeast into a small bowl with
the sugar and water. Mix well until
the yeast has dissolved, then leave in a
warm place for 15 minutes or until the
mixture is frothy.

Sift the flour and salt into a large
bowl. Make a well in the centre and
pour in the yeast, milk, yogurt and
butter or oil. Mix to a smooth dough
and turn on to a floured surface.
Knead for about 10 minutes, until
smooth and elastic. Place in the bowl,
cover with cling film and leave to rise
in a warm place for 1 to 1½ hours, or
until doubled in size.

Turn on to a floured surface, knead
for a few minutes, then divide into 6
pieces. Pat or roll each piece into an
oval.

Place on warmed baking sheets and
bake in a preheated, very hot oven,
240°C (475°F), Gas Mark 9, for 10
minutes. Brush with the melted butter
and sprinkle with the poppy or sesame
seeds. Serve warm.
Makes 6

(Picture, page 134)

PURI

250 g (8 oz)
 wholewheat flour,
 or half wholewheat
 and half plain
 white
¼ teaspoon salt
150 ml (¼ pint) warm
 water
2 teaspoons melted
 concentrated butter
 or ghee★
oil for deep-frying

Put the wholewheat flour and salt into
a bowl; sift in the plain flour if using.
Make a well in the centre, add the
water gradually and work to a dough.
Knead in the butter, then knead for 10
minutes, until smooth and elastic.
Cover and set aside for 30 minutes.

Divide the dough into 16 pieces.
With lightly oiled hands, pat each
piece into a ball. Lightly oil the pastry
board and rolling pin and roll out each
ball into a thin, circular pancake.

Deep-fry the puri very quickly,
turning them over once, until deep
golden in colour. Drain well on
kitchen paper and serve immediately.
Makes 16

INDIAN BREADS

Nān is a north Indian bread traditionally baked in a clay oven
called a *tandoor*. The leavened dough is rolled or slapped into
an oval shape, then stuck inside the heated oven so that it
hangs free; its weight stretches the nān into a teardrop shape.
It is usually served with tandoori chicken and kebabs, but is
good with any of the drier curries.

Puri are crisp and puffy deep-fried breads. They are
delicious served with vegetable curries.

Pura is a pancake made with gram flour. It is quite easy to
make in a non-stick pan. Serve with spicy vegetables and dry
curries.

Flavoured chapatis are excellent. Any kind of vegetable can
be used as long as it is mashed and spiced. Use only a small
amount, or it will break through the dough. Chopped herbs
like mint and coriander with green chillies are easier to use
and very tasty.

CHAPATI WITH ONION

CHAPATI:
250 g (8 oz)
  wholewheat flour
1 teaspoon salt
200 ml ($\frac{1}{3}$ pint) water
  (approximately)
4 teaspoons
  concentrated butter
  or ghee★ or unsalted
  butter, melted

FILLING:
2 onions, very finely
  chopped
2 green chillies★, very
  finely chopped
$\frac{1}{2}$ teaspoon salt

Make the dough as for Chapati (see page 144), adding 2 teaspoons of the butter to the mixture.

Combine the onions and chillies and stir in the salt. Put into a sieve and squeeze out any liquid. Set aside while preparing the dough.

Divide the dough into 12 pieces. Roll out each piece on a floured surface into a thin round. Put a little of the onion and chilli mixture in the centre, fold the dough over and form into a ball, then roll out carefully into a round.

Cook as for Chapatis, using the remaining butter to grease the pan.

Serve warm.

Makes 12

PURA

125 g (4 oz) gram
  flour★
$\frac{1}{2}$ teaspoon salt
$\frac{1}{2}$–1 teaspoon chilli
  powder★
$\frac{1}{4}$ teaspoon bicarbonate
  of soda
300 ml ($\frac{1}{2}$ pint) warm
  water
oil for frying

Sift the dry ingredients into a bowl. Pour in the water and beat well to form a batter.

Heat 1 teaspoon oil in a small non-stick frying pan. Pour in 1 tablespoon of the batter and spread it into a round with the back of the spoon. Fry for 1 minute on each side or until the pancake is cooked through. Repeat with the remaining batter, adding more oil as necessary.

Fold the pura in half and serve warm.

Makes 10

Chapati with Onion; Pura

BERTHA'S CHUTNEY

1 kg (2 lb) tomatoes,
    quartered
120 ml (4 fl oz)
    vinegar
250 g (8 oz) sugar
125 g (4 oz) raisins
125 g (4 oz) sultanas
25 g (1 oz) blanched
    almonds, sliced
4 cloves garlic, finely
    sliced
25 g (1 oz) root
    ginger★, finely
    chopped
1 tablespoon chilli
    powder★
½ tablespoon salt

Put the tomatoes and vinegar into a large saucepan and heat gently until the juice starts to run. Add the sugar and bring slowly to the boil. Simmer for 5 minutes.

Add the remaining ingredients and simmer for 30 minutes or until the mixture has thickened.

Leave until cold, then pour into sterilized jars and cover with a wax disc and a screw-topped lid. Store in a cool place.

Makes about 1.5 kg (3 lb)

Bertha's Chutney; Brinjal Pickle

GINGER CHUTNEY

120 ml (4 fl oz)
    lemon juice
25 g (1 oz) sugar
140 g (4½ oz) fresh
    root ginger★, finely
    chopped
75 g (3 oz) sultanas
1 clove garlic, crushed
salt

Place all the ingredients in a food processor or electric blender and work to a smooth purée.

Transfer the mixture to a small serving dish and chill until ready to serve. Eat within 2 days.

Makes about 300 ml (½ pint)

BRINJAL PICKLE

1 kg (2 lb)
    aubergines, thinly
    sliced
1 tablespoon salt
300 ml (½ pint) hot
    water
125 g (4 oz)
    tamarind★
50 g (2 oz) cumin
    seeds★
25 g (1 oz) dried red
    chillies★
50 g (2 oz) piece root
    ginger★, chopped
50 g (2 oz) garlic
300 ml (½ pint)
    vinegar
150 ml (¼ pint) oil
2 teaspoons mustard
    seeds★
250 g (8 oz) sugar

Sprinkle the aubergines with the salt and leave in a colander for 30 minutes to drain. Pour the hot water on to the tamarind and leave to soak for 20 minutes. Press through a fine sieve and set aside.

Put the cumin, chillies, ginger, garlic and 2 tablespoons of the vinegar into a food processor or electric blender and work to a paste.

Heat the oil in a large saucepan and fry the mustard seeds until they begin to splutter. Quickly add the spice paste and fry, stirring, for 2 minutes. Add the aubergine, tamarind water, remaining vinegar and the sugar and stir well. Bring to the boil, then simmer for 30 to 35 minutes, until the mixture is thick and pulpy.

Leave until cold; bottle as for Bertha's Chutney (left).

Makes about 1.5 kg (3 lb)

VARIATIONS

Bertha's Chutney is best made when tomatoes are in full season. Dried apricots can be substituted for the raisins and sultanas, but they must be soaked overnight. This chutney goes well with curries, but is also good with cold roast meats. If you like sweet chutney, use 50 g (2 oz) more sugar.

The Brinjal Pickle is for those who like hot relishes. The chillies can be reduced, but the pickle will then lose its characteristic bite.

Both recipes should keep well in a cool place.

SAMBAL BAJAK

2 tablespoons oil
3 small onions, finely
    chopped
4 cloves garlic, finely
    chopped
1 teaspoon blachan★
    or shrimp paste
125 g (4 oz) red
    chillies★, chopped
4 tablespoons lime
    juice
1 teaspoon salt
1 teaspoon brown
    sugar

Heat the oil in a small frying pan, add the onions and garlic and fry until golden brown. Add the blachan or shrimp paste and fry, stirring and mashing, for 1 minute.

Stir in the remaining ingredients and fry, stirring, for 5 minutes or until the mixture is fairly dry.

Allow to cool, then spoon into a jar. Cover and keep refrigerated until required.
Serves 4

PRAWN RELISH

1 tablespoon oil
1 teaspoon mustard
    seeds★
1 teaspoon fenugreek
    seeds★ (optional)
1 teaspoon turmeric★
1–2 teaspoons chilli
    powder★
6 tablespoons water
250 g (8 oz) small
    raw peeled prawns
    or shrimps
juice of 3 limes
1 teaspoon salt

Heat the oil in a saucepan and fry the mustard and fenugreek seeds for 30 seconds. When they start to splutter, add the turmeric, chilli powder and 2 tablespoons of the water. Stir well and fry for 2 minutes.

Add the prawns and fry for 2 minutes. Add the remaining water and simmer for 10 minutes. Mash the cooked prawns roughly and add the lime juice and salt. Simmer for about 15 minutes, until the liquid is absorbed and the mixture is quite thick.

Serve this relish cold.
Serves 4

Stuffed Bhindi; Prawn Relish

STUFFED BHINDI

10 cloves garlic, finely
    chopped
6 green chillies★,
    finely chopped
7.5 cm (3 inch) piece
    root ginger★, finely
    chopped
4 tablespoons finely
    chopped mint
1 teaspoon salt
500 g (1 lb) tender
    okra, topped and
    tailed and slit down
    one side
600 ml (1 pint) red
    wine vinegar
sugar
mint leaves to garnish
    (optional)

Mix the garlic, chillies, ginger, mint and salt together thoroughly. Stuff the okra with this mixture and arrange in layers in a dish. Sweeten the vinegar to taste and pour over the okra to cover.

Cover the dish with cling film and leave in a cool place for 12 to 24 hours for flavours to mingle.

Serve chilled, garnished with mint if liked.
Serves 4

TWO INDIAN ACCOMPANIMENTS

The Stuffed Bhindi depends for its success on tender young okra – and you really have to like garlic to enjoy it! In Bombay it is served with plain fried fish or chicken or with a dry curry.

The Prawn Relish is a delicious addition to a simple meal of rice and dhal. If you don't like the smell of fenugreek, it can be left out. Large prawns can be used but the small ones are easier to mash together. The relish can be kept for two days, covered, in the refrigerator.

FRUIT CHĀT

250 g (8 oz)
  tamarind★
1 teaspoon chilli
  powder★
salt
sugar
1 small onion,
  chopped
2 green chillies★,
  thinly sliced
2.5 cm (1 inch) piece
  root ginger★, cut
  into fine strips
1 each pear, apple
  and banana, or
  guava, mango and
  any other fruit, cut
  into small pieces

Put the tamarind into a bowl, cover with hot water and set aside for 3 hours or overnight.

Tip the tamarind and water into a sieve placed over a saucepan and, using your fingers, push through as much pulp as possible. Discard the husk and seeds.

Add the chilli powder, salt and sugar to taste and simmer gently for 15 to 20 minutes. Pour into a bowl and leave to cool.

Stir in the onion, chillies, ginger and fruit. Cover the bowl and chill before serving.
Serves 4

BRINJAL SAMBAL

1 large aubergine
1 small onion, finely
  chopped
3 green chillies★,
  finely chopped
1 cm (½ inch) piece
  root ginger★, cut
  into fine strips
2 tablespoons thick
  coconut milk★
½ teaspoon salt
juice of 1 lemon

Place the aubergine on a baking sheet and cook in a preheated moderate oven, 180°C (350°F), Gas Mark 4, for 30 minutes or until soft. Leave to cool slightly, then slit it open and scoop out the flesh into a bowl.

Mash the aubergine with a fork and mix in the remaining ingredients. Taste the sambal and adjust the seasoning. Serve chilled.
Serves 4

RUJAK

25 g (1 oz)
  tamarind★
2 tablespoons hot
  water
½ small pineapple, cut
  into chunks
½ cucumber, finely
  sliced
1 orange, divided into
  segments
1 grapefruit, divided
  into segments
1 firm mango or tart
  apple, peeled and
  sliced
2 red chillies★, thinly
  sliced
1 tablespoon fish
  sauce★ or dark soy
  sauce★
1 tablespoon brown
  sugar

Soak the tamarind in the water for 30 minutes, strain, squeezing out as much water as possible. Discard the tamarind.

Put the fruit and cucumber into a bowl. Mix the remaining ingredients together and pour over the fruit. Toss gently to mix. Set aside for a few minutes, then serve.
Serves 4

SPICY FRUIT SALADS

Two spicy fruit salads, one from northern India, the other from Java. Both are served as accompaniments and both sometimes include vegetables: add a boiled sweet potato, peeled and cut into small cubes, to the Chāt, and sliced cucumber and lightly steamed green beans to the Rujak, if liked.

Chāt can also be made with dried fruit (soaked overnight), or with a single fresh fruit – for example, banana – if no other fruit is available.

SERUNDENG

oil for coating the pan
  plus 2 tablespoons
175 g (6 oz) unsalted
  peanuts
1 small onion,
  quartered
2 cloves garlic
1 cm ($\frac{1}{2}$ inch) piece
  root ginger★
$\frac{1}{2}$ teaspoon ground
  cumin★
1 teaspoon ground
  coriander★
1 tablespoon lemon
  juice
75 g (3 oz) desiccated
  coconut
1 teaspoon salt
1 teaspoon sugar

Coat the base of a non-stick frying pan with oil. Heat the pan and put in the peanuts. Stir-fry the nuts until lightly browned, remove to a plate and leave to cool.

Put the onion, garlic, ginger, cumin, coriander and lemon juice into a food processor or electric blender and work until smooth.

Put 2 tablespoons oil in the frying pan and fry the spice paste for 1 minute. Add the coconut, salt and sugar and fry over low heat, stirring, for 20 to 30 minutes or until crisp and golden. Transfer to a small dish and leave to cool.

Mix in the peanuts and serve.
Serves 4

CORIANDER CHUTNEY

25 g (1 oz) desiccated
  coconut
1 × 150 g (5 oz)
  carton natural
  yogurt
100 g (3$\frac{1}{3}$ oz)
  coriander★, leaves
  and some fine
  stalks
2 green chillies★
juice of 1 lemon
1 teaspoon salt
1 teaspoon sugar

Mix the coconut with the yogurt and leave to stand for 1 hour. Put into a food processor or electric blender with the remaining ingredients and work until smooth. Chill before serving.
Serves 4

SAMBAL OELEK

125 g (4 oz) red
  chillies★, chopped
2 tablespoons lemon
  or lime juice, or
  vinegar
1 teaspoon sugar
1 teaspoon salt

Put all the ingredients into a food processor or electric blender and work until the chillies are pulverized. Adjust the seasoning. Spoon into a jar, cover with a screw-top and keep refrigerated until required.
Serves 4

LEFT: *Rujak; Fruit Chat*
BELOW: *Coriander Chutney; Serundeng, Sambal Oelek*

CANTONESE PICKLED VEGETABLES

250 g (8 oz) mooli★, cut into 5 mm x 5 cm (¼ x 2 inch) sticks
3 carrots, cut into 5 mm x 5cm (¼ x 2 inch) sticks
1 cucumber, cut into 5 cm x 5 mm (2 inch x ¼ inch) sticks
1 tablespoon salt
8 tablespoons sugar
8 tablespoons rice vinegar★ or cider vinegar
12 paper-thin slices of fresh root ginger★

Place the mooli, carrots and cucumber in a large colander. Add the salt and toss well to coat. Cover and let stand for 3 hours.

Drain the vegetable mixture well, then place in a large bowl. Combine the sugar and vinegar in a small bowl, then pour over the vegetables. Add the ginger. Toss the vegetables well to coat. Cover and chill the mixture for at least 3 hours or overnight.

To serve, using a slotted spoon, transfer the vegetables to a serving dish.

Serves 6–8

SPINACH WITH SESAME SEED SAUCE

SESAME SEED SAUCE:
4 tablespoons toasted sesame seeds★
200 ml (⅓ pint) dashi★ or fish stock
50 ml (2 fl oz) soy sauce★
50 ml (2 fl oz) mirin★ or dry sherry and 1 tablespoon sugar

1.2 litres (2 pints) water
salt
500 g (1 lb) young, fresh spinach leaves, washed and stalks removed
15 g (½ oz) dried bonito flakes★

To make the sesame seed sauce: crush the sesame seeds in a mortar, then transfer to a medium bowl. Blend in the remaining ingredients and stir well to combine. Cover and set aside.

Place the water and salt in a large saucepan and bring quickly to the boil. Add the spinach and cook for 1 minute, then drain immediately in a colander and refresh under cold running water. Shake the colander to remove excess water. Squeeze the spinach well to extract all the moisture then roll into a 2.5 cm (1 inch) cylinder and cut into 8 even-sized pieces.

Divide the spinach pieces between 4 small serving dishes and top with an equal amount of the sesame seed sauce. Cover and chill for 15 minutes.

To serve, sprinkle each dish with the bonito flakes.

Serves 4

ACAR

This Malaysian pickle keeps for several months in the fridge if you store it in a clean, sterilized jar and tightly seal it.

600 ml (1 pint) pickling vinegar
3 carrots, cut into 2.5 x 5 cm (1 x 2 inch) sticks
1 cucumber, unpeeled, cut into 2.5 x 5 cm (1 x 2 inch) sticks
250 g (8 oz) cauliflower florets
300 g (10 oz) salted peanuts, ground
300 g (10 oz) sesame seeds★, toasted
250 g (8 oz) demerara sugar
3 red chillies★, seeded and finely chopped
3 green chillies★, seeded and finely chopped
175 ml (6 fl oz) oil
5 cloves garlic, finely chopped
2 teaspoons ground turmeric★
salt

Bring the vinegar to the boil in a large saucepan over a moderate heat. Add the carrots and blanch for 1 minute. Using a small slotted spoon, remove the carrots from the vinegar, shaking off the excess. Place in a large bowl. Blanch the cucumber and cauliflower in the same way and transfer to the bowl. The vinegar can be saved for other uses. Add the peanuts, sesame seeds, sugar and chillies to the vegetables and toss well to coat. Cover and set aside.

Heat the oil in a large frying pan over a moderate heat. Add the garlic, turmeric and salt to taste, and cook for 2 to 3 minutes, stirring constantly. Remove from the heat and let cool completely.

Pour the garlic oil mixture over the vegetables and toss well to coat. Cover and chill overnight before serving.

Makes about 1.2 litres (2 pints)

(Picture, page 134)

FRIED SHRIMP WAFERS

oil for deep-frying
krupuk wafers★ (shrimp-flavoured tapioca chips) or Chinese shrimp-flavoured chips

Pour the oil into a wok or large saucepan and heat to 180°C (350°F) or until a cube of bread turns brown in 30 seconds.

Add the krupuk wafers. They will sink to the bottom of the pan, then in 5 seconds, triple in size and rise to the surface. Remove from the oil with a slotted spoon and drain on kitchen paper. Serve plain, with a sambal or as a garnish.

Spinach with Sesame Seed Sauce; Fried Shrimp Wafers

PARATHA

250 g (8 oz)
  wholemeal flour
1 teaspoon salt
200 ml (⅓ pint)
  water
  (approximately)
50–75 g (2–3 oz)
  melted concentrated
  butter or ghee★ or
  butter

Make the dough as for Chapati (see right) and divide into 6 pieces. Roll out each piece on a floured surface into a thin circle. Brush with melted butter and fold in half; brush again and fold in half again. Roll out again to a circle about 3 mm (⅛ inch) thick.

Lightly grease a griddle or heavy-based frying pan with a little butter and place over a moderate heat. Add a paratha and cook for 1 minute. Lightly brush the top with a little butter and turn over. Brush all round the edge with butter and cook until golden. Remove from the pan and keep warm, while cooking the rest. Serve hot.

Makes 6

Paratha; Chapati

CHAPATI

250 g (8 oz)
  wholemeal flour
1 teaspoon salt
200 ml (⅓ pint)
  water
  (approximately)
melted concentrated
  butter or ghee★ or
  oil for greasing

Put the flour and salt into a bowl. Make a well in the centre, gradually stir in the water and work to a soft supple dough. Knead for 10 minutes, then cover and leave in a cool place for 30 minutes. Knead again very thoroughly, then divide into 12 pieces. Roll out each piece on a floured surface into a thin round pancake.

Lightly grease a griddle or heavy-based frying pan with a little butter or oil and place over a moderate heat. Add a chapati and cook until blisters appear. Press down with a fish slice, then turn and cook the other side until lightly coloured. Remove from the pan and keep warm while cooking the rest.

Brush a little butter on one side and serve warm.

Makes 12

ZALATA

250 g (8 oz) ridge
  cucumbers, peeled
  and sliced
salt
1 green chilli★, sliced
1 tablespoon finely
  chopped coriander
  leaves★
2 tablespoons vinegar
½ teaspoon sugar

Put the cucumber into a colander, sprinkle with salt and leave to drain for 30 minutes. Dry thoroughly. Place in a serving dish and add the remaining ingredients and 1 teaspoon salt. Mix well and chill thoroughly before serving.

Alternatively, put the drained cucumber into an electric blender or food processor with the whole chilli, coriander leaves, sugar and salt. Add 1 clove garlic and just 1½ teaspoons vinegar and work to a smooth paste. Chill thoroughly before serving.
Serves 4

CACHUMBER

1 onion, chopped
250 g (8 oz)
  tomatoes, skinned
  and chopped
1–2 green chillies★,
  chopped
1·2 tablespoons
  vinegar
salt

Put the onion, tomatoes and chillies into a dish. Pour over the vinegar (the mixture must not be too liquid) and add salt to taste. Chill before serving.
Serves 4

ABOVE: *Cachumber; Mango Chutney*
BELOW: *Zalata*

MANGO CHUTNEY

500 g (1 lb) sugar
600 ml (1 pint)
  vinegar
5 cm (2 inch) piece
  root ginger★
4 cloves garlic
1 kg (2 lb) very firm
  mangoes, peeled
  and cut into small
  pieces
½–1 tablespoon chilli
  powder★
.1 tablespoon mustard
  seeds★
2 tablespoons salt
125 g (4 oz) raisins
  or sultanas

Put the sugar and all but 1 tablespoon of the vinegar into a pan and simmer for 10 minutes.

Put the ginger, garlic and remaining vinegar into an electric blender or food processor and work to a paste. Add to the pan and cook for 10 minutes, stirring.

Add the mango and remaining ingredients and cook, uncovered, for about 25 minutes, stirring as the chutney thickens.

Pour into hot sterilized jars, cover with waxed discs, then seal with covers and label. The chutney will keep for several months.
Makes about 1.25 kg (2½ lb)

CARROT SALAD

125 g (4 oz) carrots,
  grated
25 g (1 oz) grated
  onion
½ tablespoon grated
  root ginger★
1 tablespoon finely
  chopped mint
½ teaspoon salt
½ teaspoon sugar
1 tablespoon lemon
  juice

Mix all the ingredients together, cover and chill for 1 to 2 hours before serving.

Serves 4

Carrot Salad; Raita

RAITA

100 g (3½ oz)
  cucumber, thinly
  sliced
salt
2 × 150 g (5 oz)
  cartons natural
  yogurt
50 g (2 oz) spring
  onions, thinly
  sliced
1 green chilli★, seeded
  and finely chopped
coriander leaves★ to
  garnish

Put the cucumber into a colander, sprinkle with salt and leave to drain for 30 minutes. Dry thoroughly.

Mix the yogurt with salt to taste and fold in the cucumber, spring onions and chilli. Arrange in a serving dish and chill until required. Garnish with coriander leaves to serve.

Serves 4

NOTE: Raita can be made with other vegetables and with fruit – bananas are particularly good.

PRAWN RELISH

2 tablespoons oil
1 onion, chopped
4 dried red chillies★
2 green chillies★,
  chopped
½ teaspoon cumin
  seeds★
½ teaspoon turmeric★
1 clove garlic, crushed
2.5 cm (1 inch) piece
  root ginger★,
  chopped
4 curry leaves★,
  crumbled
150 g (5 oz) prawns
1 tablespoon vinegar
salt

Heat the oil in a pan, add the onion and fry until golden. Crumble in the dried chillies. Add the fresh chillies, cumin, turmeric, garlic, ginger and curry leaves and fry for 2 minutes. Add the prawns and fry for 2 minutes.

Add the vinegar and salt to taste and simmer, uncovered, for 3 to 4 minutes, until most of the liquid has evaporated. Serve hot or cold.

Serves 4

DATE AND TOMATO CHUTNEY

250 g (8 oz) dates,
  stoned and chopped
1 × 539 g (1 lb 3 oz)
  can tomatoes
1 onion, chopped
3.5 cm (1½ inch)
  piece root ginger★,
  chopped
1 teaspoon chilli
  powder★
1 teaspoon salt
6 tablespoons vinegar

Put all the ingredients into a saucepan and stir well. Bring to the boil, then simmer, uncovered, for about 45 minutes, stirring occasionally, until thick. Serve cold.

Serves 4 to 6

NOTE: Extra chilli powder and salt may be added if wished, according to taste.

Prawn Relish; Date and Tomato Chutney

RAITAS AND SAMBALS

Raita is a yogurt-based northern Indian salad, which is used as a cooling accompaniment to fiery curries. There are date and raisin raitas, mint raitas, garlic raitas, mushroom raitas and lemon raitas, among many others. Serve raitas in small individual bowls.

Sambal is a southern Indian speciality, a cross between a salad and a relish which can be served hot or cold, but is always pungent and spicy. Sambals are excellent accompaniments to mild curries. Guests normally take a small spoonful of the sambal and place it on the side of their plates. Morsels of food are then dipped into the sambal.

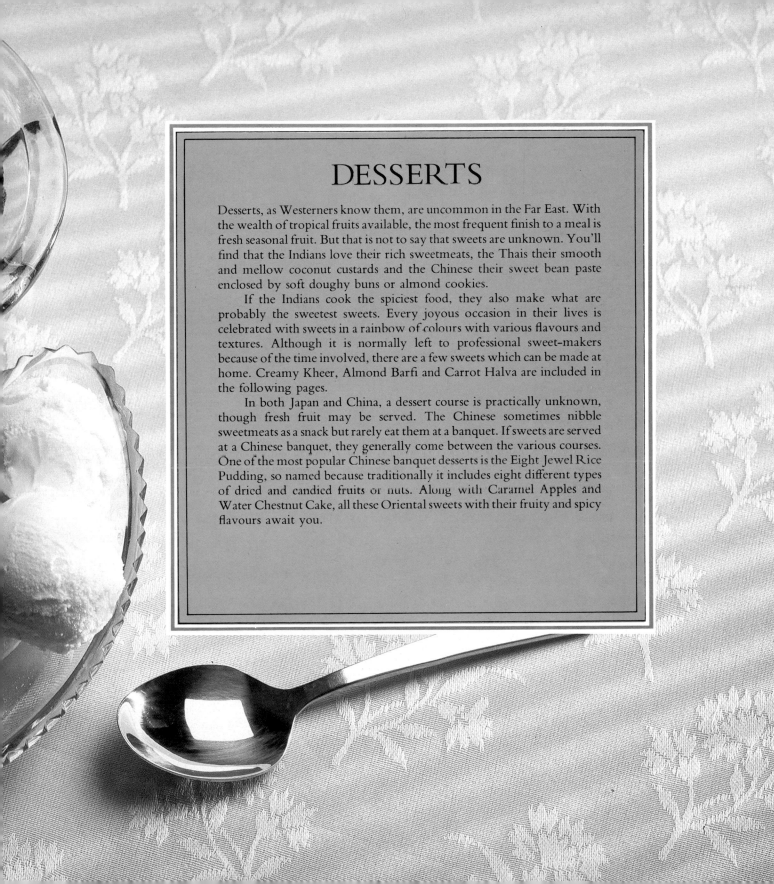

DESSERTS

Desserts, as Westerners know them, are uncommon in the Far East. With the wealth of tropical fruits available, the most frequent finish to a meal is fresh seasonal fruit. But that is not to say that sweets are unknown. You'll find that the Indians love their rich sweetmeats, the Thais their smooth and mellow coconut custards and the Chinese their sweet bean paste enclosed by soft doughy buns or almond cookies.

If the Indians cook the spiciest food, they also make what are probably the sweetest sweets. Every joyous occasion in their lives is celebrated with sweets in a rainbow of colours with various flavours and textures. Although it is normally left to professional sweet-makers because of the time involved, there are a few sweets which can be made at home. Creamy Kheer, Almond Barfi and Carrot Halva are included in the following pages.

In both Japan and China, a dessert course is practically unknown, though fresh fruit may be served. The Chinese sometimes nibble sweetmeats as a snack but rarely eat them at a banquet. If sweets are served at a Chinese banquet, they generally come between the various courses. One of the most popular Chinese banquet desserts is the Eight Jewel Rice Pudding, so named because traditionally it includes eight different types of dried and candied fruits or nuts. Along with Caramel Apples and Water Chestnut Cake, all these Oriental sweets with their fruity and spicy flavours await you.

ALMOND BARFI

750 ml (1¼ pints)
    milk
50 g (2 oz) caster
    sugar
50 g (2 oz) ground
    almonds
6 cardamom pods★,
    peeled and seeds
    crushed

Reduce the milk as for Mawa (see right).

When it is thick and lumpy, stir in the sugar, then add the almonds and cook for 2 minutes. Spread on a buttered plate and sprinkle with the crushed cardamom. Serve warm, cut into wedges or diamond shapes.
Serves 4

SHRIKAND

1 × 1 kg (2.2 lb)
    carton natural
    yogurt
1 teaspoon powdered
    saffron★
2 tablespoons
    caster sugar
    (approximately)
1 tablespoon rose
    water
TO DECORATE:
1–2 teaspoons
    cardamom seeds★,
    crushed
1 tablespoon pistachio
    nuts, shelled and
    chopped

Turn the yogurt into a strainer lined with muslin and leave to drip over a bowl for 6 hours. Put the dried curds – there will be about 300 g (10 oz) – into a bowl and beat in the saffron. Add the sugar and taste; add a little more if you like, but it should not be too sweet. Mix in the rose water, a little at a time, until the mixture resembles thick cream. Cover and chill until required.

Spoon into individual bowls and decorate with the cardamom and pistachio nuts to serve.
Serves 4

MAWA

1.75 litres (3 pints)
    milk
3–4 tablespoons caster
    sugar

Cook the milk in a large, heavy-based saucepan for about 45 minutes, until it is reduced to a thick lumpy consistency. Stir occasionally and be careful not to let the milk burn.

Add the sugar and continue cooking for 10 minutes.

Spread the mixture on a lightly buttered plate: it should be a light cream coloured, softly-set toffee.

Cut into wedges and serve cold.
Serves 4 to 6

CARROT HALVA

1.2 litres (2 pints)
    milk
250 g (8 oz) carrots,
    finely grated
75 g (3 oz) butter
1 tablespoon golden
    syrup
125 g (4 oz) sugar
50 g (2 oz) sultanas
    or raisins
1 teaspoon cardamom
    seeds★, crushed to
    decorate

Put the milk and carrots into a heavy-based saucepan and cook over high heat, stirring occasionally, until the liquid has evaporated. Add the butter, syrup, sugar and fruit. Stir until the butter and sugar have melted, then cook for 15 to 20 minutes stirring frequently, until the mixture starts to leave the sides of the pan.

Pour into a shallow buttered dish and spread evenly. Sprinkle with crushed cardamom. Cut into slices and serve warm or cold.
Serves 4 to 6

BELOW: *Almond Barfi; Shirkand; Mawa; Carrot Halva*

RIGHT: *Eight Jewel Rice Pudding; Almond Fruit Salad*

EIGHT JEWEL RICE PUDDING

350 g (12 oz) short-grain pudding rice
4 tablespoons caster sugar
50 g (2 oz) unsalted butter
125 g (4 oz) glacé cherries, chopped
50 g (2 oz) crystallized orange peel, chopped
25 g (1 oz) each angelica, walnuts and whole blanched almonds, chopped
50 g (2 oz) seedless raisins, chopped
5 tablespoons sweet bean paste★
SUGAR SYRUP:
300 ml (½ pint) water
50 g (2 oz) sugar
few drops of almond essence

Rinse the rice, drain and put into a pan with enough water to cover. Simmer for 15 minutes; drain. Stir in the sugar and half the butter.

Use the remaining butter to grease a 900 ml (1½ pint) pudding basin, then line with a thin layer of rice. Press a little of each fruit and nut into this in a decorative pattern. Mix the remaining rice, fruit and nuts. Spoon alternate layers of this mixture and bean paste into the basin, finishing with the rice mixture. Press down firmly.

Cover basin with greaseproof paper and foil, making a pleat in the centre; secure with string. Steam for 1 to 1¼ hours.

To make the syrup, bring the water and sugar to the boil, stirring. Remove from heat and add the almond essence.

Turn the pudding out onto a warmed serving dish and serve hot, with the sugar syrup.
Serves 6

ALMOND FRUIT SALAD

4 dessert apples, cored
4 peaches, skinned and stoned
125 g (4 oz) strawberries
4 slices pineapple
125 g (4 oz) lychees, skinned
ALMOND SYRUP:
1 tablespoon cornflour
2 tablespoons water
2 tablespoons ground almonds
450 ml (¾ pint) water
3 tablespoons sugar

First, make the syrup. Blend the cornflour with the water. Put the almonds, water, blended cornflour and sugar into a pan and mix well. Gradually bring to the boil, stirring, then simmer for 10 minutes, stirring constantly. Remove from the heat and leave to cool, stirring occasionally to prevent a skin forming.

Slice the apples, peaches and strawberries; cut the pineapple into cubes. Put all the fruit in a bowl and mix well. Spoon over the almond syrup and chill before serving.
Serves 4 to 6

DEEP-FRIED SWEET POTATO BALLS

500 g (1 lb) sweet potatoes
125 g (4 oz) rice flour
50 g (2 oz) soft brown sugar
125 g (4 oz) crystallized fruit, chopped
50 g (2 oz) sesame seeds★, lightly toasted
oil for deep-frying

Cook the potatoes in boiling water for 20 minutes until tender; drain and remove the skins. Mash the flesh and gradually beat in the flour and sugar. Stir in the crystallized fruit.

With dampened hands, roll the mixture into walnut-sized balls, then coat with sesame seeds.

Heat the oil in a wok or deep-fryer and deep-fry the potato balls for 5 to 7 minutes, until golden brown. Drain on kitchen paper. Serve hot.

Serve 4 to 6

WALNUT SWEET

125 g (4 oz) shelled walnuts
3 tablespoons oil
75 g (3 oz) dates, stoned
900 ml (1½ pints) water
150 g (5 oz) sugar
40 g (1½ oz) ground rice
3 tablespoons milk
apple flower (see page 155) to decorate

Soak the walnuts in boiling water for 10 minutes, drain and remove the skins; dry on kitchen paper.

Heat the oil in a wok or deep frying pan, add the walnuts and fry quickly until lightly browned (take care not to burn them). Drain on kitchen paper.

Grind the nuts and dates in a blender or fine mincer. Bring the water to the boil and stir in the nut mixture and sugar. Blend the ground rice with the milk and add to the nut mixture. Bring back to the boil, stirring, and cook for 2 minutes until thickened.

Spoon into a warmed serving dish, decorate with an apple flower and serve hot.

Serves 4 to 6

Deep-Fried Sweet Potato Balls; Walnut Sweet

CARAMEL APPLES

2 egg whites
6 tablespoons
  self-raising flour
plain flour for
  coating
4 large dessert
  apples, peeled,
  cored, and each cut
  into 8 pieces
oil for deep-frying
CARAMEL COATING:
175 g (6 oz) sugar
3 tablespoons water
25 g (1 oz) unsalted
  butter
1–2 tablespoons
  sesame seeds★,
  lightly toasted

Lightly beat the egg whites, then beat in the flour to form a smooth batter. Sprinkle a little plain flour over the apple slices, then coat with batter.

Heat the oil in a wok or deep-fryer and deep-fry the apples for about 5 to 7 minutes, until golden brown. Drain on kitchen paper.

To make the caramel coating, put the sugar and water in a heavy pan and stir over gentle heat until dissolved. Add the butter, increase the heat and continue stirring until the sugar has caramelized to a golden colour. Add the sesame seeds and apples and stir quickly until the apples are well coated with caramel.

Dip the apples into cold water to harden the caramel, drain and serve immediately.
Serves 4

Caramel Apples; Water Chestnut Cake; Fruit Custard

WATER CHESTNUT CAKE

150 g (5 oz) water
  chestnut flour★,
  sifted
350 ml (12 fl oz)
  water
500 g (1 lb) canned
  water chestnuts★,
  well drained and
  chopped
50 g (2 oz) unsalted
  butter
150 ml (¼ pint)
  milk
250 g (8 oz) caster
  sugar
sliced strawberries to
  decorate

Put the flour into a bowl and gradually beat in the water to form a smooth batter.

Put the water chestnuts, butter, milk and sugar into a large pan and bring to the boil. Remove from the heat and stir in half the batter. Bring back to the boil, stirring. Remove from the heat and add the remaining batter. Return to the boil and cook, stirring, for 30 seconds.

Pour into a lined and greased 18 cm (7 inch) square shallow cake tin and cover with greaseproof paper and foil, securing with string. Steam over high heat for 25 to 30 minutes until firm. Leave to cool in the tin.

Turn out and cut into diamond shapes. Arrange on a serving plate and decorate with strawberry slices.
Serves 4 to 6

FRUIT CUSTARD

3 eggs
4 tablespoons caster
  sugar
300 ml (½ pint)
  water
350 g (12 oz)
  pineapple, finely
  shredded
50 g (2 oz) dates,
  finely shredded
75 g (3 oz)
  crystallized fruit,
  finely shredded
25 g (1 oz) dried figs,
  finely shredded
1 tablespoon
  arrowroot or
  cornflour

Beat the eggs, 1 tablespoon sugar and 4 tablespoons of the water together in a deep ovenproof dish. Place in a steamer and steam for 7 to 8 minutes until the mixture is set.

Mix all the fruit together and spoon over the egg custard.

Mix the arrowroot or cornflour and remaining sugar together, then gradually blend in the water. Bring the mixture to the boil, stirring, and cook for 2 minutes. Spoon over the fruit and serve hot or cold.
Serves 4

KHEER

75 g (3 oz) long-
  grain rice
1.75 litres (3 pints)
  milk
50 g (2 oz) sultanas
  (optional)
caster sugar
1 × 142 ml (5 fl oz)
  carton single cream
flaked almonds or
  lightly crushed
  cardamom seeds★
  to decorate

Put the rice and 1 litre (1¾ pints) of
the milk into a heavy-based pan. Cook
gently at simmering point for 45
minutes to 1 hour, until most of the
milk has been absorbed.

Add the remaining milk and the
sultanas, if using, stir well and
continue simmering until thickened.
Remove from the heat and add caster
sugar to taste.

Leave until completely cold, stirring
occasionally to prevent a skin forming,
then stir in the cream.

Turn the mixture into small dishes
and serve cold, sprinkled with flaked
almonds or lightly crushed cardamom
seeds.
Serves 4

SEMOLINA BARFI

50 g (2 oz) fine
  semolina
125 g (4 oz) sugar
450 ml (¾ pint)
  milk
50 g (2 oz) butter
10 cardamom pods★,
  peeled and seeds
  crushed
75 g (3 oz) blanched
  almonds, halved
  and toasted to
  decorate

Put the semolina and sugar into a
heavy-based pan and stir in the milk
gradually until smooth. Add the butter
in small pieces. Bring to the boil,
stirring, then simmer for 3 to 4
minutes, until thickened, stirring
occasionally to prevent sticking. Add
the cardamom and continue cooking
for another 10 minutes until the
mixture leaves the side of the pan.

Spread on a buttered plate or dish to
a thickness of 1 to 1.5 cm (½ to 1
inch). Leave until almost cold, then
decorate with the almonds.

Serve cold, cut into slices or squares.
Serves 4 to 6

BAKED BANANAS

50 g (2 oz) seedless
  raisins
50 ml (2 fl oz) rum
  or lemon juice
4 bananas, peeled
25 g (1 oz) butter
50 g (2 oz) demerara
  sugar
50 ml (2 fl oz)
  orange juice
2 teaspoons lemon
  rind
vanilla ice-cream
  (optional)
(Picture, page 148)

Place the raisins in a small bowl, add
the rum, then marinate for 30 minutes.

Place each banana on a 20 cm (8
inch) square of foil, then dot each with
a quarter of the butter. Sprinkle the
bananas evenly with the raisins, rum,
sugar, orange juice and lemon rind and
seal the packages securely. Cook in a
preheated moderately hot oven, 180°C
(350°F), Gas Mark 4, for 15 to 20
minutes.

Serve immediately, with a scoop of
the ice-cream, if using.

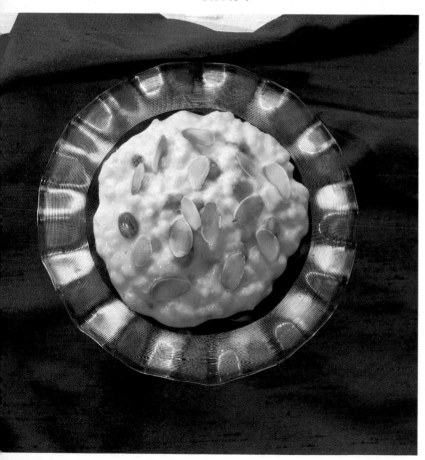

Kheer

GARNISHES

Garnishes are frequently used to add colour to Chinese dishes. Those described below are simple to make.

Radish Flowers: Trim each end of the radish. Using a sharp knife, make 'V' cuts around the top and remove the cut parts to expose the white of the radish.

Radish Roses: Cut small petals all around the radish; chill in iced water until the petals open.

Spring Onion Brushes: Trim the green top and remove the white part. Carefully shred the top leaving 2.5 cm (1 inch) attached at the base. Immerse in iced water until the spring onion opens out and curls.

Carrot Flowers: Trim the ends. Using a sharp knife, make 'V' cuts along the carrot. Cut across into slices.

Cucumber Fans: Cut a 7.5 cm (3 inch) piece from the rounded end of a cucumber. Cut in half lengthways. Cut each half into strips to within 1 cm ($\frac{1}{2}$ inch) from the end, then trim each strip, removing excess flesh, to about 3 mm ($\frac{1}{4}$ inch) thickness. Carefully turn alternative strips up to the uncut end, as illustrated. Use at once.

Tomato Flowers: Thinly pare all the skin from the tomato, taking care to keep it in one piece. Tightly curl the skin into a circle as shown. Use at once.

Turnip, carrot and apple flowers can be prepared this way.

Chilli Flowers: Cut the chilli lengthways into quarters to within 1 cm ($\frac{1}{2}$ inch) from the stem end, taking care not to remove the seeds. Shred each quarter of chilli leaving the base attached. Place in iced water for about 1 hour to open.

SALAD DRESSINGS

To make a vinaigrette dressing combine 175 ml (6 fl oz) olive oil, 4 tablespoons cider vinegar, 1 teaspoon clear honey, 1 crushed garlic clove and 2 tablespoons fresh chopped mixed herbs in a screw-topped jar, add salt and pepper to taste and shake well. This dressing keeps for up to 6 weeks.

Soy sauce dressing can also be kept for 6 weeks. To make it, put 175 ml (6 fl oz) sunflower oil, 4 tablespoons soy sauce, 2 tablespoons lemon juice and a crushed garlic clove into a screw-topped jar. Season to taste with salt and pepper and shake well.

A refreshing herby yogurt dressing can be made in a liquidizer. Combine 150 g (5 oz) natural yogurt, 1 crushed garlic clove, 1 tablespoon cider vinegar, 1 teaspoon clear honey, 15 g ($\frac{1}{2}$ oz) parsley and 15 g ($\frac{1}{2}$ oz) mixed mint and chives, add salt and pepper and blend for 1–2 minutes. This dressing can be stored for up to 4 days.

INDEX

ACKNOWLEDGMENTS

The publishers would like to thank the following individuals who were involved in the preparation of material for this book:

Photographers: Bryce Attwell, James Jackson, David Johnson, Charlie Stebbings, Clive Streeter and Paul Williams

Photographic stylists: Liz Allen-Eslor, Gina Carminati, Penny Markham, Roisin Nield and Lesley Richardson

Food for photography prepared by Nicola Diggins, Caroline Ellwood, Clare Ferguson, Clare Gordon-Smith, Carole Handslip and Liz and Pete